LIFE RE-VISION

LIFE RE-VISION

*A Journey to Rediscover
Your Core, Reinvent
Yourself and Renew Your
Future Vision*

ANAMARIA ARISTIZABAL

Succulent
PUBLISHING

Contents

Introduction

Why Do a Life Re-Vision?

There are times in which we lose the thread of our lives. We feel disoriented; we no longer know where we are coming from or where we are headed. Our current map no longer works. Our vision may be clouded by any number of problems or situations, creating a sensation of being lost. Not doing anything about this is a choice, one that comes at a high price. The old proverb says: "Where there is no vision, the people perish." In other words, in the absence of life-vision, we cannot fully blossom as human beings.

What would happen if, in those moments when we felt directionless, we knew how to rise above it all – gaining clarity and defining where to start, as well as knowing our next steps to then take up the reins of our existence again? To create a new map to orient ourselves, to develop a life vision?

To have a meaningful life, it is critical to constantly reinvent ourselves by embracing and digesting our learning experiences. Western culture celebrates the hero's journey, which portrays a person going out to the world to bravely confront challenges. Yet some of our challenges are ravaging, both externally and internally, and consume us so much that we lose our direction. We need to emphasize the importance of returning home to create an inventory of our experiences. Honoring both our pains and joys, we start to center, be at peace with our past, and unlock our designing capacity for a future full of possibility.

To start, let's recognize that we are limited if we approach life design only through an overly engineered and cerebral process. That said, our design requires a foundation and some structure to ground us as we embrace this new journey. We need both a pragmatic and poetic process to guide us, one that uses symbols and metaphors to connect our internal and external worlds. This will allow us to navigate more fluidly through the complexity of who we are individually and collectively.

The journey offered here will allow us to develop an internal compass that connects our souls with the wisdom of the world so we can learn how to read the context in which we find ourselves and create new maps that give us clarity and direction. That is what Life Re-Vision offers. The double meaning of the term "Re-Vision" invites us to review our past and Re-Vision our future. It's a metaphorical guide that invites you to gather up your experiences – the best of your past – and use all of this to connect to the integrating and creative forces within you, and from there, to envision a future of fulfillment and wisdom.

This process uses ecological principles and metaphors to help you feel inter-related and part of life, make the most of your talents and plant them in fertile ground, so you can be of service to the world and respond to its needs. You will formulate your vision and mission with clarity using a methodology that appeals to your own intuition and to the collective intelligence. With this new map, you can navigate in a much more fluid manner.

Life Re-Vision aspires to satisfy the imperative needs of the human soul: connection, meaning, a sense of direction, a sense of belonging, and contribution to others. Life Re-Vision consists of six steps inspired by natural metaphors. Each step addresses one of those profound longings:

1. **Bones.** By recognizing our creations, artifacts, treasures and sacred objects, and giving them their appropriate place, we connect with ourselves and activate our integrative and creative forces.
2. **Seeds.** By remembering our essential stories and sharing them, we see our own talents and virtues, and we recover the thread and meaning of our own life story.
3. **Winds.** By identifying the positive influences in our lives, we strengthen the confidence we have in our own sense of direc-

tion, which has led us so far and motivated us to undertake our most life-giving pursuits.

4. **Territories.** By planting ourselves in our thematic realms and sectors and making a commitment to fully inhabit them, we gain a deeper sense of belonging.

5. **Ecology.** We deepen this sense of belonging by learning to dialogue with the systemic dynamics of the territories we inhabit and access their source of wisdom, which allows for a more attuned and long-term vision.

6. **Fruits.** By visualizing our legacy, while staying attentive to our creative impulses and the context that surrounds us, we increase our focus and determination to achieve powerful and necessary contributions that benefit ourselves and others.

In summary, Life Re-Vision is an appreciative path through which we honor our multiple dimensions and gifts. With the bones, we honor our talents and our creative manifestations. With the seeds, we honor our essence and our history. With the winds, we honor our external influences and our learning processes. With the territories, we honor our place and our belonging in society. With ecology, we honor the complexity and systemic dimension of our world. Finally, with the fruits, we honor our contributions, present and future. At the end of this journey, you will celebrate a more integrated sense of who you are, feel more clarity about the direction of your creative drive and enjoy a great abundance of fruits to share with the rest of the world.

The Wisdom of the Babemba

The Life Re-Vision process is inspired by an ancestral practice that comes from the African continent. A South African tribe, the Babemba, has a custom when someone has lost their way or has done something wrong. It is known in the tribe that someone who commits an improper act has forgotten her stories and is disconnected from herself.

Instead of shaming, punishing, or isolating that person, they help her to remember, to find herself again.

The ritual is as follows. Let's imagine that a person called Inti is confused and has made an incorrect decision. The wise people of this tribe sit together in counsel with everybody who is close to Inti and perform a very important task: they remind her who she is and of all the virtues she possesses. Every person in this counsel tells stories of living with Inti, stories that show her values and her character. For example: "I remember when you and I built a house together for Mrs. Amparo." "I remember that you and I once saved Clemente from drowning in the lake." In these stories we can see her virtues and also the love that Inti has given to the world.

Her special song is also sung. It turns out that in this tribe, everyone receives their own special song the day they are born. It's their power song, sung to them by their family and the community on important occasions. The effect of hearing her essential stories and her own song is that Inti remembers who she is again. That becomes the foundation for redressing her bad decision and realigning to her own path again. She can now get back in touch with her own essence and shine with all of her light.

Let's imagine that you are a member of the Babemba tribe. At some point in your life, you are lost, you feel worn out, or you made a bad decision. You don't feel like yourself anymore; you're not happy. Allow the people in your community to remind you of your most essential stories, the stories that show your virtues and talents, and listen as they sing your song.

Reflect in Your Journal:
  - *What stories did you think of?*
  - *Write two story titles that come to you right at this moment.*

When you remember these stories, you start to forgive yourself, to remember who you are and the enormous potential you have. You are much more than the life you are currently living. You realize that you are much more than what just happened or is currently going on and has upset you, whatever it may be. You remember that your being is filled with virtues, talents, and accomplishments that you had forgotten about. It's time to remember who you really are.

Life Re-Vision is inspired by this ritual practiced by the Babemba, in which we reclaim our life stories that in turn reveal our virtues and essence. When we reconnect with our potential and create a vision of a future that inspires us, we reclaim our self-knowledge and our understanding of the world.

Stories have their own DNA, a type of deep wisdom that is tied to who we really are. We are all living out our life stories; we are weaving them at this very moment. The seeds of our current stories were planted in the past. This Life Re-Vision process helps you to collect these seeds and plant them in fertile soil so that your stories can develop with full force. Through this process, you will regain the narrative threads of your life again and become an active weaver of its creation.

How Did Life Re-Vision Come to Be?

There are crises in life that cause us to rethink who we are, who we have been, and where we are going. I lived through one of these. It was right after the end of a big love story, with a man named Steven Heller. Steven and I were engaged to be married, and each one did the impossible for us to be together. Unfortunately, despite the love, we didn't flow well as a couple. The relationship ended, and both of us wound up with our hearts broken. This breakup caused me to completely lose myself. An emotional and mental whirlwind formed inside of me that clouded my vision.

The path that I walked to get back home (to myself) was my Life Re-Vision, a process that took three years to complete. It was an anchor, a beacon that guided me to clarity. I realized that I had been looking for that clarity my whole life. This incident was a catalyst that ignited a deeper inquiry for my sense of direction. It hadn't been easy for me to find myself, because of how complex my life was at so many levels. This step-by-step process helped me to finally sort out the confusion and define a direction.

The Life Re-Vision process has been transformative for me. I feel increasingly aligned with my own self and with my path. Since I did my Life Re-Vision, I've had a tailwind that pushes me to take action in important areas once neglected or feared. This wind comes from the clarity of understanding my place and purpose. I have a better understanding of the great philosopher Socrates when he said, "The unexamined life is not worth living." This is what I wish for you: the opportunity to examine your life, so that you can fully express who you are, to the benefit of this world that needs you.

Who is Life Re-Vision for?

William Bridges, an author and lecturer considered to be among the ten most popular executive trainers in the USA, wrote an important book called *Transitions*. He says that in certain stages of life, we come across moments of deep transformation that make us question who we are and where we're going. Bridges makes a distinction between "changes" and "transitions:" external changes don't imply a great internal transformation; on the other hand, transitions make us question who we really are and what we want our lives to be about.[1]

The transition I went through asked me to envision a life on my own terms instead of following someone else's script. It made me aware that what I really wanted would take some time but that I was finally ready. This book is especially for people who are in the midst of a transition and need to take some time to process what the next stage is about. This book is also for those who know that they need to turn their lives around, but don't know which steps to take, or in which direction to take them. If this is the case, it's great that this book is in your hands at this moment, because you can see your transition as a platform into your new life – the one for which you have been yearn-ing and that awaits you. If you are currently undergoing a transition, the following description will be of interest to you.

According to Bridges, transitions have three stages: the Ending, the Neutral Zone, and the New Beginning. The Ending is the first part of the transition, where something just changed, or we know something has to change, either internally or externally. There is uncertainty about what's coming because the status quo is significantly interrupted (for example: graduations from school, college or master's, changes in marital status [married, single, divorced], living in a new place, wanted or unwanted changes in our work lives, health, relationships, family, or in any other important area of our lives). There's no going back, and these external changes make a significant impact internally. In the Ending stage, certain emotions are common, including grief, anxiety, fear, sadness, boredom, anger, disorientation, and unrest. Sometimes the emotions are so strong that we need professional help to deal with them.[2]

When we start processing these emotions, we have more capacity to adopt healthy habits. Progressively, we start to make decisions that are better aligned with ourselves and our needs. As a result, we enter a new stage, the Neutral Zone, where we feel more at ease with and open to ambiguity, although we still don't know where we are going. We are in a stage of internal and external exploration. We must set aside the need to make big decisions immediately – impulsive decisions that might be out of line with our real values – and instead take the time to explore. This moment, the Neutral Zone, is perfect for a Life Re-Vision.

This guided exploration delivers the real answer we are looking for, little by little, without rushing. We start to feel differently, and one day, we notice that we have taken important steps in an exciting and inspiring direction. We have then moved on to the New Beginning, the last stage of the transition.

Your Life Re-Vision will yield greater clarity. It won't simply calm your worries with Band-Aid solutions and leave you to live your life in the same way so that you wind up in another crisis later on. It will lead you to find your own purpose and to visualize a life aligned with this purpose.

This book will support you in your transition process, in this Neutral Zone, so that you can undertake an internal and external exploration and, in this way, reach a meaningful and fulfilling New Beginning. With this book, I want you to take full advantage of that change-energy of transition, to take a qualitative leap in your life and be filled with clarity about yourself and your path.

Conditions for a Life Re-Vision

Ángeles Arrien (RIP), a Spanish cultural anthropologist, educator, and consultant, studied more than 1,000 indigenous cultures and found a pattern of four underlying archetypes among their wise people, which can contribute to addressing the greater problems of our time.[3] Archetypes are patterns of being that influence our behavior, our way of looking at ourselves, of relating to others and of having an impact on the world. Each one of these archetypes is a way of life.

In her book, *The Four-Fold Way*, Arrien describes the four archetypes: the warrior, the healer, the teacher, and the visionary.[4] The warrior is fully present to defend her ideals with bravery and discipline. The healer focuses on that which is sensitive and meaningful and has an open and loving heart for restoring relationships and healing others. The teacher teaches and transmits knowledge and has an open mind to other points of view. The visionary is highly intuitive and defines the direction in which we are moving. We will pay the most attention to the visionary archetype.

This book is not inspired by the warrior archetype. That is, this isn't a book that invites you to take decisive and definitive action at this very moment, and it will not train you in any specific technique.

This is not a book about leadership. Although some things related to leadership are present, that is not this book's focus.

This is not a book based on the healer archetype either. The objective is not to visit past or present pain or trauma in order to heal, nor to analyze the root causes. This book will not help with the emotional baggage that can come with great transitions. To take care of that, I recommend consulting with a therapist. Although some exercises that appear in this book can be therapeutic, that is not the book's focus.

This book is not inspired by the teacher archetype. The information presented here is not the most important of the journey, nor does it aim to be revolutionary. Although you may find valuable concepts here, exploring them or analyzing those to their depths is not the objective. This book is more poetic than anything else; it uses metaphors to evoke, inspire, and invite you to experience these concepts.

This book is indeed inspired by the visionary archetype. It aims to awaken clarity and purpose. The visionary is a person who knows how to express herself, how to speak the truth without blaming or judging. The visionary is a person capable of seeing what others don't see as well as the steps to get there. In order to achieve this, the visionary creates the conditions within herself that allow her to connect to an inner guide. This means being willing to see and think differently than others, cultivate inner silence, and constantly seek inspiration.

In this book, we are going to delve deeply into the path of the visionary. To prepare ourselves for this process, we need to create the necessary conditions for our visionary archetype to be activated. These conditions are simple, but they do require commitment. The end result will be a sensation of greater clarity and direct communication with this inner source that brings us the answers. We will no longer be drowned in confusion; we will have opened a direct line of communication to our soul.

The first condition is rest. Without proper rest, we don't have any of the abilities and energy required for a Life Re-Vision process. Part of our confusion and frustration with life is just tiredness. During this process, we need to have proper sleep patterns. If we lose that rhythm for one night, it doesn't matter; we can simply get it back the next night.

The second condition is good nutrition. During this process, we need clarity. If we are drinking lots of alcohol, taking drugs, and eating lots of sugar, carbohydrates, and junk food, our brains don't function as well. Focus on eating healthy during this time, and you will see a difference in your mental clarity and in your physical energy.

The third condition is stillness. Most of us live fast-paced lives that don't allow for messages from our inner selves to be noticed. There are many ways to cultivate stillness. We recommend practicing "walking meditation," which is simply walking slowly and silently, focusing on your breath. A routine of silently walking ten minutes per day will start to open up the channels.

The fourth condition is to practice visualization. In the pages that follow, you will find various invitations to visualize. You can read the visualizations first and then record yourself reading them so that later, you can close your eyes and allow yourself to be guided by your own voice. Another option is to take our online course and use the recordings that are on our e-learning platform. At first, it may be difficult to quiet your mind and connect to the imaginary journey. But as you keep practicing, you will start to activate your ability to visualize, which is essential to activate the visionary archetype.

The fifth and last condition is to write in a journal. You will start to receive many messages along with new clarity. It's important to record all of these riches in a diary, a space to tell the truth exactly as it is. Don't worry about anybody ever reading it. If you have to, keep it a total secret from everyone. The important thing is to have a completely intimate space where you can express what you are seeing in yourself and your surroundings, without feeling any shame.

Start by writing whatever comes into your head, without any filter, for ten minutes a day. Day by day, the practice will be refined on its own. I write in the mornings, starting with describing the dreams I just had, processing the previous day's learnings, and then writing about what awaits me that day. These are moments of great honesty, inspiration, and clarity. Discover your own way of doing this, and start making this practice your own; it will be yours for life.

To start a journal, the first thing is to find a notebook that you like where you feel comfortable expressing yourself. For example, I like one that doesn't have any lines, so that I can draw freely in it if I feel like it. Look for a design that inspires you. This will be an important space where you can take refuge and express what you need to express during and after the Life Re-Vision process. You can save clippings in it if you like, and you can take it with you on trips and put photos inside it. It's your exploratory space to cultivate the visionary inside of you.

Throughout this book, you will find various questions to guide your reflection. I invite you to answer them in your journal so that you can express yourself with greater freedom and respond to them with as much depth as you wish.

Now, I ask you to define your starting point, being very honest with yourself, using the abilities of the visionary to name things exactly as they are.

Are You Ready for a Life Re-Vision?

When is the right time to begin? I went through many hard situations in my life before I eventually dove into this Life Re-Vision process. I lost many jobs, one after the other, because of my disorientation, which caused me a lot of pain. I went through many years of unhealthy relationships. As I mentioned, I almost married the wrong person. Although Steven was an incredible man and we loved each other dearly, we weren't headed in the same direction, but I didn't want to see that. The root of it all was my lack of vision. Deep inside, I heard the call for something different, but I didn't pay attention to it.

If we are smart people, why is change so hard? It turns out that there is something called "homeostasis," which is the tendency of all living beings to keep themselves stable. When we have achieved that stability, changing it requires energy. It requires a specific kind of support.

We can pretend that we can simply go on with life, things will change naturally, and we will be directed to the right path. However, it's not very likely that this will happen. Collective inertia is very strong. The structures that keep us blindly pursuing external ideals – such as money, status, and power – are constantly influencing us. Leaving it to others or events outside of ourselves, we risk missing who we are and who we can become by living our vision.

A Life Re-Vision requires energy to start. Imagine that you are at the university and you are eating at the cafeteria where everybody else is eating. You notice that the food is damaging your health. You are now in conflict because it's easier to eat in the cafeteria with everybody else. Everybody eats there and is fine with it, but you can't keep eating there anymore; it's making you sick. But you don't know what to do about it. You have to start a process. You need to get to know yourself first, to find out what you can and can't eat, to learn how to shop for food, make your own food, and start to change your eating plan so you feel healthy again.

I'll give you another analogy: You're the mayor of a city where things aren't going well. In planning to offer a new vision for the city and its inhabitants, you're probably not going to just propose the first thing that comes to mind. You're going to need to engage in a comprehensive process in order to honor the history of your city, its cultural, social, and economic identity, and the point of view of its inhabitants. Similarly, a Life Re-Vision must take into account your past, your identity, and even the points of view of people close to you.

A Life Re-Vision requires strategic thinking about the contribution you want to make in the world, but it's much more than just a strategy. Here's another analogy: If you're thinking of starting a new business, it's not enough to just go out and sell something. You need to think about your intentions and interests and whether the product you will offer is aligned with your own values, your client's needs, and the market conditions. You will want to know the context. Many businesses end up failing because of lack of motivation or understanding of their particular context.

I have asked myself many times why businesses invest so much time and energy in their strategies, but most individuals neglect this area completely. We are not used to designing our own lives or investing energy and resources to properly study who we are, where we came from, and where we are going so we can find our right place in the world. I went to business school in part to understand how strategy is crafted and then to apply this skill to people's lives. These days, the profession of coaching provides some tools to do this, but I had not found the right path for me.

A very particular type of strategy and life design is called for at this moment in history. We are becoming more complex beings these days because of the quantity of information we receive. The conventional definition of success no longer works; it is making us and the whole planet sick. There is suffering at individual, collective, and planetary levels. We need new maps and new processes to help us clarify where we are headed, beginning with each individual drawing a new map for their life.

I took years to conceive this process. As one of those people who didn't know "what I wanted to be when I grew up," I looked at others who knew what they wanted with a certain longing. However, today I'm grateful for that uncertainty because it pushed me to undertake an honest process, letting go of others' concepts and expectations of me.

This meant detaching myself from borrowed dreams that weren't taking me in the right direction (my rightful place in the world). Borrowed dreams are those that come from outside, which we internalize. Mine were to be the Minister of the Environment, to be a consultant with a prestigious international company, to be a family woman, and to have kids. Examining them more closely, I saw that all of these dreams came from outside. I had adopted them to please others, but in reality, they weren't a deep part of me.

Principles for a Life Re-Vision

There's a set of beliefs that can limit us when doing a Life Re-Vision. The German philosopher Martin Heidegger speaks of "The They," which basically refers to "what people say" or "what *they* say." These are the beliefs of the majority or the mainstream, beliefs that we often adopt without realizing or consciously choosing. Let's take for example, "They say that you can't teach an old dog new tricks" (a very unhelpful belief). Heidegger proposed that in order to live an authentic life, we need to question these beliefs and think for ourselves.

Review your beliefs before undertaking your Life Re-Vision:

Limiting belief	Life Re-Vision principle
- Only the present matters.	- We are temporal beings; the past and the future matter to us.
- Everything has been determined. I've made certain decisions. "It is what it is."	- At every moment in our existence, we are free to choose a new destiny.
- Planning and design are only for business.	- An authentic life requires design and redesign, a soulful strategic process, a constant Life Re-Vision.
- People can only operate from one type of motivation – either intrinsic or extrinsic – based on imperatives from the external world.	- A fulfilled life is in constant contact with both internal and external drivers for change.

- In order to be someone with a special purpose, I would have to live something extreme.	- The seeds for great purposes can be found in the simplest experiences.
- I need to choose only one path and identity.	- Embracing complexity will lead to fulfillment.
- I need to clarify everything right now!	- I can give myself permission to be open to uncertainty and the opportunity to explore.

Let's explore what the suggested principles imply.

We are temporal beings; the past and the future matter to us. Lately, because of certain trends, we've started to believe that the only thing that matters is the present. It's true that we need to maintain our focus on the present moment so that we don't continue suffering from the past or obsessing about the future. However, the past and the future are fundamental aspects of our identity. We need to learn how to intelligently relate to our past and our future.

In our pasts, there are important "nutrients," and when we "compost" them, they become fertilizer for the present and the future. "Composting" is letting organic material process itself to become fertilizer. The past is full of stories and lessons that define our individual and collective values. The past also carries painful memories that, if rescued and our interpretation of them is shifted, can be very liberating and helpful in orienting our lives.

The future hosts our possibilities, our longings and the forces that direct our actions. Heidegger said that we human beings are always oriented toward possibilities. If we don't have fertile future possibilities, we lose a sense of meaning. We fall into boredom, stress, and unhappiness. This process invites you to explore your past in order to reconnect with your history as well as the future you are called to live into, in order to find your inner compass.

Having a future vision is not the same as controlling the future.

The idea isn't to close ourselves off from the many possibilities that could come to us because we only have one vision and we aren't open to anything else. It's also not about becoming rigid with that vision and not being open to the spontaneity of life. There's space for everything in a purposeful life, a Re-Visioned life, and it's powerful to feel that everything is aligning around you and your purpose.

Freedom of choice. It sounds obvious that in every moment of our existence we are free to choose a new destiny. However, it's surprising how many people limit themselves because they've made a decision, are committed to it, and don't allow themselves to even question it. This could be your career, your partner, a house, a company. Obviously, we have to honor our commitments. However, we also have the right to make mistakes and go back and correct them.

Some time ago, I saw a friend who was at the cusp of a depression because things weren't going well with his partner. They recently had a baby together. He told me that the worst moments were when he told himself that he had chosen the wrong partner and now they would have to be together for life. This extrapolation of the present circumstances into the future was making life unbearable for him. If we orient ourselves toward the possibility of "everything staying the same" when the current situation is full of suffering, it can become a real prison.

We need to give ourselves the opportunity to recognize that we make mistakes and that, yes, there is a way to go back! Failures are a part of the human experience, and they give us important lessons.

A constant Re-Vision is necessary. An authentic life needs design and redesign. Heidegger speaks about human beings living either an authentic or an inauthentic life. The authentic life is one that is lived in accordance with our fundamental values, which stems from the awareness of our death and that we are here for a short time.

It's easy to have an inauthentic life. We can keep falling into following "The They" at any moment. Just remember the times that you told yourself, "I'm not eating any more sweets," but then someone you care about offers you some and you're incapable of saying no. External pressures are seductive, and we tend to follow them blindly. A Life Re-Vision gives you some tools to use to define your life on your own terms so that you can make decisions where you are loyal to yourself. It is quite easy to wind up assimilating values and beliefs that aren't really yours.

I remember a time in college, when I was full of ideals and in contact with my essence, that a wise woman told me about a phenomenon: the "undertow." Years later, I realized she was right about this phenomenon. The undertow is the undercurrent of social pressures that goes against your own ideals and eventually pulls you in. The main characteristic of the undertow is that you don't see it because it operates "under the table" dragging you along without your noticing. This wise woman predicted that many of us would be deeply idealistic in our twenties, dedicated to serve an altruistic cause. Then, in our thirties, we would lose ourselves to external pressures and ideals of individualism, money, status, stability, and image. I didn't think that it would happen to me, but it did, in a very profound way. Life-Revision helped me get back into alignment.

The need for a Life Re-Vision is constant. You may have gotten the wrong idea that planning is only necessary for companies and work-related projects. This is a mistake. How can you leave something so important as the arc of your life to chance? This is why so many people are excellent business people but have disastrous personal lives. They haven't applied their business skills to the rest of their lives. Since we are constantly evolving, we need to continuously update our Life Re-Visions. These tools are to be used over and over to recreate our life maps in line with the new understanding we have gained about ourselves and our place in the world. Therefore, this process is continuous and constant. You determine its frequency. This book will support you getting into the habit, and that habit will be with you for the rest of your life.

A fulfilled life is in constant contact with both the internal and the external drivers for change. Some people feel that in order to have a fulfilled life, you only have to figure out what you want to do and then do it. Others let themselves be guided by external drivers and sacrifice themselves to take care of these needs. These two attitudes by themselves can lead to imbalance.

The premise of this book is that in order to have a purposeful life, it's necessary to develop the capacity to explore internally and externally – both your desires and aspirations as well as the necessities of the world. This Life Re-Vision will take you to the intersection of these two drivers.

Embracing our complexity will fulfill us. You might have heard that you have to choose a single professional identity and leave everything else behind. For example, people who were passionate about horses, music, dance, outdoor activities, whatever it is throughout their childhood and adolescence often have forgotten about these passions and talents and have lost a significant source of connection and meaning. We are multidimensional beings who thrive by reclaiming all our inner diversity.

A little while ago, I found out about a school where all the children participate in different activities that complement the whole curriculum. To learn about agriculture, the children plant seeds in the garden, observe them, and experiment on them in the laboratory. They eat what they have planted together and then put on a musical theater show where they explore the lessons they learned in a playful manner.

What would it be like if all of our schools were like that? How many of us would be recovered, resulting in more fulfillment and joy? For sure, nobody would say, "I'm not creative" anymore. We would all be in contact with our multi-dimensionality. Unfortunately right now, many of us have a very hard time recovering or cultivating our innate creativity.

Brene Brown, an author, academic, and lecturer who talks about vulnerability, courage, and empathy, says that wasting our talents makes us unhealthy.[5] I have personally lived this, as well as seen it in my clients. Trying to fit into a mold – matching what we "should be" – only causes suffering. Reclaiming your richness will give you a sense of fulfillment that may even surprise you.

The seeds of the greatest purpose are often found in the simplest experiences. We often have a false belief that people find their true path only when they live extreme experiences. I wound up believing that. Listening to how purposeful people came to understand what their mission was but almost lost their lives, I ended up thinking that it was risky to ask for a life full of passion and purpose because something extreme might happen to me.

Think of a person you have seen, one who lived a traumatic experience and almost lost his or her life, and whose mission is to support others enduring similar experiences. It could have been an illness, getting lost in the wilderness, a kidnapping, an attack, a meeting with an extraterrestrial being, you know what I'm talking about. Are you comparing your life to theirs? You can think that your story isn't unique enough to deserve an extraordinary purpose, but this is false. You will see that your stories, as ordinary as they may be, are full of heart and meaning. And this discovery can be made without having to risk your life. It's enough to convince yourself of this: Reviewing and designing your life deserves the same level of seriousness that you put into your professional career.

Openness to uncertainty, giving yourself the opportunity to explore. Many of us grow up in educational and social contexts that favor certainty and "arrival" at a clear destination. Once we have achieved this "clarity," we are rewarded and no longer need to question. In fact, it is often considered that exploration – and its implied uncertainty – is a waste of time, a sign of incompetence, immaturity, or even a downright mistake. For example, in many of our schools, we are rewarded for giving the correct answers and punished for "not knowing."

I remember that it was very uncomfortable for me when people asked, "What do you want to be when you grow up?" At that time, it was very favorable to be one of those children who immediately said, "I'm going to be a doctor/engineer/manager/economist." I honestly didn't have any idea what I wanted to be. I looked at my classmates who seemed to know with a certain envy.

Today, I'm very happy to have been the one who didn't have a clear outlook, because this motivated a serious inquiry. With time, I've been able to learn and carry out a more diligent exploration of my vocation, full of misses, hits, and uncertainty. This has taken time and dedication. Today, I'm noticing that this process is never over. It's ongoing and requires building a "muscle" of self-knowledge and self-definition that many never develop but which leads to extraordinary results.

Perhaps you are at a point in your life where you don't know where you are going anymore, and you are asking yourself, "Now what do I do?" You may lack the tools to undertake a self-discovery journey, and so you don't know how to start or where it will take you. I've met a lot of people who, at those times in their lives, instead of confronting the uncertainty of their exploration, prefer to take solace in just about anything, especially things that aren't very healthy.

Some people hide themselves in their work, by staying busy. They are the so-called "workaholics." This addiction to work is rewarded by society, which can cause us to be trapped there for a long time. I have certainly been a victim of this avoidance tactic. Although I wasn't happy with what I was doing, I worked until very late and didn't give myself time to reflect on or explore my true path. Besides, my anxiety about making money made me feel like the work I was doing was never enough and I needed to produce more. In this vain search, one can waste one's whole life, leaving nothing but emptiness.

Others hide themselves behind distractions: television series, movies, the internet, video games, sports, and other distractions, which may be healthy up to a certain point. The risk is that we spend too much time on them and wind up not confronting the real questions about our lives, or being with the discomfort and uncertainty that come with them.

Others hide themselves behind dogma. By dogma, I mean an ideology that gives certain solid answers to every single aspect of life and provides a sense of direction beyond the spiritual. We certainly need a spiritual anchor for our lives; however, there are many cults that inhibit our human faculty of self-determination.

Running away from uncertainty and keeping ourselves busy with productive or unproductive tasks are risks that we take every day. With so much information and the challenge of navigating all of life's variables, it can be tempting to seek out a person who gives us all the "answers," or simply to avoid even asking the questions. But this comes at a very high cost: our freedom of choice, our self-determination, our autonomy, and our greater potential. To claim our freedom requires developing a considerable tolerance for uncertainty and an openness to not knowing, to exploring and embarking on a new path. Your own path. That's why we are here.

Respond in Your Journal:
- *Which limiting belief, habit, or excuse would you like to leave behind?*
- *Which principle is especially relevant to guide your Life Re-Vision?*

I

The Starting Point

Some time ago, I had a dream that brought back the longing and the imperative to do a Life Re-Vision. I dreamed that I was late for an early class at my university. I managed to find transportation to take me there, but it was very far away. When I got there, I saw that I had forgotten my class schedule for the semester where I had all the information on each class, including the location and timing. When I realized that I was lost, I asked for help, but nobody was able to help me. Nobody had the information I needed. I started worrying about losing the money I had paid for the semester because of not showing up for classes. I started wandering around the university without my bearings, watching everybody else who knew exactly where they were going. I felt disoriented and frustrated.

On top of everything, a classmate in the dream offered to have an affair with me. I considered it, as a distraction from feeling lost and empty. I felt admiration for this man and thought it would be a good way to feel valued and pass the time. However, a voice inside of me called out, "Hey! You have a partner!" At that moment, I woke up and felt guilty about having considered getting involved with my classmate, even if it was only a dream.

Upon reflecting for a moment, I realized that I really did live all of that in my past. That was my starting point. The disorientation, the emptiness, the falling into temptations for a temporary distraction, but it ended up taking me away from my purpose and my commitments and later on, left me feeling guilty. After breaking up with Steven, I remembered I started to date a lot of people in order to forget my pain and disorientation and, for a moment, I could hide from myself. Those were nights of intense passion, but the next day left me feeling even more longing, more emptiness. I remember spending entire afternoons browsing social media, vicariously living through other people's posts, because I had no idea where my own life was going. I also remember not being able to sleep, waking up at three in the morning feeling anxious with a sensation of incompleteness, regretting many mistakes and not knowing how to get back on track again.

In those days, I wrote some poems expressing what I was going through. My coach at the time, Sarita Chawla, assigned me the exercise of looking at myself in the mirror and telling the truth about what I was feeling: sadness, emptiness, fear, desperation. It was a cathartic way of letting it all out, seeing it face to face.

Sad and Lost

I see you in the mirror, Anamaria
I see your sadness, your disconnection,
Sometimes despair
Your longing for something...
Starting the day off lost,
And how you grab onto something
To not completely succumb
To the void

Everything that you find is a mismatch
A wall, a bottomless barrel
What is that look crying for?
What injustice violated your perplexed psyche?
How are you looking to be compensated,
Amended,
And find your way home from exile?

Fragile

I want, I need
Protection
From my fragility

I open a path
To feel, to not hide
From sadness

Open wound
Volcanic eruption
Of tears

Empty

An abandoned countryside
Desolate
Mute ruins

In the distance
A bird's complaint
Lost and hungry

Desert bush
Ignorant one
Meditates on water

Intelligent structures
Of other epochs
Host absence itself

Alone

Orphaned, family–less
Wandering the streets

I forage my belonging

With traces of hope
I sniff the corners
For the promise of union

But nothing... nothing...
Gangrenous with rage
Upon contact with garbage

Hopeless

Winter
Of the soul and the sky
Snow falls inside of me

Death
Lost aspirations
Buried avalanche of dreams

In these poems, you can see how deep my crisis was. I'm sharing these because for some people it's important to understand that they aren't the only ones to hit rock bottom. In my work as a life coach, I've seen hundreds of people pass through painful transitions like this, moments that they have turned into opportunities for transformation.

What is Your Starting Point?

It could be that you're experiencing some of what I'm about to describe. These are examples from participants in Life Re-Vision workshops who shared their starting points in the first check–in conversation. Read the following paragraphs to see if any of them relate at all to your current situation. There could be many statements that apply to your present circumstances, or none at all; it doesn't matter.

What I'm offering are some ideas for you to connect with yourself and see what applies.

- You are hungering for something new, but don't know exactly what. Everything seems "fine" but something inside is looking for change. Maybe it's a desire to take yourself more seriously.

  "I want to take a break to see who I have been so that I can value myself more. Who am I right now? I want to be honest with myself so that I can plan my life more from the heart."

  "I'm stable, maybe too stable. I'm afraid of change, but I know I need one."

  "I have been in the same job for nine years. I'm not happy, but I'm comfortable. Many people tell me I'm stuck in the comfort zone. I know that I need a shake–up so that I can make changes in my life and do something different, and that's why I'm here: to take that step and make a decision."

- You're feeling a light or strong sensation of being disoriented, lost, anxious, and of not knowing exactly what to do, how to use your time and resources.

  "I say 'Yes' to everything, and I'm overwhelmed. I don't have any criteria to decide what to do and what not to do. I don't have a clear direction."

  "I have too many responsibilities, and I feel frustrated, bored, and discontent."

  "I'm a fearful person. I feel stuck. I've been working on the same things for a long time now and I don't make any progress. I stay right here. I don't know what I can do about it. I want to be myself and not who people say I am; I'm trying to free myself."

- You're anxious because a big change has come or is coming and you still don't know how to deal with it; you don't have clarity to make the decisions you have to make.

"I'm a student; I'm going through a period where I need to make many decisions, and it's key to know myself (my strengths and weaknesses) and review what I've lived so that I can orient myself and decide what I want out of life."

"A big change is coming in my life. I'm no longer the mom; I'm no longer the entrepreneur. But I'm not clear on who I am. I need to understand who I am now."

"I don't know who I am, nor where I'm going. I just got back from living abroad; I was forced to leave. I wanted to make my life there, but now I find myself back here, and I don't know where to start. I feel completely lost. I need to feel comfortable in this country again, to feel OK with what's happening. To accept and understand why I need to be here, and for what. I need to find my sense of direction."

- You're bored; you've lost your passion. You do what you're supposed to but without pleasure or zest. You accomplish tasks mechanically and repeat them over and over again. You feel numb or frustrated and get easily irritated with others, which stems from a deep dissatisfaction with your life.

"I've lived for many years on autopilot, the rat race of studying, working, getting married, having kids, acquiring material things, and not focusing on myself. I'm in the process of becoming conscious. I've decided that my life decisions should be not by omission but rather with intent; I should make my own decision. I yearn for a space to reflect on where I've come from and clarify where I'm going. No more autopilot, I want to touch the ground of my conscience. I'm motivated to keep evolving."

"I want to make the most of the unique situation I find myself in, reset myself. Like in the movie *Boyhood*, I've seen that there are patterns in life that keep repeating. One keeps on repeating oneself in many behaviors, until all of a sudden one says: 'Wow! I'm forty-five years old, and I've spent so many years repeating myself. Am I condemned to just keep repeating myself or is it possible to reset myself and change the direction of my existence, without losing the good, but changing that which I wish to change? I want to plan a generous, abundant, and most importantly healthy second half of life for myself in all dimensions of being: spiritually, relationally, creatively, and artistically."

- For a few years you've had questions about your sense of meaning and direction, your talents, and your vocation; and those questions just can't wait anymore.

- You're not comfortable with your life as it is. You need to feel like you're making a greater contribution, one that's more fulfilling and relevant to the world. You want to leave a more meaningful legacy, to leave your mark. It's time to tackle those questions.

"I want a more integrated life. I want to accomplish important milestones this year: leave a legacy, not just go unnoticed. I want to explore my talents and use them in the service of others."

"I feel like I have an important calling in life, and it's getting stronger every day, but I'm not sure what it is. It's a good thing, but it's also overwhelming because I feel an enormous weight on my shoulders, and I need to get the weight off and find out what it is. I need to find my essence, find myself, and turn to whatever is calling me."

- For a few years, you've felt very lonely. You might be passionate about something, but you've pursued it on your own. You feel like you need to belong to something bigger, where you feel companionship and a collective force that powers and motivates you.

- You are going through a period of mourning or breakdown, because of losing a relationship, a person, a job, something material, or your image. Maybe you've experienced a painful failure. These are tough emotions that are hard to manage, or you feel like you are numb and don't have any emotions at all.

"I feel like the world has come down on me. I have lost my ideals, or they never really existed."

"Life is super capricious. There are events that turn your existence upside down, but they are very important. One sees them as tragedies, but they are events that push you into being the person you are called to be, so you learn, grow, and change by means of suffering. This year started off with a super abrupt change in my life. I had been together with my partner for twenty years sharing a perfect life project that was exactly what I wanted. Yet everything ended up turning around in the most heavy, hard, and dramatic way. It caused me to completely reconsider everything I had planned for my life. I want to find out why this happened and shift accordingly in order to achieve my life's purpose."

"The last few years have been difficult in my relationship with my partner, and that struggle has left me feeling stuck. I've been living for others; I don't think I have been really living for myself. I'm nearing the point of having an empty nest. I want to get organized so that I can plan, to take stock of my fifty-six years of life on every level and say, 'OK, this is what I have, how can I direct it? Where do I want to go?'"

"I'm undertaking a Life Re-Vision because I've been through a process of shattering. All of my options and possibilities connected with academic life have vanished. I was convinced that this was going to be my path, but it is not. I am living this process with lots of humility and with openness, because I know that my life is in service of knowledge, but it's time to reconsider my perspective."

- You have intense worry or even rage and despair regarding what's happening in your family, in your work, or in the world at this moment. Maybe it consumes you to see so much reactivity, hate, poverty, environmental destruction, violence, inequality, vice, suicide, or any other unfortunate realities at the family, social, or planetary level. You need to do something about it but you don't know how to start or what your role is in all of this.

- The economic, social, or cultural structures around us don't make any sense to you anymore. You no longer want to follow other people's models. You want to define your life on your own terms.

"I'm here to question my social roles. I know this is not me at the deepest level. I need respect for the way in which I want to live my life. I want a plan of action. I don't have clear goals."

"I thought I wanted to follow in my father's footsteps, but I'm finding out that this isn't for me."

"I'm thinking about going to school, but I don't know if I'd be doing it just to meet a standard. I'm not really sure who I am or what I want."

Or maybe you are feeling something entirely different. The question is: What is your starting point? All starting points are valid. This is a moment to be honest with yourself and candidly express what's happening to you and why you need a Life Re-Vision. You'll be surprised to know how many people are in a similar situation. Have faith; "the journey of a thousand miles begins with a single step," and this is the first step.

> **Reflect in Your Journal:**
> - *What is your starting point?*

Just Start!

Once we have challenged our limiting beliefs, adhere to new principles, and understand the necessary conditions for a Live Re-Vision, we can start. Once we get started, something will keep moving us forward. This is intuition. Our intuition will be a guide throughout this process. Upon accepting uncertainty, we open a channel so that our intuitions can speak to us.

Our intuitions tell us the truth, and we need to have the attention, the courage, and the persistence to listen to them. Intuition takes different forms for everyone. I'm going to tell you a story about intuition called "Vasalisa" from the book *Women Who Run with the Wolves*, by Clarissa Pinkola Estés.

In this story, the protagonist, Vasalisa, in a similar fashion to Cinderella, is bullied by her step–sisters, who send her to "fetch fire" from the house of a dangerous witch in the middle of the woods. Innocent Vasalisa does her best to pack up and immerse herself in the forest. Luckily, she was given a little doll to guide her, which does send her messages of where to turn and how to get to the house of the witch.

The witch promises to give her the fire in exchange for performing some tasks. However, if she fails in these tasks, the witch will keep her forever. Vasalisa doesn't have any other option but to accept the deal and get to work. The tasks are objectively impossible to accomplish: such as sorting grains of rice from a huge sack in one night.

Anybody would give up on such a task, but Vasalisa's doll (representing her intuition), along with, miraculously, a supernatural force, help her finish the task before dawn. The same thing keeps happening with all the rest of the successively more difficult tasks the witch puts before her. Finally, the witch gives in and provides her with the fire. The fire allows Vasalisa to open her eyes, and transforms her from innocent to wise.

I had a witch just like that; she lived inside of me. She kept ordering me to do unusual and apparently impossible tasks, and I diligently performed them. Something inside kept whispering to trust and finding the way to finish each task. Steven and I broke up on December 4, 2011. The first task was to document in a journal everything that happened every day. Those were roller–coaster days; I took it one day at a time. I didn't know whether to laugh or to cry or if I felt good or not; my only anchor was the present moment and to write down events that happened as they were.

Christmas and New Years came, and I didn't want to go anywhere. I stayed home alone for a week in order to carry out the second task: to reorganize my living space, to throw a bunch of stuff out, and start to create a nest for the new me in gestation. This emerging being needed to be nourished by my past. I saw that I had thirty–nine journals stored away, and I knew the third task would be to read every one of these, and even though the task seemed Herculean, I started in on it and eventually finished it.

We are ready for a Life Re-Vision when we are willing to listen to the voice of an internal witch (or wizard) that knows what to do, or to a little tiny voice of a doll that whispers where to go. We stop questioning and start following its guidance obediently, even though it may seem arbitrary. We know that something has to change and we are ready for whatever it takes, even if it doesn't have logic or meaning at first. But there's an intuition that guides us to explore and to keep going until the end.

Are you in touch with your intuition? One way to awaken intuition is through the use of visualization. The following is the visualization that describes the whole path we will undertake with guided imagery. The best way to work with this is to read it out loud and record yourself and then listen to it, allowing your imagination to take flight. It will give you another entry point to the Life Re-Vision journey you are about to undertake. If you're ready, let's get to work!

VISUALIZATION:

The Complete Path

Breathe, relax for a moment, and put your worries aside. Connect to your body and take three full breaths, exhaling with your mouth. Close your eyes. Now, imagine that you are traversing a desert, the desert of forgetfulness, of oblivion. At first glance, there's nothing in sight, just sand and sky. You feel the warm wind on your face, the light of the sun in your eyes, and the heat all over your body.

At first, you walk around without knowing where to go. There is a sensation of being lost. Suddenly, a guide appears in the distance to help you. You can call it your Inner Guide. This guide, at first, is a formless energy, but as it gets closer, it transforms into a being you can see and with whom you can interact. Imagine how your guide looks, their face, their features. Your guide has a sixth sense and an otherworldly knowledge of where you need to go.

Before starting your path together, your guide looks at you with love and gives you a blessing to start your journey. These are just the right words you need to hear to encourage and inspire you. To make this blessing more tangible, your guide gives you a gift. It is a symbolic expression of what you will need for this journey. Receive this gift and feel the gratitude of being connected to your guide.

Your guide will now take you to the right places in the desert: where your bones are buried. Your bones are parts of you, forgotten and scattered all over the landscape. Imagine that you have a big bag where you will put all the bones you will be collecting. When you get to one of these places, focus on the sensation of putting your hand in the sand, finding a bone and pulling it out so that you can store it in the bag. Repeat this many times, selecting your most meaningful bones. Keep on walking, following your guide, gathering more and more bones. Your guide will know when you have gathered them all. You take a moment to look at the sky and appreciate the beautiful sunset.

After a moment of contemplation, you walk toward your campsite and pull together what you need to start a fire. Night has fallen, and it's cooler now. You sit at the fire, accompanied by your guide. You take the bones out of the bag and lay them out in front of you. Your guide now asks you to assemble them together. You connect with an age–old wisdom, which helps you to assemble the bones together into a complete skeleton. It's a very specific skeleton, that of an animal (or combination of animals), which you slowly start to discover.

Upon seeing your completed skeleton, you know exactly what you have to do: sing. You sing from your soul, spurred on by the fire, surrounded by the night and her stars. In the middle of this song, you cry, and continue singing. You sing from the bottom of your soul. You let it all out. And in the middle of this cathar-sis, all of a sudden, you see that because of your song, you notice that there is still life in these bones. The bones are beginning to take on flesh and come to life right in front of you.

Amazed, you watch this rebirth happen. The animal comes to life, opens its eyes and looks at you. You look back. You both know that you are family. This is a part of you that you are reclaiming. It takes care of you, and you of it, and from now on you will not abandon each other. You are in contact with a wild being that wants to run free. This wild being is your Daemon. We're going to talk more about the Daemon later.

Before letting it go free, you see that it has embedded in its fur some very special seeds. You take these seeds and put them in a bowl. The seeds are of all types of sizes, colors, and textures. When there are no more seeds left, you let the Daemon run free in the desert, and it couldn't be happier.

Dawn is now breaking, and you watch your Daemon with great joy. You put the seeds in the sun to dry them out on a white fabric, and throughout the morning, you admire their colors and forms. You ask where they have come from and where these beautiful seeds are going. You feel nourished just by looking at them, and you are filled with energy. You see so much potential there; they are full of life.

Afternoon comes, and with it, a strong wind. This wind begins to lift your seeds up to the sky. You know that the seeds need to go on a journey. These seeds are not from the desert, and they need to find their right environment. The wind takes them up in the air and across different landscapes: mountains, oceans, *forests, and rivers. The seeds keep on traveling, driven on by not just one wind, but many winds, all over the planet.*

After a long trip, the winds start dying down. The seeds naturally start falling into territories. These are just the fertile territories for these seeds to germinate and flourish. It could be that not all seeds fall in the same territory. They do end up falling in adjacent territories, territories that share borders.

By your own means, you arrive at this confluence of territories, accompanied by your guide and Daemon. You are just in time to care for the seeds and provide them with the water and nutrients they need. Time speeds up. You see how the seeds planted there sprout and grow. They have found the right place to manifest all of their potential.

It's now time for the harvest, and in the whole landscape, there is an unprecedented abundance. You feel inspired to invite your family, your friends, and your whole community, in other words, your "tribe," to celebrate this abundance. Imagine that you choose a sacred site to have a great feast, the harvest. Your whole tribe comes from all over to celebrate this momentous event with you.

These people you love have come to celebrate your legacy. You're sharing all the fruits that you have grown in your life and now harvest to enjoy them with the world. They are tangible and intangible fruits: things you can see, like achievements, organizations, works of art, writings, and others you can't see, like values manifested, love, happiness, your own transformed being.

Imagine the scene of this celebration. Imagine that everybody there is happy with you honoring your legacy. Imagine how you have inspired others with your fruits and how they have made a necessary and meaningful contribution to the world. You have made a difference. You feel happy, fulfilled, grateful, and actualized.

Reflect in Your Journal:
- *What came up for you in this visualization?*

Welcome to your Life Re-Vision. This is where I hope this process takes you – to that same internal and external abundance.

2

Bones

The book *Women Who Run with the Wolves*, which I mentioned in the previous chapter, tells an ancestral story from the Mexican culture. In this story, we meet the Bone Woman, an old and wise wild woman whose job is to gather bones. The Bone Woman does this without stopping, without asking questions or hesitating. She's sure of what she is doing; she keeps looking for bones all over the desert, all over the region, until she has all the bones she needs.

Once she has gathered all the bones, she goes to a camp and lights a fire. She starts to organize, clean, and assemble the bones, putting them together in a structure. Once she has a complete skeleton, she sits in front of it, admires it and starts to sing. She sings from her soul, expressing all her emotions, everything that comes up in her heart upon seeing those bones. After a while, this skeleton starts to take on flesh, becomes an animal, comes to life, and starts to run downhill, celebrating its rebirth. This story inspired the beginning of the visualization you read in the last chapter.

What Are Bones?

At the beginning of your Life Re-Vision, it's possible that you are feeling lost or fragmented because of one or more circumstances in your life. If so, you may have a strong resolve to integrate yourself, to assemble your scattered pieces. This Bone Woman symbolizes the part of us that is looking to reunite us with ourselves, our integrating force.

Gathering bones is the metaphor for the first step of a Life Re-Vision. This step consists of finding, unearthing, organizing, and valuing your "bones," that is, your relics, sacred objects, artifacts, trophies, and other physical manifestations of your contributions to the world up until now. Bones are traces of your creations, your interests, your accomplishments, and your history. These relics are testimony of your creative potential. Gathering these bones is accomplished with the integrating force and the persistence of the Bone Woman.

Gathering bones isn't always an easy task, but it's worth it. Upon gathering them, you will recognize the richness of your life up to this present moment. It's easy to forget the multiple talents, experiences, and accomplishments that we've had since childhood. We are all creators. Gathering our bones shows us the creative works and contributions that we have manifested, sometimes without even acknowledging them.

This step is an important first step because, in the middle of confusion, boredom, depression, mourning, or other strong emotions, we need an anchor. Connecting with the physical and historical part of our existence—recognizing it and putting it in order—grounds us. This intuitive process is done alone and in silence. It's an introspective that connects us with our past through special artifacts. Contact with meaningful physical objects brings a certain peace and activates our imagination and memory, which is very useful for our Life Re-Vision.

The Bone Woman helps us find our bones, and gathering the bones connects us more closely with that integrating force, the Bone Woman. Heidegger says that external pressures are constantly scattering us, disorienting us, and distancing us from our values and our core. This philosopher says that external factors beyond our control are constantly "throwing" us into situations alien to our essence, pulling us in multiple directions away from our center.

This is where the Bone Woman comes in. An authentic life requires that we constantly work to re-integrate ourselves, consciously returning to the center. Therefore, activating the Bone Woman's integrating force is fundamental for this continuous Life Re-Vision journey. The exercise of gathering our bones is perfect for practicing this.

Examples of Bones

In our Life Re-Vision workshops, after explaining what bones are, we give people some time in silence so that they can remember and list their most important bones. Then, the participants share what they have found in a circle.

For Adriana, a business consultant, artist, and dancer at heart, these are her bones:

- drawings she made as a child stored in boxes at her parents' house
- presentations and projects from her school and college days on subjects she was passionate about
- costumes from folk dance shows in which she had participated
- her academic diplomas and letters of recommendation from beloved teachers
- publications and documents produced in her consulting jobs
- her general collection of music, especially folkloric dance music

Now, let's look at the bones of Raul, a professional pianist:

- photos and albums from different moments in his life
- programs from his piano concerts
- recordings of his concerts
- a collection of quotes he has been putting together in a notebook since he was young
- souvenirs from his trips that he has saved in boxes
- writings from his trips

Imagine that the bones of each of these people were put on display in a gallery in two different rooms to rediscover the identity of these people by means of these physical relics, or bones. What would these two exhibits look like? Visualize yourself going into both of these rooms. What impact would the displays have on you? How much would you be able to connect with the soul and creative potential of these two people? Revealing, isn't it?

As you connect with your bones, you will feel something similar: you will touch upon something essential in yourself. As you start to physically assemble the bones and see them in front of you, they will start to speak to you. Eventually, you will assign them a special and dignified place in your life and space. Oftentimes, we have cast our bones aside, inside boxes, basements, and storage spaces, and put them in places where we don't see them, may even forget them, so they collect dust and deteriorate. We are no longer aware of them.

Gathering your bones means having them in view, appreciating them, taking care of them, and displaying them for yourself and others. This can mean putting them on a shelf in your bedroom, the living room, or ordering them in a drawer that you open at special times. Decide where you wish to keep them; you will know the appropriate place.

Let's Talk about Bones

Recognizing and gathering your bones isn't always easy. For some people, starting this step brings up many emotions, and it's important to be in communication with others to process them so we can complete this task with dedication. In the Life Re-Vision workshops, we hold space to listen to each other and prepare each other for what is to come.

Mónica, a filmmaker and mother of two college age kids, started her reflection:

> "Gathering bones makes a lot of sense for me, and I've arrived at the perfect moment to do so. I'll tell you my story: Three

years ago, I went to live abroad, and I stored all of my belongings in a storage unit. I didn't even pack anything myself. Can you imagine the disconnection I had with my things? I paid a couple of men to come to my house and pack everything; I didn't want to have anything to do with it. I was very jaded at that time. I wanted to go far away and only take a little suitcase with me, leaving everything else behind.

"Those were three years of adventures in which so much happened. When I came back, having matured a lot, I was ready to confront my old life again. That which centered me the most and gave me the best re-connection with myself were those objects. They are few, because I have few possessions: my photos, my films, some furniture, my decorations...for example, a particular vase that I adore. Everything I own has value; these things hold memories of life for me. I started valuing those things again. I can testify that this anchor to the physical world can bring peace and clarity."

Lizette, an entrepreneur in the fashion and women's empowerment industries, added,

"I don't have many possessions because I have traveled a lot during my life. I'm always going, going, going. I had a storage space with all of my things, and I left them there for years. When I came back to Bogotá, I went to the storage space, and it was like life itself, full of memories. I found something very important: the death certificate of my brother who had died ten years earlier. Before, I just saw it as an ordinary document. But now that I have been going through this Life Re-Vision process, I can see that I want to preserve these relics, print out my photos. I felt the deep need to start to have a record of my life. If I die tomorrow, I'd like to leave a story. This is part of reconnecting with yourself and understanding that this all has to do with leaving a legacy with immense emotional value."

Angela, a political scientist who is passionate about women's and spiritual issues, commented:

"I also had a radical change in my life. A little while ago, I went to live as a hermit in the countryside. I made a decision to only live in the present and not to recall the past nor plan the future. I confess that the idea of gathering my bones seemed very difficult to me. But that's what Life Re-Vision invited us to do – to go back to the past. I can see that this is very important for me right now. Maybe I'm now ready to receive this invitation to relive, review, and heal some aspects of my life.

"I'll give you some examples: when I came to Bogotá from a very small town, I came for a scholarship. I was not a city girl; I was a small–town girl...Where I come from, we had a different concept of family, warmer and more caring, in contrast with what I had to live and deal with in the city. I moved all over the place, looking for the affection that I missed. I was a nomad. I went from one place to another, because that's your life in college when you don't have any family in the city. You have to pick up and move, they throw you out, they give notice in another place, one day you're out of money so you have to go and live with a friend. Because of this, it was always a case of "don't have too much stuff; if you have too much stuff, it's going to be hard to move the next time." I took very poor care of myself at that time. I can now see that my life was directed toward others, sometimes at the expense of myself.

"Throughout this whole journey, there are relics, I'm sure. Only now am I ready to look at them and gather them up. Before, I wasn't even looking at myself. Now I want to know where my bones are. Possibly in my mother's house in my hometown, I kept some things. I'm remembering at this moment that Dani, a friend, has an old box of mine, and I've just made a note that I have to go and pick it up so that I can do this exercise. There are many more of my things in my friend Berta's place, since I left to become a hermit. I'm here doing this exercise of asking myself: Where are my little relics? How can I recover them and reconstruct my life?"

Rocio, the mother of two children and an executive, commented (reflecting some resistance):

"My life revolved around my children; everything I kept is related to them. I didn't keep anything of mine."

Angela makes an invitation to Rocio:

"The idea is not to deny yourself or resist, but rather to notice that a part of who we are now came from before, and make the decision to start. To start, do this task with some deep breathing and an assertive intuition that guides us to find these relics. Rocio, use your maternal intuition to find your bones. I assure you that it will come to you like an epiphany. 'Ah! I kept that one thing over there! This picture represents the following...' Even if it's just a few things, I can tell you that those few things will have something to say about you."

Mónica identified in part with Rocio:

"As women, we blur ourselves out when we start a family. We become extensions of our spouses and children. When all of a sudden, life asks us 'Who are you?' and 'What do you like?' one doesn't even know which way to go. Constantly, many women sacrifice themselves fully for their families, giving them everything, including what they didn't get as children. Eventually one begins to feel like something is missing, like one wants to re-cover oneself. I've seen so many women in that situation."

There was a silence and, with her filmmaker's mind, Mónica added:

"With this exercise of finding our bones, I can see an image and it's like there was an earthquake. An earthquake or a tsunami passed through one's life, shuffling things around. Gathering the bones is like being an archeologist and going in, outfitted to gently dig, investigate, and analyze what's worth rescuing. And from all of these items that you manage to rescue, you can make a jigsaw puzzle. Suddenly, a mental and physical map emerges revealing to you where your essence is. It will surely be very therapeutic."

Lizette shared:

"This is aligned with the message of Pope Francisco. I'm not a mother, but I read a message he wrote a little while ago. It said that one has to love their children and their family very much, raise and teach them, but one can't let the family become the only purpose in life. It was really a warning to not lose yourself. Don't forget that you are also a woman or man before anything else and that you have talents and necessities, and if you don't acknowledge them, it will eventually cost you."

Rocio started to open up and commented:

"Listening to all of you, I realize that I do have my own bones. I remembered some writings of mine that I no longer have."

To contribute to the conversation, I added a piece of my personal history:

"It's valid to remember bones that we no longer physically have, that we have lost. I remember that I had written a book in 2003 on eco-neighborhoods based on my college thesis. It was an almost finished book that talked about various examples in Bogotá and in the world of ecological neighborhoods. It was a great book (in my opinion), but one of those tsunamis in life came, and now I can't find it. I lost it. Now, I'm writing another book. At least I know that the book existed, and this is evidence that something in me wants to create, wants to write."

Mónica must have picked up the melancholy in my last comment and added:

"It's likely that your loss motivated you to write this Life Re-Vision book, and later on many more books, because a loss like that causes you to mourn and conclude, 'I'm not going to sit around lamenting, I have to take up writing again.'"

"Exactly," I said. "I'm never going to abandon my creations again."

Angela got inspired and said: "Our divinity is expressed in our bones, with our creations. We are creators."

Lizette, excited, said:

"Yes, what you do or make has enormous power. This bag, [pointing to an accessory she was carrying] was made by me, it has my brand name, and when I put it on, I feel proud – as if it were something I bought in Paris in the best stores, because I made it myself, with the sweat of my brow and my two little hands."

Angela remembered something similar:

> "I found a piece of writing of mine from college days, from a literature class about *One Hundred Years of Solitude*, by Gabriel García Márquez. I started to read it, and it didn't have my name at the beginning, and so I thought it was from another student, whose paper I had graded as a teacher's assistant. When I finished reading it, I saw my name at the end, and read it over and over again and said to myself, 'I wrote that!' It was actually very good."

There is laughter all around, probably because we can all identify with being surprised by the greatness that lives inside of us, which we sometimes don't recognize.

Angela reinforced her point:

> "I was very surprised that I was able to write that. I had completely forgotten about it, and this demonstrates that we can easily abandon our creations and that we underestimate ourselves a lot. Especially as Latin Americans, we tend to compare ourselves and believe that others are better than us. We underestimate that which we create, as if there's always someone better, a better country. But we don't notice the potential that we have."

Mónica noticed something important:

> "What you said reminded me that one can't just gather things without reflecting on them. It's important to stop with every bone and see it as a treasure: read it, see it, reconstruct it, and rescue the hidden potentials that are still alive in you. If you were capable of writing that text, you can do it again now, just

like you with your book" she said looking at me and referring to my lost book about eco–neighborhoods.

I reinforced that idea:

"Exactly. This exercise reconnects us with our own potential. You can honor your bones even if you don't have them physically with you. Like your writings [referring to Rocio] that aren't here anymore, but you can invoke them with a symbol (like a new notebook), or some way that represents them. This will begin to signal something about yourself that you have left behind. When you have your bones in front of you, a force of life and creativity is activated."

Lizette pointed out an important theme regarding bones, which is that we sometimes don't appreciate them:

"This happens to me with my degree, I feel like it didn't do a damn thing for me. When I see it, I feel betrayed, and I say to myself: 'What was this piece of crap good for? Probably nothing.' I left university totally directionless, more lost than when I started."

Other participants from Life Re-Vision workshops expressed similar feelings of disdain toward bones from a part of their life they'd like to leave behind. This is a great opportunity to make peace with that stage of your life and rescue its value and its lessons.

In one of the workshops, a Spanish woman named Fatima, who wanted to leave behind her life as a law professor, was ready to discard many articles she had written. According to her, they "came from a place that wasn't authentic." She went on to realize that, even though she didn't want to keep writing about terrorism, that subject was connected with her Palestinian roots and her relationship with her father. She had learned a great deal through her writing.

I made a suggestion to Lizette before sending the group to the exercise where they listed their bones:

> "There's some work to do there, Lizette. The idea is to learn to value every bone for now, to find its contribution and gifts to your life. For example: the fact that you felt so lost could be the gift. Now that I know you a bit [I was her life coach for a time], I know that you now want to help women find themselves and their professional path. This motivation possibly came from that sense of being lost at that moment." She looked at me and nodded her head softly.

The recommended attitude for the bone–gathering exercise is to be appreciative. Look at each one of the bones and the combination of all of them with an appreciative lens, make them yours again, and listen to what this collection of objects reveals about your essence and potential.

Reflect in Your Journal:
- *How does the idea of gathering your bones make you feel?*
- *Who could help you process these emotions or sensations?*
- *Has there ever been a tsunami for you? What was it? (It could be your family, a heavy workload, moving, moving out of the country, a calamity of some sort, any situation that tore you into pieces.)*

After reflecting alone and making a list of bones, the people attending the Life Re-Vision workshops came back to share what they found.

Rocio, who was distant and resistant regarding her bones in the last section, opened up and generously shared:

> "I have photos that capture my special moments. I don't have them in physical form, they are stored digitally, and I'll have to look for them. At one time, many years ago, I had a collage in

my bedroom, with all kinds of pictures of my friends. At some point, I got emotional and threw them all out. Now I think it's important to value those types of things, since they were my experiences and that was how I gave them form."

I create training manuals for my work, but I've never kept a single one of them. I make them, I print them out, and I give them to the attendees of the trainings and don't save them for myself. That would be another important bone. I love wristbands and necklaces, and I've made some. I write my thoughts down in notebooks, and then I lose the notebooks. It would be great to gather them all together and keep them."

What Rocio is saying about notebooks disappearing is true. She left her notebook in the workshop room, and even though I called her to tell her to come and get it, she still hasn't come. The way we treat our bones shows us patterns in the way we relate to ourselves. The invitation to Rocio is to start giving more importance to her bones and to activate the integrating force that assembles and cares for them.

María Pía, an anthropologist that works for the government, shared in another workshop:

> "I went into shock and became very nervous with this exercise. I had to focus on breathing; I felt very sad and then I calmed down. I classified my list according to what's there, what was there, and no longer exists. The stuff that was lost: at one point I made lots of drawings, I painted a lot, wrote journals and poems. I wrote down my dreams, I woke up and had a notebook beside my bed, and recorded everything in it. Because of all the moving around, I didn't keep them. I didn't realize how valuable they were until now."

She paused, and some tears rolled down her cheeks. The group held her empathetically. Many of us have gone through the sensation of losing something valuable. The most appropriate thing to do is to feel the sadness. To give ourselves permission for the emotions to flow through us and run their course. As we do this, we might discover, liberate, and recognize something important within ourselves.

After a few moments, María Pía picked back up the thread of what she was saying:

> "What's left from all this? I have photos, letters, and postcards. The correspondence with others when one is far away or has someone far away is beautiful. And I have recipes! I love to cook; at one time, I had a little food business. I kept the recipe book, and I still love to make and share those dishes."

María Pía shows us what gathering your bones can be like. At first, she had a very strong reaction because of having lost so many of her physical bones. But after a few moments, she started to calm down. She realized something important: although some things can't be recovered physically, you can remember them, honor them, and change your current attitude toward your bones. At the end, as she talked about the recipes, one could see her eyes shining because she now valued and intended to care for her new creations.

The Life Re-Vision is a learning process that requires us to experience and value our strong emotional reactions without repressing them so we can be compassionate and patient with ourselves and, little by little, accept where we are. This implies forgiving ourselves and bringing understanding to those moments in our lives when we didn't take care of our bones.

Angela shared with us:

> "The men in my life have clearly marked the stages of where I am now. Each one has left gifts that say something about them: letters, poems, songs."

Angela paused and self-corrected. She realized she fell again into the habit of valuing others more than herself. Many of us define and value ourselves through our life partners, or our children. We wind up blurring ourselves out by means of pouring ourselves out over them. Sometimes it's hard for us to look at ourselves, and we avoid it by concentrating on others. Note that gathering bones is a personal and individual exercise; the bones are our creations, not those of others.

Angela began again:

> "Before that, there were drawings from school; I was very good. In college, I took several drawing classes, and I know that many of these drawings are still lying around somewhere. My mother could be the guardian of my bones, of who I was in school, and then in college. She's kept every little thing; I'm sure that she has a drawer full of all my diplomas, awards, report cards (because I was really a very good student in school).

> "In my meditations, I've tried to leave my ego behind and leave behind everything associated with my accomplishments. I forgot about all those examples of my skills. But now, I can see that my bones can help in providing some closure. To see a diploma or a medal for the half marathon is to notice that you've made it to the end of something. There's a symbolic interpretation of every object; I have interpreted it as my ego, versus allowing myself to see my achievements for what they are."

It's been hard work for Angela to acknowledge her own achievements. She had an automatic reaction of rejecting any possible feelings of pride, believing it's pretentious. She ignored our shared necessity as humans for recognition, achievement, and self-esteem. Angela had an opportunity to integrate this aspect of herself that she previously rejected automatically and to learn to embrace and celebrate her successes so she can find closure and take care of her sacred objects. Her mother had been playing this role for her, but now she is ready to own this responsibility for herself and become her own guardian.

Life Re-Vision considers that it is our personal responsibility to keep a material record of our achievements, talents, and gifts. Just by doing this, we start to understand the power of taking our rightful place as individual creators.

Juliana, a business consultant, also had some difficulty in gathering her bones:

> "I'm also conflicted because for a long time now, I've been focused on living in the here and now. I feel I have been neglecting the material world. I've been thinking about how my living space has changed. I went from having a house overflowing with things to a minimalist house. I gave everything away. I didn't value anything and now I ask myself, 'How did I just throw all that away?'

> "But finally, I realized that I did have all my files from college on my computer: all the assignments, presentations and projects. I also have many notebooks that I was about to throw out and decided not to, notebooks full of to–do lists. I have diaries, but I'm not that dedicated. I have *Harvard Business Review* magazines that I collect and no longer have room for at home."

Juliana reminded us that it's not a bad thing to do a deep cleaning where we live so as to live a life less burdened by stuff. However, it's recommended to practice discernment. Knowing what to throw away is key, and the distinction between what is a bone and what is clutter will prevent us from throwing away our treasures.

When Emiliano started the Life Re-Vision workshop, he was studying industrial engineering in college. This is what he said about his bones:

> "Unlike many others, I have tons of things, so I had to filter a lot. I have spent lots of time on music. I've made many playlists that represent me. They are designed for special mo-

ments with certain people, and show how important my relationships with others are.

"I've played rugby for many years now, since 2007. It's a sport
where one really has to prove oneself and 'win your uniform.'
One uses the team shirt in the matches, but it's not yours at
first, you have to earn it over time. There are injuries every
tournament – you get hit, you give your all – and at the end,
you end up with the shirt that's now rightly yours. The cup or
the medal won't ever be mine; many times they even wind up
lost. But the shirt is mine to keep. I have all my shirts in my
closet as important achievements.

"At some point in my life, I liked to paint. I have a folder
where I keep all my drawings, and I know I can never throw
them away. They are also part of my bones. As a little boy with
my brother, we were big fans of LEGO. We have an enormous
box full of legos that helped form my creativity. Those toys I
will never throw away. If I ever have children, I'd like them to
play with them. Since I've always lived in the same house with
my parents, I've never had to throw anything away."

We share a friendly laugh thinking about all the times the rest of us
have had to move. Those who have always lived in the same place and
have never felt the urgency to throw their bones out have the good
fortune of getting guidance about how to value their bones on time.

The majority of young people tend to value their bones. Very
young people have come to the workshops, sometimes people as young
as sixteen years old. They remind me of that innocent spirit and enthusiasm for their own creations. It seems that we lose that innocence
at some point in life, replacing it with a cynicism that our creations
aren't really worth anything: "it's all garbage." Gathering bones invites
us to recover an innocence that sees the beauty in simple treasures created by our own hands.

Ricardo, a technology and organizational change consultant, shared with us:

> "Like you, Emiliano, I keep the shirts of events from my Agile community. Agile is a management framework full of practical tools for projects. Those are like the shirts from sports teams. They're symbols that nobody can touch. I have a songbook of Cuban songs that I used in my college days all the time, and it's intact. I could take up the guitar again at any time. I have souvenirs from the trips I took over the past seven years – I didn't travel before that – including a whole lot of pictures. My dancing shoes! I grew up in Cali, and dancing was essential. I work in technology, but I don't have many tangible things from that. If you go to Homecenter (a big store in Colombia), you will see an electronic purchase system. I made that."

Ricardo stopped playing the guitar for a long time. However, something in him feels hopeful of taking it up again. Life has stages, and you can't always attend to every dimension of yourself at once. However, taking care of our bones helps us remember more easily what we have been passionate about. That way, when the time is ripe, we know how to re–ignite those passions.

Mónica, from her experience and life story as a filmmaker, shares her bones with us:

> "I realize that as time passes, you have more and more bones. You have to sort them, and this can be done by life chapters. Places, homes, schools, country homes, where one has lived, and which have a dramaturgical participation in one's life story; they represent different chapters of our life. Those settings are helpful for remembering. You can't 'keep' them, of course, but you can take pictures of them or paint them. Photos are key obviously, which I don't always properly store, but

with my sister and others from my family, I can reconstruct those memories. I have texts; all my life I've been a writer. What happens with many of us creative people is that we don't always value what we make. We keep throwing things away that later we wish we could recover. I still have some articles, essays, and scripts. I have documentaries and films that I have made. I also keep recipes (food generates so much family union); these are also bones for me."

Mónica reminded us again how hard we can be on ourselves. We are always evaluating our creations as if we were our own worst grade school teachers. Instead of having such a judgmental attitude, we should be like parents that receive gifts from their children and are thrilled. For example, a child's drawing of a cow that a mom put up on the fridge so she can see it every day. It's an attitude that values every creation and finds its rightful place to honor it.

Luis, my father, came to a Life Re-Vision workshop. Having spent many different chapters of his life in different professions, he listed his bones:

"I have many bones, but I will share the most meaningful ones with you. I went on a long trip at one point in my life and took many photos in Europe and Asia. They are in old photo slide format, which I have shown to my family and friends when I had the opportunity. I also shot many family videos that show our relationship and communication during those times. At some point, I'll have to convert them to a format that we can easily see again. The motorcycle has been very important in my life, since I was very young. I just started riding again. Also, I have my scuba gear. I loved going to an island and living off of what I fished. This reminds me of something I wanted to do again; I want to get connected again with that spirit of adventure.

"It's also important to mention all the bones related to the art gallery, the internet portal we put up and where we document all the exhibits and some works of art that I have been acquiring. One of them, which I keep in my office and makes me laugh, is an aquarium, and the interior of the aquarium is the Louvre Museum, and the fish swim through it. In the house, I have a painting with the text of "El Retrato," a famous song by Colombian composer Rafael Escalona, outlining the face of Cathy, my spouse. This was a very meaningful and important gift for the family. We also have a photo of a very good artist with his hands stretched out representing the Last Supper, hanging in our dining room. Lastly, another different kind of bone: I have planted many pine trees on our country property. I've thinned them out, and I hope that future generations will receive a beautiful forest."

Luis was very clear about his greatest passions at this moment, close to retirement, where he will have even more possibilities to incorporate them into his life in order to live the next stage in the fullest manner. Life Re-Vision gives us tools to reinvent ourselves at any moment by activating our integrating force and remembering that which we have been and what gave us so much connection to ourselves, our essence, and perhaps our soul.

Bones and Mourning

One participant called Mercedes expressed her reaction to the exercise of gathering her bones:

"I have to confess that gathering my bones creates fear and a feeling of rejection; I don't want to think about this. I have to find out why. [She goes silent for a few moments, which the group respects, and then continues.] Because of my mother's illness, we had to vacate her house and unearth her bones, which that was incredibly painful. I've lived through episodes of confronting physical objects that bring up painful memories and feelings. This exercise evokes something strong and not very gratifying; I don't want to have to do it."

It could be that you are feeling the same thing, and we will respect that emotion without forcing anything. However, let's reflect for a moment. What Mercedes shared with us brings up something important about the exercise of gathering bones. It has to do with confronting our own mortality and that of others around us. The bones remind us of the fragility of life and that we could lose it at any moment, leaving only a trace of our existence in our bones and that intangible something of our essence in other people's hearts.

Gathering your bones is preparation for passing on and helps to leave everything organized. It's recognizing that you could leave this planet at any moment – and a way to leave a physical legacy for the people that you love. There's great maturity in the solemn and humble act of gathering your bones. At first, it can be painful and difficult because we may not want to confront this harsh reality. But with time, we notice the value of this exercise: to rescue that which is valuable in our past, celebrate our physical memory, and feel the satisfaction of a life well–lived. This reminds us that life is a precious gift to be appreciated and lived fully in an awakened and purposeful state.

Reflect in Your Journal:

Close your eyes for a moment. Imagine you're not here anymore. Imagine that people close to you have cleaned your house and gathered up everything valuable that represents you.

- *What are these objects?*
- *What does it mean to you that these people are keeping these objects as memories of you?*
- *How is it for you to imagine your loved ones feeling joy, connection and closeness to your spirit by being in contact with these objects that were meaningful to you?*

Record in your journal everything that came to you from this reflection as it is also a valuable gift to recognize your gifts.

And there is grief. Life itself is full of joy and also pain. Gathering our bones has us confront all that we have left behind, perhaps without understanding who we were then or the impact it had on our future potential. If you feel strong fear or rejection toward this exercise, it's possible that there are episodes in your life that you have suppressed or not completely digested. In my experience, that which we deny and don't wish to see in ourselves or in our past, fragments us. Aspects within us that we have buried lie in secret, sucking the energy out of us and hiding our pure essence. They silently inhibit us, limiting the expression of the totality of our being.

I felt this as I was gathering my bones. When I came upon forgotten aspects of myself, I felt regret and remorse. The sensation of having lost the thread of my life overcame me. When I saw my writings, songs, and other bones, the message was overwhelming. I was confronted by a very strong sense of self–betrayal. How was it possible that I had left these parts of myself behind? I had to properly mourn this loss and forgive myself for decisions I had made.

Over time, I began to understand. It's very easy to neglect oneself and be lured by the external world at the expense of our true path. It's also easy to believe that our own undertakings "aren't really special." Our multiple insecurities and challenges can cause us to devalue our bones, bury them and leave them behind. This happens to almost everyone! You are not alone. I have seen countless people experience this feeling of regret. Acknowledging this is the first step toward forgiving ourselves and reclaiming our essence and purpose. Whatever path we have taken, we have many lessons to uncover. It is never too late to pause, reflect, center, and return home to ourselves, thereby reclaiming the capacity to make decisions that honor who we are and where we are on our journey.

With this exercise of gathering our bones, I invite you to be sensitive and aware of what mourning is yet to be done. Embrace yourself and allow yourself to become vulnerable to feel the pain of the past in order to process the grief and be available to support your ongoing rebirth. Grief could be stored and suddenly show up as deep sadness, anger, regret, disappointment, or even hate. The idea is neither to get stuck nor to act from that place – that would be very destructive. Rather, to allow these emotions to come out, like waves that come and go, to run their natural course until they are released, leaving us with acceptance and peace. Upon doing this inner work, internal aspects of us will be revitalized and resurrected. Seek professional help if you need to. Don't lose out on the richness and regeneration possible from this exercise.

Reflect in Your Journal:
- *Do you have any grief in your heart right now?*
- *How would you like to tend to it?*
- *What support do you need?*

What Is the Daemon?

Our bones can connect us to death, *and* they also definitely connect us to life. As we gather our bones, activating the integrating force of the Bone Woman and healing broken parts of our past, we connect with another very powerful internal force, the Daemon.

The Daemon is a mythological creature from the ancient Greek world that represents the guardian of your talents and potential. This part of you, your natural genius, knows the call of your destiny. This part of you is aware of unique gifts that were given to you; its role is to make sure that you express and manifest these gifts for the benefit of others.

After having gathered the scattered bones of your creations, the sum of these is your creative force, symbolized by your Daemon. Let's describe how the Daemon fits in the Life Re-Vision mythology. We are going to imagine that the skeleton you assembled in the initial visualization is your Daemon.

The Daemon is a wild part of you that ferociously protects your talents and has an appetite to move, create, and manifest itself in the most authentic way possible. The tranquility and silence of gathering your bones and starting to connect with forgotten parts of you gives the Daemon its opportunity to appear before you. No matter how much time has passed, it arises again, and here it is before you. Embrace your Daemon, a very important part of you: your creative force.

Your Daemon understands perfectly how valuable your bones are, and guards them. At the same time, the Daemon is the life force that, once freed, drives you to fulfill your mission and vision. (We will touch upon this later with more detail.)

I guide participants of the Life Re-Vision workshops to connect with their Daemon using a visualization.

VISUALIZATION

Connecting with Your Daemon

Close your eyes. Breathe deeply. We're going to invoke a being that's inside of us, the guardian of our talents. From the time we were children, it has pointed us toward what we like, what drives our instincts, and what makes us unique and passionate. It's very persistent and doesn't rest until our talents are developed and expressed. Imagine you're in a beautiful, natural place. It's a place where your Daemon likes to spend time. Now, imagine your Daemon – what does it look like? It is either an animal or combination of animals that feels and moves. This Daemon is the unique and wild expression of your being. It is the entity that guides moments of maximum vitality and spontaneity.

Let your Daemon present itself to you. Trust what comes. Don't censor anything. Open your perception to your uninhibited and pure nature. Observe its eyes, its appearance, its body. Connect with its energy. Let it know that you will be relying on its instincts and energy many times throughout this journey. Thank it for everything it has already shown you. Say goodbye now with a "see you later."

I always ask participants to draw their Daemon, to record what they see in the visualization. This is a key exercise to start connecting with our imagination. Then the participants talk about their experiences. One does not always see the Daemon in the first visualization. Some people, like Mónica, have already worked with their Daemon, so the image comes clearly:

"We have already worked on the Daemon with Ana. My Daemon is a huge creative force, a horse, a free and strong animal, vigorous, capable, that has the ability to run, as well as to fly. That's why it has wings. A story that my grandmother made up comes to mind. She told this story with all the drama in the world to her grandchildren. It was called 'the story of the horse of seven colors.' It's a horse with a magical mane, a mane that turns to wings, that turns into the sea, that turns into speed, wind, movement, strength, and color. The sun is always behind it, keeping it company. My Daemon is full of the magic of childhood and playfulness – something that I never want to lose."

As you make your first attempt to connect to your Daemon, you might not get the full picture but an important clue. Alexandra, one of the participants shared: "I didn't see a whole animal, but I did see its eyes, like those of a bird or a wolf. Blue and purple around them." The eyes she drew were very evocative, and the group pointed out that you could clearly see her inquisitive and determined nature in them.

Cathy got a clue about her Daemon that is a bit more abstract than the previous person's:

"I see a kind of energy like a hurricane. It's turning around and around, and it has many colors. When I was little, people couldn't follow my pace. There's was a lot of nonconformity. I was in love with revolutionary and leftist ideologies. I was the rebel of the family. Now I see that at the bottom of it all, there was a need to communicate with my mother, since because of her mental illness, we couldn't connect. This caused me to never connect with myself either. I've been in an eternal search for contact with my own center. I've dedicated my life to others as a result, and now I want to start to think about myself."

We can see that Cathy's Daemon is hiding behind a whirlwind. We don't see its face, but we can see its wake. Cathy says that the energy of her Daemon is so strong that sometimes she can't see clearly. At the same time, we can see that her energy has been generative as well; it has taken her to meaningful political, social, artistic, and personal inquiries.

For many people, the image of the Daemon doesn't always come immediately. But eventually, upon persistent exploration, an image starts appearing, as was the case with Fatima:

> "The first thing that appears is a book, but it turns into a butterfly. Then, in the center, in what would be the body of the butterfly, a leopard's face appears. There's a force that comes out when I'm centered. It's surrounded by nature; being in contact with nature is fundamental."

Fatima's Daemon combines the lightness and delicacy of the butterfly and the strength and passion of a leopard.

It's common that Daemons are the combination of two or more real or imaginary creatures, as Angela also shows:

> "I tried to evoke the wild woman within me in my imagination. It was difficult to give it form. My Daemon embodies feminine power, the spiral that takes you to the center, the wind that evokes movement, things transforming that aren't fixed but rather are in constant change. I painted a feline face with a deer's horns. The feet have roots that go in and out of the ground. It's a huge accomplishment to depict this image. I'm not sure what it all means, but it's a start."

Our Daemon is a mystery, and the process of discovering it can be exhilarating. With great clarity, Luis saw a bird:

> "My Daemon is an eagle that sees the world from above. It's engaged in a search for freedom and a wider perspective. It wants to develop a good relationship with the world. It takes the good from the world. I live my connection with the world through an eagle's eyes."

In his very clear image, we can see the maturity of someone who is in contact with his Daemon and has followed its instructions. One can feel it in the drawing of his eagle, full of harmony flying the skies.

It's important to understand that our Daemon is not a god. It's imperfect, idiosyncratic, and rebellious. It needs to be reined in and slowly trained by us. Sometimes people confuse it with the Inner Guide, and they consider it to be a wise one, a mentor or an elevated spirit. Those are other parts of our being; they are not the characteristics of the Daemon. Our Daemon is more primitive. It has raw strength connected with our primordial nature. It's wild; it cries and throws tantrums when we don't pay attention to it. But when we give it its place, it surprises us with its force and beauty, like an animal can when it's in its natural habitat.

It can be difficult for us to reconnect with our Daemon. The responsibility to own up to the energy, the idiosyncrasies and the gifts and talents protected by our Daemon is great. It requires catering to its special needs, learning new disciplines, and even going against the social norms that imprison our creative nature. This is why many people fear their Daemon as being the wild, uncontrollable part of who they are: they are afraid of not belonging or feeling rejection.

As a result, some people may quiet and suppress their Daemon instead of appreciating, nurturing, and guiding it with their spiritual connection. They may ignore their Daemon and choose what they believe to be a comfortable and socially acceptable path, which leaves a void in their souls and extinguishes their passion for life. But the cost of doing this can be very high. The Daemon is a creative force that, in unfavorable circumstances can become destructive, and in favorable environments, can serve as our genius. Lizette, a participant in one of the workshops, saw this very clearly:

> "When we manage to gather all the bones, everything we have created, we can then integrate and welcome our Daemon. To begin, take ownership of your bones and give them their proper place, their dignity. When you turn away and leave your bones

to the side, you are ignoring your Daemon, and it's like having a skeleton in the closet. It becomes a demon inside of you."

I responded to Lizette and the others:

"That's right: it's not a coincidence that the words 'Daemon' and 'demon' are so similar. A Daemon that's boxed in can turn into a demon, since you haven't given it a habitat in which to live, anything to eat, or given it any attention. As a consequence, it gets agitated and makes your life more difficult. This can cause physical illnesses, depression, panic, aggression, and dysfunctions at every level. This is repressed energy, not properly channeled. In some corner of your psyche, you know that you're not honoring essential parts of yourself, you're turning your back on them, and this sucks energy from you and also generates a lot of internal and external noise."

Connecting with your Daemon opens a new horizon for you once you are in contact with your wild and creative force. But the story doesn't always end like a fairy tale: "and they lived happily ever after." There needs to be a readjustment to open up space for this wild creature in your daily life, and so you can learn to channel this sometimes overflowing energy. You need to learn how to care for your Daemon: to feed it, nurture and discipline it, and give it what it needs so that it can manifest its potential.

My Bones

Gathering my bones has been one of the most gratifying and important things that I have done for myself. Like many other participants in the workshops, I've also traveled and lived like a nomad at points in my history. Many tsunamis have changed my inner and outer landscape in material ways. My default approach had been to accumulate things and then store them away. I had endless possessions packed in boxes, spread out among my mother's and father's houses and my own. I had to use my discernment to decide what to throw out and what to keep. I spent mornings, afternoons, and nights working straight through, digging through boxes, creating mountains of things to throw away, give away, or keep. In the course of this, my sacred objects started to emerge: artifacts and relics that really meant something to me and had the imprint of my Daemon.

Throughout all of this, my intuition was guiding me. Having my bones in front of me, an inner voice, similar to the little doll in the Vasalisa story – kept on telling me the next thing I needed to do, which often sounded absurd, but that slowly led to a greater inner and outer order. This voice told me things like "Open up this box," "Put these books in order," "Put them in the bookshelf," "Throw all of this out," "Number these diaries," and "Start reading them."

I found all types of bones. Since I was ten years old, I had been writing in journals, narrating events and feelings that I had since forgotten. Once I started my Life Re-Vision, these journals became a treasure to me. Taking ownership of my bones meant giving them a rightful place (instead of storing them in some dark closet), numbering them, and re–reading them. Because of this, I was able to remember many life experiences that I hadn't ever before integrated or put into perspective.

From the journals, which are bones themselves, other bones surfaced: my poems. I was surprised by how many poems I found. I didn't remember that I had written so much poetry. The poems were inside the journals and other notebooks.

Other scattered bones were my albums. My parents didn't make any picture albums of me when I was growing up. There aren't many records of my childhood. My parents getting divorced when I was two years old, moving to other countries, and the resulting emotional turbulence surely contributed to that. As an adult, I started to fill up this empty space. From the time I was nineteen, I started collecting memories to make scrapbooks and photo albums that told visual stories. Suddenly, when I was twenty-five, I suspended this activity, as if the celebration of my life had stopped. This left me full of questions about why this happened.

Other bones were songs that I had written since 1999. I had forgotten them and felt a little bit ashamed of them, since they expressed emotions that I was afraid to confront. Collecting those bones meant remembering those moments, feeling my emotions, assembling my songs in one place, and starting to practice them again, healing the painful events associated with the songs and opening a space up for them in my heart.

Finally, other bones I found were my personal notebooks, which I have had since I was little. These notebooks are like works of art since I consider myself a student of life. There are notes on subjects I discovered in my youth that I am passionate about, like the environment, personal and social evolution, and creativity. Many of these notebooks were stored in many different houses and in my own garage in boxes, gathering dust. Collecting these bones meant going to pick them all up, dusting them off, identifying the bones I wanted to keep, and giving away whatever I was willing to part with.

To be able to appreciate and reflect on my bones, I designated part of a room in my apartment as a gallery. When I sat in front of my bones, I saw many things. First, that I am very passionate about writing. I didn't write literature, but I did write reflections about life, my personal development, my trips, and learning experiences. Second, that poetry and music have been a constant throughout my life. I used them to connect to and express my emotions. Third, that I am passionate about social and environmental issues. I not only want to write about personal issues but also about social innovations and trends.

I saw my Daemon's face months later. It appeared for the first time while I was painting a stone I had found in a river. I had never painted a stone before. It was an unusual activity proposed by a participant of a workshop I was facilitating. It was weird to express myself on such a small "canvas." It took some time for me to get used to using the brush on such an unequal surface and decide how much color to use, how thick to make the lines, and what types of shapes were good for this medium.

It was a sunny day, and our group was chatting among each other as we were painting, talking about the film *The Hunger Games*.

"What a crazy society where one group oppresses another," Lauren said. "That game in which children and young people have to kill each other to survive is savage: just like animals!"

"That reminds me of the time Jesus lived in, when they put people in the Coliseum and others gathered to watch them being eaten by lions," Greg added.

"We have evolved as a species; we now have ways of stopping those abuses. But the animal part of being human hasn't gone anywhere," said Lauren. "We still have high rates of violence in many parts of the world."

I started to reflect on the fact that humans have inner animals, with their good and bad attributes. "If we knew how to channel the animal force we all have, it would be very different," I added, dreamily.

There was a moment of silence. I was concentrating on my painting. I painted and painted until I had no more ideas. Then I said out loud, "I don't like what I've seen up until now. I'm going to let the shape of the stone guide me." The others stayed focused on their own paintings. I felt the color blue calling me and the face of an animal started to define itself, similar to a dragon. It really captured my attention. I showed it to my companions and said, "This is my inner animal! The one I need to train, as suggested in the film *How to Train your Dragon!*"

I then understood that this blue dragon was my Daemon. It has the strength of an animal and the magic of a mythological being, with an exotic and unusual color, and it will need special attention. Confirming this by communicating with it in a meditation a few weeks later, my Daemon started speaking to me through creative impulses:

> "You need to organize your poems, songs, and writings immediately. The first thing is to make a book of your poems that you share with others at the event you are going to in two months. You have to complete your photo albums from your twenty-five year mark (2003) until the present, filling in the empty spaces of the jigsaw puzzle, mending holes in the quilt. Then you will start to practice your songs again and make a CD. Eventually you will write a book with all of the stories you have collected over the years. It's time to substantiate all that creative energy!"

Writing this book was one of the creative impulses from my Daemon. I went along with it, understanding that, like Vasalisa, it was important to follow those intuitive instructions without trying to question or rationalize them. Receiving those messages wasn't something that happened all of a sudden. It was a slow process that unfolded as I was patiently gathering my bones. I learned about my Daemon by reading books about an authentic life and understanding what was happening inside of me. I opened space for this new part of me to have its voice.

A book called *The Desire Map* by Danielle LaPorte helped me to understand a bit more about the Daemon. She writes about our basic desires. At a certain level, we all operate by seeking a certain feeling or sensation to fulfill a desire. This comes from a vital instinct, from our basic drive to live and flourish. I associate this primordial capacity for desire and moving toward our desires with the Daemon. It's not our spirit or our higher self, it's our wild instinct to create and procreate.

I discovered that the basic desires of my Daemon are vitality, expression, connection, and discovery. This is what my Daemon desires and toward which it is constantly moving. Finding these words helped me to understand my Daemon better and to start taking care of his primordial needs. It is by this process of getting to know my Daemon that

I have been able to reconnect with my creative force. I now invite you to do the same.

> **Reflect in Your Journal:**
> - *How would you describe your Daemon?*
> - *What are your Daemon's basic desires?*

How to Find Your Bones

At the time I was writing this chapter, I went to a museum of ancient civilizations, the Musée du Quai Branly in Paris. There was an ancestral culture in Africa that left a collection of dolls that women carried with them as a magical totem for getting pregnant. From this symbol, I could imagine the importance of life, fertility, and reproduction for the women in that society. They saw their power to gestate new life as a fundamental value. I instantly connected with something essential from that culture.

This is the power of bones: to reveal the Daemon of a person or even a whole society. I was able to see how that bunch of objects in a museum transmitted the creative force of different cultures. I had a fresh look at each object, appreciating the intention and values they represented.

I've always liked to visit people's houses. Their objects and decorations say a lot about their interests. It's particularly interesting when they exhibit their creations, photos, and other personal relics. These objects are a window to the Daemon.

If an archeologist were to come upon your "bones" in the future and put on an exhibit in a gallery to show people who you are, what would that reveal? Which objects would they choose to represent you? What would we learn about your Daemon? Start to think about these questions while we explore the subject of bones a bit deeper.

Let's make clear what bones are and are not. Bones are physical objects that demonstrate your unique contribution to the world. It's important to differentiate between our bones and our other stuff. Our stuff is objects without much significance that we sometimes get attached to. In contrast, a bone is charged with meaning to the point that it becomes a sacred object. Bones have significant emotional value and reveal something about your history, creative force, gifts, and potential.

For the majority of bones, you are the artist or author. For other bones, you are the curator of a collection of objects made by others. For example, in the list at the beginning of this chapter, Adriana is the artist who created her drawings and photos and the curator of the collection of her folk–dance costumes. Raul is the author of the recordings of his concerts and the curator of the quotes of the authors he likes.

At first, you might have difficulty or resistance listing your bones and then going to gather them. This is a new skill we are learning, and we will build the muscle over time. As you keep at it, you will feel a natural rhythm and joy more and more. We will examine the roadblocks so that we recognize them, and address as well as nurture the openings we discover. Bottom line: we will unlock and empower this stage of your Life Re-Vision.

It's possible that you are undervaluing your own bones. You may possibly say something like, "I don't have any bones of value or creativity, those are just a child's drawings that don't have any relevance," "Those photos aren't important," "That diploma isn't worth anything because I don't work in that field," or "Those writings are worthless." Don't listen to any of that! Stop the judgment and welcome the unfolding and recognition of who you were at a time in your life so you can see the past and thread it to the possibilities of your potential. Honor the history and gather your bones to see what is here and what you can learn from that.

You may say, "I have a very bad memory," and feel a block, and absolutely nothing comes to you. Let that be. Don't try too hard; ideas will start to come. With the examples we have below, some light bulbs may be turned on. Don't judge yourself if it takes some time to remember them; respect your own rhythm in this process. You can also ask your loved ones to help you remember what your bones are and where they might be found.

It's possible that you feel significant resistance when looking back on your past. As we have mentioned above, some current thinking may focus only on the present and disqualify the past as something already complete and unimportant to your development and even ask that you disregard the past, which you cannot change; however, the past has formed who you are and may have valuable hints about who you are becoming. There are pains and also gifts. The pain of the past needs to be released and burdens unleashed so we can see the treasures and gems in our bones, pointing to our creative potential.

If there are painful things in your past, this process will help you identify the essential things you need to heal and give you the strength to keep moving forward. If you feel a strong resistance to go there, it's probably because there is something you still need to process to find a deeper peace and plan for the future more freely.

It's possible that your bones are physically scattered all over the place and you will have to work to bring them all together. In my case, I had boxes with important relics in them – like my notebook from grade school with the first songs I learned – in my parents' houses. There were things in boxes buried in my basement, like my journals. Find the resolve to gather these bones and take ownership of them.

It's possible that it won't be easy to discern what your bones are among the multitude of your possessions. Trust that bones have a "sacred object" quality that makes them stand out. They are objects that represent you, that carry your energy. Only you can tell what your scattered, sacred bones are. They help you remember something fundamental about yourself. In order to distinguish them, we need to use an internal thermometer that qualifies our connection with that object.

Part of the process of gathering your bones could involve a deep cleaning of your spaces. You might realize that you have accumulated a lot of "trash," which makes it difficult to focus on what's most important. Strive for simplicity, but be careful of impulsive urges of "throwing it all away." Follow your instinct on this. Keep in mind that it's very freeing to get rid of things that aren't essential; however, some people have thrown things out and later regretted it. Use your discernment here.

You could have many bones or few. There are no rules here. Some have very few bones, which isn't necessarily a problem. But if you see that you have less than six types of bones, ask people close to you what they might include in your bone collection. It's possible that you are not fully aware of your own physical legacy and need others to support you in seeing yourself more clearly.

It's possible that you have very few bones in part because you have lost everything, thrown everything out, or due to an external disaster like an earthquake, fire, or theft. There are internal and external phenomena that can destroy our physical relics. As I have already said, this happened with a book of mine that I had started (I had written 100 pages!) several years ago but never finished. I would have liked to finish that book, but I can't find it. It's gone, and I am pretty sure I will never be able to recover it.

Confronting this can stir up some grief and a moment of acceptance and detachment may be required. You could do a ritual, make an altar or other tribute of some sort for these lost bones. At any rate, the traces of these bones still live in you, and your awareness of their past existence can still provide information about your own creative potential. The most important thing is that, from now on, you will be more caring with your bones and give them their rightful place.

Reflect in Your Journal:
- *What do you feel when you think about gathering your bones?*
- *Are there any obstacles you need to address? How can you address them?*

Declaring Your Bones

I invite you to be resourceful when identifying your bones and making them visible. If you are studious, rescue your diplomas. If you are a politician, collect your speeches. If you are a policy maker, list your policies. If you are a storyteller, list your stories. If you are a concert performer, recover your recordings, pictures, and mementos of your concerts. If you are a chef, document your recipes. If you are an academic or a consultant, record your works.

> **Reflect in Your Journal:**
> - *What are your bones?*
> - *Where are they located?*
>
> *Make a list of at least six types of bones you found in your exploration. There could be more; use your journal to make a complete list of all.*

The next step after listing is to start looking for them and gathering them together. Try to reserve a space in your home for displaying your bones. Take in the visual impact of having them all together in the same place for some time.

Most people feel empowered when they do this. Through these objects, we can start to see our own identity and interests. They show us our passage through the world and what we valued at various stages of our lives. We are made aware of our great creative or co–creative abilities. Often, this visual proof of our bones invites us to appreciate our life up until this moment and gives us hope for what's to come.

If you see that you have too many bones and feel a bit overwhelmed, allow yourself to feel that way. This is telling you something. Could this be the moment to let some of these bones go? Maybe your connection with these bones isn't as strong as it was before. Could it be that this is showing you your life needs to take a new direction? Listen carefully. If you see that you have very few bones, how does that make you feel? Could it be an invitation to start materializing and creating?

When you connect with some bones of your past, you might feel nostalgia, sadness, or even deep mourning. Let yourself feel those emotions. This is part of the work. Opening up to these emotions allows you to notice what was and is important for you. Sadness is a sign of something meaningful that has been lost. Your Life Re-Vision will take you closer to these forgotten parts of yourself.

Reflect in Your Journal:
- *What do you feel when you see your bones?*
- *What are you connected with as you realize what you have created?*

Now, try to draw your most important bones in your journal. Make six squares in two rows of three. Paint a group of bones in each one of the first six squares. Don't try to make them perfect, just do them in your own way. Let your hand be loose; let it guide you.

Great, now, look at them again. We're going to go into a sacred ritual space. Open your heart and allow what comes next. Give yourself the time and space necessary so that this magic can occur. How do you wish to celebrate this step of meeting your bones? What is this special moment asking of you?

You can stay in silence for a moment with your bones, appreciating them and permitting the soul behind each one of them to come forward for you to feel, sense, value, and experience. Create a ceremony if you like, light a candle or some incense and sing, or play your favorite music. Being in this receptive state might reveal the image of your Daemon. Paint it on a separate page with as much space as you need.

Let the strength and energy of your Daemon fill your whole being. Connect with the wild and uninhibited part of you. Listen to your deepest desires. What are these desires and longings?

When you have connected with your Daemon and its desires, you can ask it: Now what do I do with these bones? Let your Daemon speak. It will tell you in your ear what you need to do. Finish and publish the book? Frame the diploma? Cook and share your recipes? Frame and exhibit those photos? You don't have to decide right now. Also, learn to listen directly to the bones themselves. The first thing is to recognize them and give them a special place in your heart and home. The next steps will be revealed at their proper time. Promise yourself that when the bones tell you what must be done, you will listen and obey. That's where the part of Vasalisa's story comes in, when she has to obey the witch and do the seemingly irrational tasks put before her. Don't resist.

> **Reflect in your Journal:**
> - *What message does the Daemon have for you regarding your bones?*
> - *What does your Daemon tell me to do with your bones?*

Giving Life to your Bones

Gathering, appreciating, and listening to our bones offers us a set of learning experiences. Receiving this learning is one way of giving life to your bones. Every step of this Live Re-Vision is an opportunity to deepen your self–understanding. What relationship do you have with your past? What is your relationship with the physical realm? How connected are you to your integrating force (one of your inner guides represented by the Bone Woman)? How connected are you with your creative force (represented by the Daemon)? It's time to harvest these learning experiences and nourish ourselves to keep walking through this process.

Some people feel joy when they rediscover themselves and their forgotten but meaningful past; it's like they have new blood running through their veins. Take Roberta, a lady who, in one of the Life Re-Vision workshops, recalled some revolutionary pamphlets that she wrote in school, criticizing her education saying that it had "turned into a simple banking transaction." In her college run by nuns, Mother Superior put her on probation but did not expel her due to her intelligence. She told us the story with lots of joy and discovered she still has a revolution inside of her that she wants to revitalize.

Others wind up feeling prouder of themselves because of this exercise. For example, Lucia noticed that one of her bones is her doll collection. When she speaks about her dolls, she describes how each one represents a feminine archetype (like Aphrodite, the sensual woman, or Athena, the warrior woman) and how having her dolls in a visible place invites her to feel proud about different aspects of her woman-hood.

Some people find out about their unique ways of processing life events. Catalina said in one of the workshops, "When I go through something painful, I dedicate myself to writing. I've written stories, plays, and other texts, and they help me to learn and accept what happened." Catalina also likes to send messages to herself about learning experiences she's had in her relationships and has a collection of these words of wisdom.

Other people uncover forgotten passions that open up new questions. When remembering her collection of recipes, Roberta asked: "What could I do with this passion of mine? How could I combine it with my line of work, psychology?" It wasn't necessary to answer this question right then – the process eventually took her to an answer – but the question came up through connecting to her bones.

Alejandro realized that he was at war with his past and had thrown everything away. Presently, it will be difficult for him to recover all of his bones; however, he noticed that he could still recover some objects that were representative of his bones and indicated his creative potential. In this way, he could make peace with his past. With this new attitude toward his past, he saw new ways of valuing himself and integrating what he's doing now with the various ways he expressed himself in the past.

We can also learn from our life cycles. Situations may have interrupted our creative pursuits. For example, I noticed that I stopped making photo albums when I was twenty-five years old, the same time I went to get a master's degree. It's as if at that moment, my Daemon had become frozen. Upon reflection, I discovered that was a stage of my life where I forgot who I truly was and turned my attention to society's expectations.

When I realized this, my Daemon spoke clearly to me: "You need to finish those albums." I followed its instructions. I also count this as a learning experience; I learned that I'm susceptible to external pressures, which can make me forget my creative projects and my passionate pursuits.

A few days ago, I was feeling anxious about the possibility of a large and very prestigious project that could have stopped me from finishing this book. The self-knowledge I gained from the importance of gathering my bones and honoring them helped me center myself and understand that I could not allow anything in the world to interfere with finishing this book. Finally, the project was much less intense than I thought, and I felt at peace respecting my own creations.

Like many people, I didn't value my bones enough; I didn't give them an important place in my house or in my life. It made an impression on me that, since I started gathering my bones and giving them their rightful place, many aspects of my life started to find order. It was amazing how I was able to clean up my physical space, and since then I've been able to keep the same order, prioritizing my creations and letting everything else go. For example, I bought some shelves to hold my journals and photo albums, and while I was doing that, I threw away and gave away papers and books that I no longer needed. Upon organizing my songs in a folder, I threw away sheet music and papers from my music lessons that I no longer use. Upon finding and filing my diplomas from various courses I have taken, I seized the opportunity to organize my file cabinet and recycle many documents that were obsolete.

In any case, I learned that I'm still prone to devalue my bones and leave them buried. Now that I make yearly photo albums, I find that sometimes I haven't included important bones from the year. It's like a little self-sabotage I do unconsciously, neglecting my own creations. This learning experience has made me more aware of this tendency and I know that I have to pay special attention to my bones every year so that I can recognize them, document them, and give them their place in my memory.

Now, ask yourself: What have you learned from gathering your bones? How important has it been to make a record of your history? In what moments are there records, and not? What happened? How attentive have you been to giving your bones a special place? When did you stop shooting photos, drawing, inventing recipes, dancing, or any other activity important for you? What kind of relationship do you have with your past? What do you need to throw out and let go of? What other learning experiences did you have from this process?

Reflect in Your Journal:
- *What did you learn about yourself from gathering your bones?*
- *How would you describe your relationship with your past?*

Completion List

In a personal development workshop called "The Landmark Forum," I learned the concept of "completion." Completion, as I remember it, means that something has been processed, worked on, and has been completed. There are no more loose ends. This applies to physical tasks, conversations, relationships, and life events.

As we reach back to our past, unfinished business can come up and may require an effort on our part to bring it to completion. As I mentioned, my photo albums were incomplete; there was a big empty space, and I saw that those bones were important to me. If the photo albums weren't bones, there would be nothing to complete.

Your Daemon's instructions are essential as you create your completion list, so you don't feel overwhelmed. Your Daemon will always prioritize what makes you feel most alive. It's not about leaving everything in your past in perfect order but rather tackling the most relevant tasks and bringing them to a satisfying closure. We will continue to make our completion lists in the next part of Life Re-Vision – seeds – that also refers to the past. The idea is to be at peace, as much as possible, with your past.

In your journal, I invite you to make a list of works, conversations, relationships, or anything else that may need completion so that it can bring you more peace.

Closing of Bones

I suggest that you use these recommended practices to root your learning experiences of this chapter. Go for a meditative walk to integrate what you have received from this stage and what is still pending on your Completion List. Draw your Daemon and write the messages that you received from it when you started gathering your bones. Give yourself a moment of silence to thank yourself for having done this important work. Find a space to share your bones with people in your community. If you are inspired, curate an exhibit of your bones and invite people to visit them and converse with you on what they experience and how they see new sides of you. If one or more of your bones prove to be unrecoverable or there is an aspect of your life that awakens and causes you pain, do a ritual to honor it, create a symbolic way to complete an aspect of your life. These are all ways of symbolically and elegantly closing the subject of bones.

In this chapter, we met the Inner Guide, the Bone Woman, and the Daemon. We have listed our bones, visualized our Daemon, seen the relationship between the bones and the Daemon, identified the root desires of our Daemon, listened to its instructions on what to do with our bones, and finally, harvested the learnings from gathering the bones, including starting on our Completion List.

I congratulate you for having taken the first step on your Life Re-Vision!

Declaration for Closing Bones

When you are ready, declare the following:

I'm now in contact with my Inner Guide, my integrating force, the Bone Woman, and my creative force, the Daemon. I listen to their messages, and I diligently take care of them. I commit to constantly honoring my creative assets, gathering and dignifying my bones, and taking care of my Daemon.

Reflect in Your Journal:

- *Upon connecting with my bones, I find that my legacy/contribution up until now has been centered on...*

3

Seeds

I remember having many of my bones in front of me, including my journals, and feeling overwhelmed thinking about my Daemon's order to "read all of them, as soon as possible!" My living room had been invaded by the thirty-nine journals and by other bones such as photo albums, the most important school notebooks from my childhood, and other relics that were crying out to be placed somewhere visible and important in my home. Anyone who would have come into my apartment during those days would have seen a physical manifestation of my inner state: *chaorder* (the combination of chaos and order). Upon seeing the mountains of journals, photo albums, notebooks, and sheet music, I could see my fertile confusion, and inside, faith that everything was going to be made clear.

With courage, I confronted this conglomeration of objects to let them speak to me. In the middle of all of this, I connected with a childhood notebook – a bone that I had never wanted to throw away – from a Spanish class taught by an unforgettable teacher, Bertha. As I could see on the first page, it was from the year 1989; I was ten years old at the time. I was studying in the French Lycée of Bogotá, and this was one of the few classes taught in my mother tongue. Bertha designed this class to teach us about our own culture through traditional Colombian music.

I opened the notebook and saw the lyrics and my drawings illustrating every song. I remembered the magic of those classes; with every song that Bertha Olga taught us, she told us the history of the composer and talked in a very colorful way about the era when the song was written. We discussed the song's lyrics, relating them to history and culture. She had us draw what we were imagining. Then, she took out her guitar and had us sing the song over and over again until we had all learned to sing together by heart.

These moments were sacred and are engraved in my heart forever. During those lessons, worries were forgotten, differences with my classmates disappeared, and we were one singing together – connected through our voices. I felt as if I was flying, happy, light, and powerful – singing with all my strength. As I sang, I let out a whole chest full of emotions restrained by the formal Cartesian education I was getting. My Daemon was free, singing and dancing. I felt acknowledged for my voice and intonation, and my singing opened the gates to express my repressed energy in those times of hierarchical education and strict discipline.

I remembered my uninhibited passion, my memorizing the words and recording myself singing the songs. I even taught my childhood best friend, Thalia, the songs on the school bus. She was patient with me; I didn't leave her alone until we could both sing the song from beginning to end! Years later, upon remembering those times, Thalia told me, "With crazy people, I just follow along," as we both burst out in laughter.

My eyes watered.

Reading this little notebook, I connected with something essential in me. It's not every day that I recall such important memories as that one, which showed me who I am and what sparks my passion. Clearly I love music; it moves me that a song can depict a person's feelings and, at the same time, evoke an era. I am motivated to connect with artistic creation (and creation in general), and to understand its psychological and cultural background. Also, when I find something I like, I'm an obsessive student. I immerse myself completely, and then I teach others so that I can share the bliss of what I've learned. I'm a ferocious learner and also love to teach. I could see what makes my Daemon come alive and express all its splendor. I made a note of that.

What Are Seeds?

The second step on a Life Re-Vision are seeds, or essential stories. These are stories in which a signature trait of our Daemon is expressed, where we discovered something new about ourselves, overcame something, learned something, or made an important decision. These stories mark the origin of a fundamental aspect of our lives; that is why they are called seeds. I knew that seeds had to be the second step in a Life Re-vision once I got more involved with my bones and started reviewing my past. Certain memories came up that helped me see parts of myself that are still alive, but perhaps buried. These newfound parts illuminated and oriented me. I was not so lost anymore. These stories highlighted traces of my being, my Daemon, and my virtues. In short, I saw myself, and because I saw myself, I fell in love with myself again.

A Life Re-Vision needs to be grounded in self-appreciation. This is the fertile soil in which we can sow new possibilities. When we reconnect with our essential stories, or seeds, we start to remember valuable and neglected aspects of our beings that, for many reasons, we have forgotten.

Just like with the Babemba tribe I mentioned in the last chapter, our stories help us remember who we are. We realize how our character and our values took shape to make us who we are today. Because of this encounter with our seeds, our self-love will shine more brightly, along with an appreciation of our essential qualities. Seeing many seeds together, we can see the relevance of many situations, the purpose of certain decisions, and the connection in between occurrences that we had not previously seen. This provides a deeper meaning in our lives and helps us to take back the thread of our own stories again.

Reframing Our Seeds

It's possible that exploring our seeds can bring back painful memories. However, in doing this exercise, we start to turn the most emotionally charged events in our lives into seeds (essential stories). This happens because these difficult situations left us with valuable lessons that marked our lives. The work we can do is that of "connecting events" and "editing our life stories," as defined by Chistina Baldwin, writer and facilitator of personal writing workshops. Baldwin says that "linking" is what actually makes the story – bringing to light certain memories and connecting them together – and "editing stories" is the constant process of updating "who we think we are and how we speak about our histories and ourselves."[1]

These painful events could be in the past or in the present. In my case, the exploration took me to the past to a difficult incident I lived in middle school. Remembering and sharing it helped me link events and edit the way in which I tell them to myself and to others, and I began to see the event as one of the essential stories of my life (a seed).

The story happened in Boston, Massachusetts, in the United States. I was living with my mother, who was working on her doctorate degree, and Paola, an exchange student who was living with us. Paola was working on her English and became an indispensable companion, like a sister to me, in a year marked by difficulties. I will now narrate the critical point in this story:

> I was thirteen years old. The public school Paola and I attended was very diverse with students from various backgrounds. As an inner-city public school in the US, one could say it had social complexities that I was not accustomed to. It was not easy for me to navigate that environment. Despite being able to speak the language, I was unable to establish connections with many of my fellow students.
>
> For some reason I didn't understand, I started to become the victim of bullying by some of my classmates. They made fun of

me day after day and pulled pranks with my belongings. For example, if I left my hair-tie out on my desk, it would suddenly reappear soaking wet.

This situation reached a boiling point the day I couldn't find my backpack. After looking all over for it, I found it hidden in a closet. It was recess and everybody else was out of the room. I was alone. I had identified two suspicious people, possibly responsible for these acts. I judged Malden, an African-American teenager with a stocky appearance as the worst offender. Full of hate, I completely wet his jacket despite it being the middle of a Boston winter. But the most brutal act of all was when I took everything out of his backpack and threw it all around the floor and, like a human shredder, ripped up his papers and destroyed his textbooks and notebooks. It was an arduous task because he had a lot of stuff. An explosive rage carried me all the way through to the end of the task.

I wound up feeling tired and liberated at the same time. As I sat on a staircase by myself to get my breath back, my mind was blank. Several minutes later, the class returned from recess, and I heard them talking about the mess all over the floor. Like a wild animal, I went back into the classroom, looked for Malden, and punched him in front of all the students and teachers. I punched him as hard as I could, activating memories from action films. That was the finishing touch to my implicit message of "Don't mess with me, motherfuckers!"

That behavior could have been worthy of expulsion in many contexts. But since this was a public school, they couldn't kick me out. Instead, they called my parents, my mother (a feminist with a strong character like mine) said, "Don't worry, Ana, that moron was asking for it." Malden's parents didn't show up. Since the teachers had no idea what to do, they just let me go. It wasn't surprising because the teachers, although generally nice people, were lacking in tools; the education was generally very poor.

My retaliation took care of the bullying. Nobody bothered me again the rest of the time I attended that school. I was treated with a certain deference. Not surprisingly, it wasn't the best year of my social life. Fortunately, my friend Paola stayed with me through this crisis; at least I had one friend to be with during lunch and recess.

The story I told initially ended here, on a sour note, showing how far my aggression could go, celebrating my vengeance and "an eye for an eye" culture. But, when I did my Life Re-Vision, I gave myself an opportunity to reflect and edit my story. I was then able to draft a new and more meaningful ending, connecting it to the next major event.

At the end of the school year, there was a graduation as we finished middle school. I remember that in the middle of the ceremony, I felt relieved to be leaving such a hostile environment. I clearly didn't have the tools to handle it. That day, at fourteen years of age, I communicated to my mother the first big decision of my life. "Mom, I don't want to keep going to public school here. I'm going to live with my dad and his family in Colombia."

"Why?" my mother asked, disconcerted.

"I don't like what I'm turning into to survive here. Hitting people isn't right. Violence isn't the solution. I also don't like being in a school with such low academic standards. I want to be challenged. On top of all this, my stepmother just had a baby, my little sister Sophie, in addition to my brother, Julián. I want to experience family life with siblings, which is something I haven't had."

At that moment, I saw the sadness in my mother's eyes. Being separated from her only daughter was devastating. I can imagine how divided she must have been at that moment, wanting to give me freedom but afraid to let me go. I know she must have thought, "I'm her mother and I'm the one who makes decisions for her until she turns eighteen." However, from a place of great trust and generosity, she decided to support my decision.

When I tell this story, I start to cry. I experienced the pain of that time again, of being bullied, of punching somebody, of feeling totally socially isolated and deciding to leave my mother in the last years of my adolescence.

I also feel the pain that my mom must have suffered at that moment and throughout my teenage years when we were so far apart. But at the same time, I felt proud. I recognized that going back to Colombia was the best decision I could have made. I returned to an environment that was more appropriate for me at that time, in my own country, with a family and a school that provided more emotional stability.

This event had been buried in my memory, covered with layers of shame and pain. When I dusted it off, I realized that what I had done made sense. Defending myself, even if not in the best way, allowed me to be empowered and demand respect. I started to understand that our cultures punish women severely if they express their rage. When anger is repressed, many women get stuck and become depressed. Breaking free of the bullying was a very important step for my development, and it was empowering to declare myself deserving of respect.

That force that defended my dignity is part of my Daemon. My Daemon has very little tolerance for situations where there is no respect or justice. It's impossible for it to stay silent. At those moments, my fear disappears and a volcano explodes so I can correct a dysfunctional situation. I began valuing that aspect of myself. Being able to defend myself has been useful in numerous ways, including getting out of undesirable situations, exiting disempowering situations, and letting go of an abusive relationship.

However, this unchecked Daemon can do a lot of damage. I saw that I had to do something about my strong character. This event, with its new ending, was the beginning of my great sense of responsibility. Starting to make such important decisions at such an early age – like going to live with my dad in a different country than my mom – gave me the ability to take up the reins of my life.

This is something that continuously comforts me, knowing that it's in my hands to make my own decisions and orient these decisions toward greater peace and possibilities. My good friend Silvana said to me one day, "It seems like you have an illuminated inner compass that guides you." Having lived through such a difficult situation, one either continues in the spiral of violence, or their inner compass awakens to create better alternatives.

Writing this story revealed several things. Besides seeing the power, we have to reframe our events; I realized that these essential stories never end. They keep sprouting and branching out endlessly toward new futures since they are charged with the DNA of our essence. This is why these stories are like seeds, since they have an infinite potential and can keep germinating. The effects of these important events in our lives that were sowed in the past keep expressing themselves in the present.

Looking back at my life, I can see that I incorporated the lessons from that story in many ways. After the bullying I experienced in school and my violent reaction, I became conscious of my strength and courage to stand up against disrespect. At the same time, I recognized my commitment to dialogue and worked toward peaceful resolution of conflicts. This commitment is continuously present in my life, in particular when my Daemon wants to explode and destroy.

Alongside my commitment to dialogue and peaceful resolution, building communities became a pillar for me. I learned to co-create with others and acquired skills in nonviolent communication. Another pillar, my personal development, has enhanced my capacity to build harmonious relationships and manage my reactions. Years later, I became a professional life coach and made the vow to constantly observe myself and act from my wise self. Working on my emotions and being present instead of just reacting is now my daily bread.

Having been a witness to war in Colombia – and the amount of "recycled violence and hate" as Father Leonel Narváez says (whom I will speak about more later), and the resulting cycles of revenge – I can see things with more understanding. I know what it feels like to be the victim of an insult, having rage boil over, and exploding with a vengeance ten times worse than the initial offense, which can generate an endless spiral of violence. But I know that doesn't resolve anything. I'm a firm believer in forgiveness and dialogue as a way of resolving conflict. I have faith in our ability to heal deep wounds. This requires a personal commitment to work on one's inner self, let go of anger and resentment, and cultivate inner peace, which is essential for a fulfilling life.

My Seeds

The stories in one human life are infinite, but I believe that the essential stories – our seeds – are not. Sometimes we tell funny stories about things that happen to us in our daily lives and laugh about it, and that's it. Or we tell stories about difficult situations and feel heartbroken about it at the time, but once we resolve the situation, we forget about the subject. On the other hand, certain stories resonate with us more than others because they have a special force and meaning. Our eyes start to shine when we remember them. We may start to cry or our heart skips a beat because of the poignancy and emotional connection to our souls and what we value in our essence. Others can see who we really are when we tell these stories. Furthermore, they unite us and create community; they bring us closer to each other through our humanity and soulfulness.

Looking for my seeds evoked the practice of the Babemba, the African aboriginal people who tell a person meaningful stories of their life when they lose their way. Although I didn't have a tribe telling me my stories, I was doing the same work for myself. Every story contributed to integrating my scattered inner fragments so that I could start to see myself as a valuable and worthy human being.

I yearned for my community or "tribe" to be able to tell me these stories one day. But first, I had to remember them myself and recognize them as seeds. I started getting more and more motivated to remember them through an appreciative lens, to gather a multi-colored basket of seeds. To become a "storycatcher" as Christina Baldwin invites us to be. Various stories came to my memory, of which I will tell you one more:

> In 2003, I went to India to learn about solutions to social and environmental problems in a developing country, like my native Colombia. I was inspired by Gandhi's legacy of nonviolence and the mystique I experienced in that society. I traveled with my boyfriend at the time, Andrew. We had connected originally because of our common desire to travel and our interest in socio-environmental themes. Andrew was a filmmaker, photographer, and writer. Before going to India, we took a cross-country roadtrip in the US: camping, taking photos, listening to music, and talking. The next stop on our adventure was India.

> We took a flight, crossed the oceans, and landed in New Delhi. I got a job that lined up perfectly with my interests, which allowed us to stay there for five months. It had to do with researching environmental issues in India for a nonprofit called Ashoka, which led me to meet environmental leaders and participate in innovative projects all over the country.

I met people like Vandana Shiva, a great environmental activist who valiantly stood up to corporations such as Monsanto. I met the lawyer who sued the Indian government that resulted in all taxis in Delhi switching from diesel, which was literally choking the population, to natural gas. I met a famous writer, Arundhati Roy, who defended the rights of vulnerable populations.

I also interviewed a great number of social entrepreneurs working on socio-environmental issues in an innovative way. The most memorable experience I had was in a place that neither appears in Indian guidebooks nor is a priority for Indian tourism.

I'm talking about Kanpur. It was in this unattractive, medium-sized city – one of the most polluted on the planet – that I met Rakesh, an unstoppable activist, completely committed to the health of the Ganges River. With the strength and enthusiasm of one of the Hindu deities, Rakesh had created a citizens movement to protect the river.

Rakesh made our visit to Kanpur unforgettable. He introduced us to a large number of stakeholders so we could understand the issues regarding the Ganges: dysfunctional water treatment plants, tanneries poisoning the water with chemicals, "spiritual guides" throwing cadavers into the river, farmers using poisonous chemicals that leach into the river, companies selling chemicals to farmers, people bathing in the river fouled by excrement, and the media, among others. We continued to learn and meet amazing people and visit incredible places.

Rakesh used our visit to strengthen his campaign. In those days, we appeared in the city newspaper as "environmental experts worried about the Ganges." We felt like participants in this environmental epic struggle (which involved a whole constellation of characters with their interests and their beauty) in the thick of things, playing out the human and environmental drama.

This incredible and heart-wrenching visit full of learning experiences inspired Andrew some years later to write his first book on a new type of ecotourism to the world's most polluted places titled *Visit Sunny Chernobyl!*

Immersing ourselves in this environmental tragedy, communing with its relentless and very human heroes, I connected with what would be my destiny. It happened upon meeting an enigmatic character, the caretaker of a Jain temple I visited. I asked him some questions about his faith (the religion of Gandhi, as he let me know). He answered my questions and then wanted to know about me.

"And, what is it that you do?" he asked me.

"I work on environmental issues," I told him politely.

"What do you mean by environmental issues?"

"Those which have to do with the relationship between human beings and nature. You know, ecology."

"That's very good," he said, with a teacher's tone of voice. "Protecting the ecology is a part of our philosophy of nonviolence. But the most important work out of all the work that you do is that of the inner ecology – the ecology of your own being."

"The inner ecology of my own being?" I repeated the question, trying to digest this new concept.

"That's right. There's an external ecology, and there's an internal ecology. Dedicate yourself more to the internal, which is the source of everything." With these last words, he gave me a book on Ahimsa, or nonviolence, which is, according to the author, "the supreme religion." In the first pages, it explains what this man was trying to tell me: "We hope that we can use the two principles of Ahimsa and Aparigraha (nonviolence and nonpossession), to protect the Boat of Life so that it may not sink."[2]

This brief encounter left me deeply marked. I thought, "This is what I came to India for, to connect the external and internal ecologies." More and more, I could feel the call to discover the "inner ecology of my own being," as my anonymous teacher called it. After this conversation, the trip became a spiritual journey, fueled by a hunger and aspiration that is still alive within me today. The great lesson taking shape inside of me was that spirituality would be the foundation of my being and acting in the world. I understood that this inner ecology is what will bring about the transformation of the external ecology.

What adventures I had lived! How joyful is it to remember this treasure trove of experiences! I kept at the task of finding the stories that definitely showed the most important parts of who I am. A chronological list came into being, which I started to edit, giving each story an evocative title. This was the result. As you review it, consider how you can do the same with your own stories.

My Debut as a School Diva. This is the story I told at the beginning of this chapter about the songs I learned from Bertha and taught to my classmate, Thalia, on the bus. I discovered my love for music, learning and teaching.

The Queen of the Spelling Bee. This story tells how I learned English, applying myself to conquer the world of spelling bees in order to break the language barrier, thereby discovering my tenacity, focus, and desire to participate and belong.

Punching Malden. This story is about being a victim of bullying and giving back the violence ten times over, which led me to make my first big decision to go back to Colombia and live with my father, discovering my ability to make good choices, my desire to build communities, and knowing when to get out of an unsustainable situation.

Breaking the Taboo of Maternity. This is the history of the assignment given to me and my classmate by a professor that influenced me greatly, Madame Beucler. The task was to study the subject of maternity through a radical feminist perspective claiming that the maternal instinct is not existent. I discovered my inclination to question existing structures, and I started to explore freely whether I wanted children or not.

The Yellow Carnations Bomb. This is the story of when I received a hate-token from my classmates. This time, instead of lashing out, I co-created a space for dialogue with a teacher. This led not only to restoring relationships, but also to finding my place as the class valedictorian. I discovered my resilience and bravery to confront a difficult situation without resorting to violence.

Teatime with Rodrigo. Drinking tea with Rodrigo Escobar Navia, a great Colombian intellectual, academic, and politician influenced the arc of my life. He told me that we were going through a big paradigm change from universe as machine to universe as living being. I decided to become an eternal student of nature and contribute to the great paradigm change.

Circle of Stones. This is the story of creating a spirituality group whose purpose was to nurture the transformation we were living as women at Mount Holyoke College. Here, I saw my deep aspiration for inner growth and bringing in the feminine principle.

Ecobarrios Take Over Bogotá. This is the story of my undergraduate thesis which became a part of the city government's policy, impacting two hundred neighborhoods, which made me discover my commitment to a social transformation, beyond the personal.

The Spiritual Pilgrimage to India. This story tells of my journey exploring socio-environmental innovation in India, followed by an exploration of the internal ecology of my being. By means of different

Eastern spiritual paths, I was bathed with the richness of the world's wisdom. I discovered my ability to take the best from every path.

Another World Is Possible. This story talks about my social pilgrimage to global events where social movements explore different directions for civilization, such as the World Social Forum in Brazil and the World Summit on sustainable development in South Africa.

My First Child, Aldeafeliz. This is the story of co-founding the Aldeafeliz ecovillage on the outskirts of Bogotá in 2006 and the many years we have spent building a utopia of ecology and community.

My Conversion to Judaism. This is the story of the reconnection with my Jewish ancestry, learning new rituals, and reconciling with patriarchal religion.

I Get Fired and Find My True Calling. This story is about how I got fired from a prestigious job. I got off the train of conventional success, and eventually life-coaching became the backbone of my life.

I Meet the Love of My Life. This is the story that I told to my tribe on my wedding day of how, once I got clear on what I was looking for in a man, he came into my life and fulfilled my dream of living a deep and authentic love.

Making this list and telling these stories took a long time. In fact, this was what took the most time out of anything in this book. I went into what Christian Baldwin called "the editing of our history." When we do this, we aren't changing our past, we're changing the links between events and their interpretations. We have the freedom to constantly update our self-image and the way we narrate our own story. This is a faculty that we can count on when it's time to define who we are, rather than letting other people or external events define us.

Leonel Narvaez calls this the "right to hermeneutics."[3] Hermeneutics is the branch of philosophy that studies the multiplicity of interpretations that any given story or concept can have. Reviewing our personal narratives invites us to give new interpretations about what happened. It allows for a type of "personal hygiene" that helps us get rid of burdens and pardon the past. If we don't do this, we keep making ourselves and others sick with unresolved emotions. Coming to terms with the past and turning the page opens up a new chapter of our life.

Connecting with Our Essence

After playing with all of these stories, delighting in their joys, having fun with their nooks and crannies, seeing the interconnection between stories, tasting their bitterness, and being inspired by their lessons, I had a very special sensation. Disorientation and emptiness were dissolving and giving way to a deeper acknowledgment of myself and the meaning of my life. Each of these stories were weaving into a tapestry whose threads were specific elements of my essence. My heart started opening up to an appreciation of myself and a gratitude for everything I had experienced.

Around the same time, I found a letter from Madame Beucler, an unforgettable French literature teacher from my high school years. It was a recommendation letter that I had asked for as part of my college applications in 1995. I had read the letter before, but after connecting to my seeds, or essential stories, her words had a profound echo in my soul because now I was able to see myself.

She said, "Anamaria is characterized not only by a great intellectual *curiosity* and an attraction to knowledge, but also and undoubtedly, an almost inflexible *imperative* to completely comprehend something. As long as she hasn't completely understood a piece of knowledge, she will not let go; she will fight tooth and nail to achieve her understanding. I have never known such an *impetuousness* linked to such a *determination* for knowledge. She doesn't scatter; she absorbs."

The letter went on to say, "Her preferred subjects of conversation are above all ethical: the values to lead one's life. What fascinates her is her relationship with others. Who is one for others? What do we know about each other? ... To conclude, the words imposed upon me to describe what I feel from Anamaria are *curiosity, ardor, intensity, passion, energy, determination, rigor*. And also, a light: that of her shining eyes and her great smile, open to life itself and to every space to be explored."

I was surprised how vividly this teacher captured what she saw in me – a picture of my Daemon. I felt completely seen. I understood that humans are an open book; our essence emanates from our inner light and is perceived as the aroma of a flower, when we are open to it. We can all reflect that light to each other, just as Madame Beucler did for me. It requires a commitment to preparing ourselves in the art of recognizing and naming essential qualities.

In New Ventures West, the coaching school where I trained and now work as faculty, recognizing and naming the essential qualities of our clients is something we teach and practice. To learn how to do this, we make a list of all kinds of essential qualities, which we write on a board with the help of the students. To the list made by Madame Beucler (curiosity, ardor, intensity, passion, energy, determination, rigor) we could add a large number of qualities that exist in human beings to widen our repertoire. For example: generosity, compassion, warmth, tenacity, commitment, responsibility, tenderness, receptivity, happiness, sensitivity, creativity, integrity, honesty, humor, respect, serenity...We could continue this list for quite some time.

One of our biggest needs as humans is to be seen. Seeing someone else or seeing ourselves is one of the deepest ways we express love. When we feel that someone else is genuinely seeing us, something within us relaxes; our heart opens. It's almost magical. It was what I felt when I read Madame Beucler's letter again, a sensation of existing, being, occupying a valid space in the world. It's as if naming these essential qualities brings the deepest parts of us to the foreground so that we can stop hiding and show all of our splendor to the world. This magic is described in a poem:

It felt love
How did the rose ever open its heart

And give to this world all of its beauty?
It felt the encouragement of light against its being;
Otherwise, we all remain too frightened

Hafiz

Fear and insecurity keep us hidden, separated from our essences, and forgetful of our light; however, we are the first ones who need to see our own light. Otherwise, we won't connect with it. We will reject or deflect other people's appreciation, judging it as ungrounded compliments. This is why the seeds, or essential stories, give us a solid base from which to see and appreciate ourselves.

The power of the seeds is that, when you narrate them, your essential qualities or virtues can be easily perceived. It's like when you can see the bottom of a crystal-clear lake. Seeds are a direct channel to your essence, where you can see yourself, and others can see you as you are. The first step is to perceive your own virtues. Before then, others' reflections won't land. When you fully see and appreciate yourself, the reflections from others become a true gift. A gift that will nourish your spirit, like the letter from Madame Beucler did for me when I read it years later, because I was first able to see myself.

How Do You Find Your Seeds?

I now invite you to connect with your own seeds. Doing this will help you understand your main storylines, signal where your story is going, and recognize your virtues. We are constantly weaving our own stories at every moment. The understanding of where we come from gives us plenty of "wool" for designing and weaving our lives. At the same time, when we connect with our own history, we are able to digest various aspects that haven't been completely digested before.

When unearthing some stories, you may feel difficult emotions. This is part of the process, and you need to be brave to confront them. The beautiful part is that if we dare to see and feel the most painful stories in life, very powerful intentions can emerge. You start to see these episodes as fundamental in your life, full of colors and textures.

In one of the Life Re-Vision workshops, a woman told us that she had been sexually abused as an adolescent. Because of this dramatic event, she went on a journey to heal herself and find meaning. Today she dedicates herself to helping other women with similar episodes to rise above the trauma and convert these events into a source of growth.

These tales of reclamation, and in some cases redemption, give us hope and faith in humanity. There are innumerable examples of people taking charge of their stories and refusing to turn their back on feeling emotions by asking, "What does this mean in my life?" and "What can happen from here?"

Sometimes other people's seeds remind us of our own stories and aspirations. Identifying these inspiring stories that have impacted us the most and that we tell often can help us find the narrative threads of our own lives.

I will share one of these stories that touches my soul. I tell it regularly because it inspires enormously. I heard this story in the US at a conference I attended in graduate school. The keynote was the author of a book on entrepreneurship, Steve Mariotti, who told us how he came to be interested in this subject, springing from a particular incident that happened to him. When he was an executive at a marketing company he had created, he would end his workday by going for a run. One evening, he had his headphones on and was wrapped up in the music as his feet hit the pavement. Then he was assaulted by a gang. They demanded his wallet. Instinctively, he resisted and started fighting with the young guys. After hitting him multiple times, they left him bleeding and injured on the road, having taken his possessions and leaving many broken bones and serious wounds. His recovery took a long time, first in the hospital and later at home. Although he improved physically, his spirits were still in the dumps. He took an extended leave of absence from work to try and figure things out.

Steve searched deeply within his soul and saw that he couldn't go on living as he had before the attack. This incident connected him to the ongoing social tragedy in his city. People were capable of almost killing him just to get at his wallet. He started to ask himself, "How could I have been so blind? And now that this has touched me personally, how can I just go on with my life as if nothing happened?"

Having ruminated over these existential questions through many months of depression, he finally found his bearings. He decided to quit the company, sell his shares, and dedicate himself to teaching in a high school. Surely, he would be able to positively impact the youth there. He started out teaching history with a sociological focus in order to transmit positive values and empower the kids to write another story and hence create another history. This helped him get out of his depression, and the experiment sowed the seeds of a really exciting possibility for his life.

One day after class, his students were asking him about his past life as a business executive. At first, Steve experienced some internal resistance to talking about that stage of his life, which he considered "egotistical and blind." But the kids insisted, so finally he relented and began talking about how he created his company, his clients, and the company's achievements. He talked about the challenge of maintaining a business, along with the satisfactions and rewards he experienced at an economic and social level. His students were mesmerized, more than in any other history class he had taught. In fact, they insisted that he teach them how to start a business.

At that moment, a light bulb went on in his head. "Maybe my past as a businessman could be useful for these kids. Maybe it could help them achieve better self-determination and economic independence. Maybe that's my mission – not neglecting my past but taking advantage of it." Without a second thought, he started designing an entrepreneurship curriculum for youth in public schools and a nonprofit organization called the NFTE (the National Foundation for Teaching Entrepreneurship). He put the curriculum to work and adjusted it constantly to make it more effective. Steve found his voice in doing this work and the most effective way to get his message out.

The impact of his curriculum and courses was so powerful that he wound up writing a book that became a best seller. That book is now used even by the faculties of business schools all over the United States, which is where I discovered it.

Ever since I heard this story, I couldn't forget it. I now understand why it touches such a deep spot in me; this is an essential story, a seed that has the DNA of this man, along with his values, talents, and commitments. I felt eternally inspired by this person and infused and connected with his essence.

This is the power of an essential story or "seed" as described in the previous section. By means of these stories, we can immediately see the most important parts of someone. In this case, we see that this man had the ability to create a business (because he had already created one), perseverance and resilience (to maintain it), the ability to forgive (to not be resentful of the past), a sense of social responsibility and compassion (wanting to do something to fix the root causes of his attack), honesty with himself (to not stay in his comfort zone once he had a new clarity), and lots of courage (to risk changing and exploring a new direction).

We all love these stories. They show us what's possible, who we can become, and more inspiring ways of leading our lives. The essential qualities or virtues I saw in him (compassion, forgiveness, resilience, and responsibility) captured my soul.

Without a doubt, this story helped me process the tragic news I received on March 29, 2015: the murder of Steven Heller, my fiancé. Three young people killed him to steal his bicycle. On top of that, it was in the same municipality as Aldeafeliz, the ecovillage I co-founded and love so much.

Immediately, instead of blaming the murderers and filling myself up with hate, I remembered Steve Mariotti's story. I put myself in the shoes of those kids and thought empathetically about their pain, frustration, and disorientation, which must have brought them to commit such an atrocious act.

I didn't turn my back on the intense pain I felt. The torment was indescribable, the sleepless nights, the panic, the confrontation with my mortality, the danger all around us, the rage, the infinite sadness, my broken heart from losing a dear friend, the pain of his family. Colombia lost a man of infinite generosity. How destroyed is a country where things like this can happen! At the same time, I took refuge in my family and in the wisdom of Judaism and its grief rituals, which helped me get ahold of myself in the most painful moments of my life up to that point.

Little by little, I came out of the black hole. Several months later, life gave me an opportunity, just like the one Steve Mariotti had, to perform a restorative act. I was offered a job to facilitate a series of conversations about getting along and building peace among people in the educational community in towns throughout the region of Cundinamarca (in central Colombia). I deliberately chose San Francisco (in Colombia) and other municipalities close to where Steven's murder took place. The day that I was facilitating the discussion in San Francisco, I was able to feel the root causes of the violence that ended my friend's life.

I discovered that there was a huge disconnect between parents and their children, and between teachers and students. The spaces we opened for dialogue and empathetic listening didn't exist at home or in classrooms. The youth were full of rage, and this led to them becoming conflictive and violent among themselves. This seemed fertile ground for violent acts.

Our facilitated dialogue was generating consciousness about this type of behavior. The youth's final presentations before the whole group included comments like "I don't want to be so belligerent anymore, I want to learn to address things differently." Others made signs with images of unity, friendship and holding hands. The students were attentive; they participated and talked among themselves and proposed alternatives.

At the closing, I asked them a question: "What do you want to do after what you have discovered today?" One student responded, "I want my class to become an example of how to get along." Everyone applauded. A rain of ideas poured down illuminating how to support the work of this class to achieve its purpose. I was hopeful for the possibilities of what might happen if we responded to violence with peace, and grateful that I could contribute my grain of sand to help restore the social fabric in that part of the country.

As we can see, other people's stories can inspire our own stories. Steve Mariotti's story influenced me at the time of my own tragedy. When we become aware that we can choose the end of the stories that we live, giving them a necessary twist reclaims and redeems us, restores our faith in ourselves and humanity, and opens up new possibilities. That's when we become the authors of our own stories.

When you listen to other stories, observe what you feel. Don't let yourself be intimidated by the most heart-wrenching stories. Part of what keeps us quiet about our own personal stories is that we think they aren't sufficiently inspiring or valuable. Each story shines its own light because it shows us another dimension of our shared humanity. Every human life has innumerable examples of overcoming challenges, of ingenious or bold ways of confronting our limitations and creating new possibilities. You, without a doubt, are not an exception. Your story matters, and the world needs you to take ownership of it and share it.

Become a Seed Collector

Remember the Bone Woman? She's the one who goes all over the desert collecting bones – creative manifestations. She's an integrating force inside of you that you can also call on to help collect your stories, or seeds. Because seeds are not always visible like bones are, we are going to appeal to memory. Memory can be slippery; we can't force it. What you can do is be attentive when a story comes into your mind, whether because of an exercise, a dream, hearing someone else's story, an anecdote from the past, etc. Like a butterfly catcher, use your net to capture the story, look at its beauty, and then let it go free.

Becoming a seed collector has various advantages. It helps us see more clearly the direction our lives are taking. In her book *Storycatcher*, Christina Baldwin says, "Only by telling each other our authentic stories will we come upon our wisdom and make the new roadmap we need for survival." Seeds are an essential element to illuminate our navigation map so we can see where we are going.

Besides Christina Baldwin, many other authors talk about the importance of telling our stories. In the book *Playing Big*, Tara Mohr claims that "playing big" in life always includes, one way or another, taking the next step on our own stories, giving a voice to our own inner questions, and sharing our basic and simple truths. Mohr is able to detect the many ways we hide from ourselves. We hide behind others' ideas or theories, keeping our own essence behind the scenes. This also keeps us confused and doubtful about which decisions to make.

Owning our own stories gives us strength and clarity. When we recognize our essential qualities, we can see even more deeply into the nature of our Daemon. We see the adventures on which this internal creative force has taken us as well as the luminous qualities of our souls.

The seeds don't just enrich us at the individual level, but at the collective level as well. The book *Sacred Economics* by Charles Eisenstein, tells us that we live in the "age of separation"; we have been losing what keeps us together because the current economic paradigm and system only makes monetary things visible. According to the author, the relationships within a community are made by gifts and stories. He affirms that when community life is built with these fibers from a place of love, we are connected by a web of stories to the people with whom we are acquainted and live an abundant and nourishing life. Otherwise, a monotonous and impersonal life drives us to meaninglessness.[4]

Another great advantage to becoming collectors of our stories is to integrate them and heal. There are difficulties in life that are hard to swallow, and silence makes them ferment and rot inside of us. According to many authors, these rotten seeds can later manifest as health problems, relationship issues of every type, or even accidents. Giving a voice to these difficult events and finding the meaning and the lessons in them help us to process these traumas and repurpose them. This is what happened with the story of me punching my classmate. Writing it down and telling it helped me understand the meaning behind what I did and see the connection to other positive events, leading to a restorative ending.

This is the foundation of the work of the incredible man, Michael Lapsley, who created the Institute for Healing of Memories in South Africa for people to process the traumas of apartheid. In a safe and compassionate environment, people are able to open themselves up and tell traumatic stories, which helps them to get rid of the emotional burden they are carrying. People also realize the lessons learned from their experiences and the possibilities for individual and collective healing. These spaces for telling stories are very valuable. They can be collective or with a therapist who knows how to listen. Telling our stories in a safe environment gives us the wider perspective we need to take back the reins of our life story.

To generate more intimacy with our own stories, we must invoke them consciously. Some people have a gift for that and do it naturally without effort. The rest of us, for whom it's not so easy to collect our stories, need practice. We can use techniques to improve our ability to collect stories. In the following section, we will share some of the techniques we use in Life Re-Vision workshops.

Exercises for Collecting Seeds

There are lots of exercises you can use to help you find your seeds. Just like the bones, you will use an internal compass and guide to detect which of your stories are most charged with meaning. The quality and intensity of your emotions are a good indicator. Some stories are full of pain, others are full of happiness, others are full of many other feelings in our emotional palette.

Attention, please! We are going to focus here on stories that elevate us as people, that highlight our essential qualities. These could be stories about great difficulties, or even about huge blunders we have committed; however, they show how you recovered from these incidents, what you learned, and how you were able to transform your life. At the end, the story should highlight your dignity and make you feel good about yourself. If there's a story about which you feel particularly strongly but don't feel ready to confront yet, leave it aside for now and seek therapy. Don't judge yourself. Wait for a moment when you are prepared or have the necessary support to unpack it.

What I'm about to say is also very important. There are stories that are better to let go of, so as not to give them any more power. Those are the stories where you strayed from your essence; remembering them won't bring anything positive or edifying. Did you do everything possible to fix the damage done? Did you learn the relevant lesson? Are you at peace? If not, clean up your messes responsibly, become more self-aware, and seek inner peace. After that, let it go! Use your wisdom and focus your attention on stories full of potential and life for you and for others.

Below, I will offer you some exercises to help you identify some of your most important seeds. Some of these exercises may be fruitful and others not. For this reason, I will offer several ideas to help find your seeds in the hope that some of them will work for you.

Review your bones. These are objects that carry your history. When having some of your bones in front of you, it's very possible that they will evoke essential stories from your past.

Write in a journal. For Christina Baldwin, writing in a journal is like "practicing your scales on the piano: it helps us to get to the fundamentals of our own story." With this practice, we are in contact with our own voice. As we narrate our lives day by day, we are likely to remember defining moments in our past, moments when there was a big change, and we will learn to keep the connection to our narrative threads alive.

Free association. In Life Re-Vision workshops, I make use of various objects, which include postcards, images of archetypes, talent cards, and cards denoting values and virtues. Everybody chooses an object that reminds them of some important story in their lives and then they tell the story to one of their companions at the workshop. Many relevant stories come out of this. You can even make an altar of evocative objects, explore what memories they bring you and then share them, even to just one other person or by writing them down or speaking them into a recorder.

Another version of "free association" is everyday conservations. People naturally tell stories, and hearing these evokes memories of essential stories. Christina Baldwin asks us, "What could we learn from the story of others that helps us to see our own story?" Other people's stories activate our memories and our imagination. Take note of these memories. Make an effort to share that story, whether it's at that time, later with someone else, or for yourself in your journal.

Also, take note of the new ideas that come up when you listen to other people's stories so you can use them as a resource to help nourish your own story. Christina Baldwin says that one of the healing properties of sharing stories is the potential to reinforce positive decisions and give an example of options and ways of living that we had not thought of. An example of this is the story of Steve Mariotti being assaulted and his inspiring response, which later inspired me when Steven was murdered. Something like this could happen to you too, so be attentive.

Milestones in your life. I learned this exercise in a workshop with Father Jorge Julio Mejía in Colombia. He had us choose key milestones in our lives in chronological order. I found the first list I had made in 1998. The milestones keep growing and, in some cases, have changed, with more emphasis in some areas and less in others. Try to make a list of your milestones because they are probably very connected to your essential stories, or seeds.

Life-walking. One of the practices discussed in the introduction of this book is walking meditation. Life-walking is a variation of that practice, focusing on contemplating your life. It's very simple. Find a park or a natural area, like a beach, a forest, the edge of a river, or another place that inspires you. Take a twenty-to-forty-minute walk meditatively, associating every step with a year of your life. Without forcing it, let memories of this era come to your mind.

To keep your mind from wandering, return to your breath while walking. You can use a recurring phrase like "I recall the first year of my life" or "I open to the first year of my life," then "I recall the second year of my life," and likewise, to keep your attention focused on the exercise. If you need to, take note of what comes to you in a little book you take with you. Open yourself up to store the memories that come; be ready to be surprised and to accept anything that happens with the exercise.

List of questions. Another technique is to respond to questions. This reminds me of the job interviews I have had where they ask similar questions. It also reminds me of the processes for applying to universities where they sometimes ask you to write essays on similar themes. I always loved these interview and application processes because they connected me with my stories and gave me the opportunity to write them and reflect on them. I hope these questions are equally evocative for you.

- When was a time(s) that you felt like you shined in front of others?
- What have been the biggest difficulties in your life and how did you overcome them?
- What are your fundamental values and how did you arrive at them?
- What are your virtues and strengths and how did you discover them?
- What dreams do you have and how did they get planted in you?
- What event(s) marked the way you see life?
- What story are you living now?
- What important, magic, or difficult moments have you been living lately?

Autobiographical tale. When you live an important event, you can capture it by writing a tale you keep for yourself or share with others. In this tale, include details of what happened, the challenges you faced, the results, the learning experience, and how this transformed you or your surroundings. Later, you will be thankful to have these written memories, for yourself and your descendants.

Make photo albums. If you like photos and collages, you will enjoy making albums or scrapbooks with them. This activity invites you to organize your memories and show them in a visual and creative manner. You can add souvenirs from your experiences like cards, airplane tickets, napkins from restaurants, newspaper clippings, and inspiring quotes to give it a spiritual touch. When you show your albums, it will naturally flow from there to tell your main stories of the year, and you will see how that will strengthen your relationships with those close to you. Others will get to know you more deeply and understand that which impacts, attracts, and transforms you from year to year.

Make art. There are people who record their stories with art, music, altars, or special objects. Many of the bones we saw in the previous section are ways of giving shape to these stories so that we can remember them later. I don't necessarily recommend that we become compulsive object collectors. There's an art to knowing how to choose the best way for each person to collect and preserve their valuable life seeds.

Creative introductions. A practice to help you become a story collector could be to attend meetings or workshops where they ask you to introduce yourself. Instead of just highlighting your resume, you can respond differently to the question "Who are you?" by sharing one of your seeds and how it made you who you are today. In my coaching school on the first day, we ask everyone to introduce themselves differently from the traditional introduction. The prompt is "What do you want to be known for this year?" The point of this exercise is to leave a clearer trace of our lives, illustrated with stories. Even with a simple prompt like "Tell us who you are," you can still share one of your seeds.

Appeal to your ancestors. In this process of recognizing your seeds, there could be stories that go beyond your personal life. Some of these stories involve your ancestors and a greater family or even historical context. In this inquiry, sometimes a deeper meaning of life is found. It could be that you discover ancestral seeds full of meaning. They could be stories about your ancestors that have great relevance for your own path. This point deserves a wider illustration with the case of Alejandra who went into a deep Life Re-Vision that included ending her marriage and her prestigious government job.

In this Life Re-Vision, she reconnected with the story of her maternal great-grandfather, which confirmed essential aspects of herself: a rebelliousness against the status quo and an insatiable thirst for creative endeavors. At first, he was a very conventional man. He was a lawyer, married, living in the city in an era where the typical thing to do was move from the country to the city. Later he rebelled, going to live in the country and giving up his profession in order to dedicate himself to reading and projects that captured his imagination. His wife and children begrudgingly followed him.

He didn't have any support and his projects failed; he lost a lot of money. In spite of all that, he kept on with the path that his soul was telling him to take. He died in an accident, but it would seem that he died more from exhaustion and sadness because of not being able to find the support that he needed to fully live out his creative potential. After his death, his wife, full of rage, threw all of his books into the river. From that moment on, she decided to forget about him and tried to make her family never speak of him again.

Alejandra noticed that this unresolved chapter of her family history was still with her, pushing her to reinvent herself. She also felt a deep and incredible longing for an artistic life and to be able to live it fully but not in isolation and silence, as was the case with her great-grandfather. Following her longing pushed her to transform her current life and jump into the unknown with total uncertainty. Connecting with her family seed gave her the courage to choose a path more aligned with her soul.

This started to change her life. Alejandra dedicated several months to taking care of her Daemon, which insisted upon her recording a music album. She took the request seriously and publicly released her album. I had the privilege of attending the album release and saw how happy and proud her mother was of the steps Alejandra was taking. It seemed as if Alejandra was generating a type of collective healing in her family by dedicating herself to her art. Also, instead of throwing her talents and aspirations in the river, she put them in service of her community by creating a project that supports and celebrates feminine creativity. When she opened herself up to this generational seed, Alejandra connected with the narrative thread of her own life and that of her ancestors, which led to untangling family issues and brought her to her purpose.

Reflect in Your Journal:
- *What generational stories have not yet been resolved in my family that perhaps it's my turn to bring to a happy ending?*

Declaring Your Seeds

We have already mentioned the custom of the Babemba, the African tribe that orients people who are lost by retelling their essential stories so that they can remember who they are. Apparently this works much better than any other way of correcting, punishing, or isolating people. When these stories are shared, something magical happens; there is an auto-recognition, a moment of truth, of being able to say, "that's me," and stand up with dignity and start to remember one's authentic path. Like Christina Baldwin says, we reconnect with "the best part of ourselves."

I have experienced this myself; I bet you have too. In very hard moments in my life, people around me have said things about me that help me, that give me encouragement. The times it has helped me the most have been when they add a story, a seed, that proves what they are saying and shows that their appreciation is real. Sometimes, I had forgotten about the event they are recounting. Knowing once again that other identities live in me, latent strengths give me the courage, experience, and impetus to rediscover and nurture those forgotten parts of me.

When I wrote down, reread, and later shared my stories or seeds, I found myself again. The ones that I shared helped revive me and are those that my tribe can remind me of in a dark hour. In my Life Re-Vision, I was my own tribe when I told myself these stories, remembered them and recognized who I was again. We don't always have someone to do it for us. But it's worth it to cultivate this type of tribe, in case we ever lose the capacity to remember or wind up totally lost.

I hope you understand how important it is to identify your seeds and share them with the people in your life. These stories can't just stay buried in your private life. Their purpose is to be shared with your tribe so they can use them when needed. You will need them in difficult moments and also in joyful moments, when seeds will bring a special light.

We all have meaningful stories that carry the DNA of our essence. They are stories that, when we tell them, cause something to light up inside of us. We feel like we are in contact with something sacred. At the same time, this reinforces our self-image and shapes the image that others have of us. They can be short or long stories, simple or complex. Everybody has their own style. These stories are powerful; they have an important lesson and make an impact on your life and on the lives of others.

For you, what would these essential stories, these seeds, be? I invite you to list your most representative stories, those which you want people who love you to know about you and remind you of your most difficult moments and your joyful moments. Try to remember at least six seeds, hopefully ten or more. Try to give each seed an evocative title, such that anybody would want to know more about them. Have each seed title sound like a chapter of a great novel because our lives really are fantastic novels with great miracles and great blessings.

Reflect in Your Journal:
- *What are my seeds?*

Giving Life to Your Seeds

Once you have made the master list of your stories, the first thing to do is savor them. What do these stories reveal about your essential qualities? What do they say about your Daemon? Remember your Daemon is that creative force that wants to express your talents. Get to know your essence, your aspiration, and the desires of your soul. The next thing is to give your seeds evocative titles, as if they were chapters of a book you want to read. This will give the seeds some "spice."

The third thing is to ask yourself, "What story still needs to be resolved? How can I resolve it?" With this question, you are reclaiming the narrative thread of your life. Fourth, write down your stories or tell them to people close to you. Take note when a new ending might be in order, or a connection with another story, so that you can assimilate and highlight the learning experiences and redemptive nature of each event. Christina Baldwin says, "Whatever isn't integrated or resolved keeps repeating itself until it is."[5] When we edit these stories, we are digesting and integrating them into our inner world so we can evolve. The flavor at the end of this should be sweet, hopeful; it should taste like celebrating life and the great learning journey we are all in.

You could be in the middle of a story that hasn't yet been resolved. This connects with your *Starting Point* of this Life Re-Vision. In this case, take a deep breath and leave this current story on the back burner. There is no need to force anything. The inspiration will soon come to take the next step, like the poet Rainer Maria Rilke says,

> "Have patience with all that which isn't resolved in your heart. Do not despair if the answers don't come immediately. Try to love the questions themselves, like locked rooms or books in a

foreign language. Do not look now for the answers. They cannot now be given to you because you would not be able to live them. And the point is, to live everything. Live your questions now. Perhaps then, someday far in the future, you will gradually, without even noticing it, live your way into the answer."[6]

You will keep finding more tools to navigate your unresolved questions in the rest of this book.

Another interesting fact about stories is that they have patterns. According to Christopher Booker, the English author and journalist, there are seven kinds of plots that make up stories. These plots have a structure that keeps repeating and keeps us captivated century after century. These are: comedy, tragedy, overcoming the monster, from rags to riches, the quest, voyage and return, and rebirth.[7] Each of these plot types has its basic structure with innumerable variations. The stories that we see in the movies, on TV, or in books are composed of one or more of these plot types, as we can see below. I will share here a summary of each of these types:

Comedy. Stories where the heroes/heroines enter into a state of confusion for various misunderstandings, which generate funny situations, until the problems are resolved, identities are cleared up and couples get back together again. (*A Midsummer Night's Dream* or the TV series *Friends*)

Tragedy. There's a gruesome challenge to resolve, and temptation presents itself, usually by means of an evil character. The hero/heroine falls into temptation to achieve a goal at great cost, usually death. (*Romeo and Juliet*)

Rags to riches. Stories where the protagonist starts out with few resources and dreams of the possibility of a better life, which they obtain through their efforts or their charms and good character. (*Cinderella*)

Overcoming the monster. The life of the community is in danger because of the presence of an evil monster. The hero/heroine is called to confront it, which is done successfully. (*Superman*)

The quest. The protagonist is called to go on a dangerous and unpredictable journey, which implies overcoming a great number of challenges and being transformed as a human being. (*The Odyssey*)

Voyage and return. Stories where the hero/heroine, without looking for it, finds themself in the middle of a strange world that is fantastic at first and becomes more and more bizarre and frustrating, until they finally manage to get free and return home. (*The Wizard of Oz*)

Rebirth. Stories where the protagonist enters into a period of lethargy or quasi-death because of an evil spell cast on them, which is counteracted by the power of love. (*Sleeping Beauty*)

As you can see, all of these types of plots include a challenge that has to be overcome. In the majority of cases, this happens. The big exception to this is the tragedy. In tragedies, the characters succumb to their dark side, and they wind up being driven by their conditioned patterns or blindness. In general, it ends in death, or paying a high cost for their mistake. Christina Baldwin says that "part of the creative tension in novels, movies, and reality is that integration or resolution isn't guaranteed. For many reasons, many people get stuck in periods of discombobulation."[8] A prolonged state of being stuck could happen because of not listening to the hidden opportunity that presents itself or not being open to evolving.

Baldwin also declares that "the gate to any new period of growth or maturity in our lives requires a period of discomfort and disorientation. Out of this experience, we eventually create a more deeply integrated story."[9] This explains the significance of the *Starting Point* that we explored in the introduction. We usually start a Life Re-Vision because we don't really know where the plot of our lives is going; we are disoriented. Although there may be lots of confusion, there is a way to pay attention to how the plot is unfolding. Nobody wants their life to be a tragedy; we all want stories with a happy ending.

Baldwin gives the key in the following paragraph:

> "Plot is set in motion by some detonating event that discombobulates us, shakes up the status quo, and sets us off on the journey. When this happens in real life, we may try to reestablish our former life, but eventually we realize that is impossible. Plot carries us forward into new territory; there is no going back. The only resolution is to reorient our lives so that we can integrate this experience into who we are...If we think we are in a period of discombobulation, we can gain perspective by seeing our crisis as an inflection point of the plot of a novel – after all, our lives are stories and stories follow certain structures."[10]

We can see that these periods of imbalance are opportunities to recreate ourselves, reinvent ourselves, turn our story around. When we realize this, we take the narrative thread of our stories in our own hands, assuming the lessons that life brings us in the most empowering way possible. Michel Lapsley, who I mentioned previously, says that this is possible even with the most heartbreaking stories, like the one that happened to him. He was the victim of a letter-bomb that destroyed one of his eyes, an ear, and both hands back in the apartheid days of South Africa. He doesn't hide his injuries; he goes around with hooks in place of his missing hands, similar to a pirate. Because of his experience, he became a healer of others. He declares in his book *Redeeming the Past* that we can go from victim to victor when we do an internal cleaning and repurpose our stories.[11]

Once you have clarified the narrative thread of your stories, the next step is to share them as much as possible. These stories are an important part of your personal legacy. Maybe you still don't fully value their importance. If you feel an internal or external obstacle when you tell your stories, be patient. At first there could be some reluctance. Act like a compassionate parent, giving yourself the encouragement and support that you need. Look for appropriate contexts where the story can be well-received. When you feel ready, experiment. Start with people you trust or people you don't know at all, whatever works better for you.

If you are like me, you don't have an innate talent for storytelling. I had to learn. There are techniques for telling good stories. According to Charles Vogl, a colleague, author, trainer, and storytelling expert, the basic elements of a good story are specifying a place and time for the events so you can transport the listener to a specific scene, well-described characters, a challenge that is difficult to resolve, a climax moment that leads to an outcome, a lesson to be learned, and a significant impact in your life and the lives of others.[12] When you tell your story, it's important to be connected to the sense of surprise and magic that your story carries. This magic will be contagious for others and give strength to your story.

The next exercise can be useful. It's the equivalent of putting your seeds in water so that they will start to loosen their shells and activate the life that they have within them. Start by writing those evocative titles of the stories on index cards and "play cards" with a friend, pulling a story card randomly and telling it. If you can, write these stories down somewhere or record them and share them with your tribe. Sharing the stories generates conversations about them, which then deepens your relationship with yourself and others.

It's helpful to create a fertile soil for your seeds. In other words, we need to learn to promote environments that are conducive and favorable for telling stories. Do you have some stories that just flow and others that don't? What are these fertile contexts for stories? How can we generate them so that we can enrich ourselves with our seeds and those of others? There is one determining factor: listening.

When we learn to listen, people open up. When we listen, we can reflect back to somebody the essential qualities we see in them when they tell us their seeds. You can see it happen; it's powerful. This can also be applied to yourself, learning to listen to yourself. When you tell a story, you can see your own essence; you can be attentive to when your soul and your essential qualities appear.

Remember that telling your stories strengthens your identity and your relationships. When you remember and tell them, you give them life and start to notice narrative threads or plot lines you may have forgotten. Like bones, they were buried in the desert of oblivion. To have others know your seeds benefits you just like it does in the Babemba tribe. It means that one day, people close to you can rescue you from a difficult situation by reminding you who you are. It also means that when you start to doubt yourself, you can evoke these seeds and remember your own essence.

Preparing to share our seeds invites us to think more about our tribe. Who are these people that know us intimately, with whom we can be ourselves and who support us in our most difficult moments? That is your tribe. It could be five people or sixty. There is no ideal number. They are the people with whom you feel comfortable when it's time to do an experiment like this one, your Life Re-Vision. They are also the people who help you heal dark periods in your life's story and get back up again.

Francis Weller, psychotherapist and author of *The Wild Edge of Sorrow*, says that without a community who reflects our value to us, we have to live the difficulties of life alone, in an empty space, and may come to an unfortunate conclusion that "I deserved that bad luck." In his book, he talks about cases where people who were abused recover their dignity thanks to their community helping them see their intrinsic value and their essence. Weller recommends going back to what our ancestors did: forming circles to tell stories, performing rituals, and singing songs together. According to this author, with time, this community becomes internalized and a source of inner compassion. "Self-compassion is the community, internalized."[13]

The result of creating these spaces with our tribe, as well as healing us, is generating within us a type of very special empowerment. It's a different kind of empowerment than that of obtaining degrees, making money and becoming your own boss, which are still important. This kind of empowerment comes from being able to be oneself in front of a group of people, being fully seen and valued for who we are, without achievements or masks, knowing that one can count on the support of our tribe during tough times.

I experienced this a little while ago with my family on my birthday. That day, I wanted to create a ritual to celebrate life that at the same time would strengthen the tribe and the sharing of seeds. I told everybody about the custom of the Babemba and said to them, "You are my tribe. Let's pretend that I've lost my way. What stories would you tell me to help me remember who I am?" Everybody told a story that confirmed the essence I am now in touch with, giving me an even stronger sense of identity.

What I felt when I heard these stories is hard to describe. It was as if my heart was expanding, my being melting, and happiness bubbling up all throughout my body. I felt seen. I felt that I existed in the hearts of my people. Those stories that bring us together have enormous significance. I recognized a level of connection and intimacy with my family that had been built up over the years by creating spaces for conversation and listening attentively so essences can flourish. I even saw spaces where my divorced parents, my stepmother, and the children from my father's second marriage could exist together, where we all considered each other family.

It's very clear to me that I was able to open up this space for others to see me because I saw myself and listened to myself first. The Life Re-Vision process brought me to value my seeds and share them with my tribe, which then came back and multiplied, creating a fullness and a feeling of communion. I invite you to leave your shame behind and do the same with your tribe. The stories can have a beginning and an end, but their repercussions keep touching our lives like waves with ripple effects that keep expanding. These seeds are continually sprouting and producing new shoots, enriching these essential stories.

Sameet Kumar, a clinical psychologist and the author of *Grieving Mindfully*, invites us to imagine our identity as a necklace full of precious stones that falls apart and needs to be re-strung. If some stones are lost, they will be replaced with new ones. This invites us to recognize and thread the stones that are there right now, so that we can show them off proudly like a luxurious necklace. As life goes on, we will keep adding new colorful stones to the necklace, treasuring each one of our memorable moments.[14]

We never know what might happen as a result of telling our stories. The effects can be beyond our imagination. Think of stories people told you years ago that they have influenced you positively and the memories you have from them, even years later. There's an anonymous saying, "Everybody knows how many seeds there are in an apple, but nobody knows how many apples there are in a seed."

It's difficult to estimate the power of seeds, which is why it's so worthwhile to share them. A friend of mine says, "el cuento que no se cuenta no cuenta." *The story that isn't told cannot unfold.* I invite you to tell your essential stories! I invite you to spread your seeds through the whole landscape. Think about a cottonwood tree that can release more than twenty-five million seeds, which the wind transports to germinate at great distances. You are like a cottonwood tree, full of seeds that will be released and need to fly, finding fertile ground to sprout and grow in the minds and hearts of other beings.

Closing of Seeds

The key ideas in this chapter are the following: we easily forget the narrative thread of our lives and wind up living on automatic pilot. In order to have a meaningful life, we need to learn to reinvent ourselves constantly, using the learning experiences of our lives as a base. Our culture focuses on the path of the hero: going out and confronting challenges with courage, but there is less emphasis on returning home, in taking an inventory of our experiences, digesting them, and coming to terms with the past so that we can design a future that resonates with our beings. By remembering our essential stories and sharing them, we see our essential qualities, talents, and virtues; we reclaim the thread and meaning of our life stories.

When we collect our stories, we reintegrate within ourselves and also with our tribe, which one day can rescue us from a difficult situation by reminding us who we are.

Use the recommended practices in this process to deepen your learning and understanding of your life. Go out and do some walking meditation to assimilate what you have received from this step and what is pending on your completion list. How does it feel to get reconnected to your seeds? The next steps: make your list of seeds, write them down on cards, start sharing them with your tribe.

Reflect in Your Journal:
- *What did I learn about myself when I remembered my seeds?*
- *What do I think are my essential qualities?*
- *When I connect with my seeds, I discover or affirm that I am (write your essential qualities down)...*

Declaration for Closing Seeds
When you are ready, declare the following:

I am now in contact with my seeds, with the narrative thread of my life and with my tribe. I have become a collector of my own seeds and those of others that inspire me. I commit to honoring my life stories, constantly collecting and dignifying my stories, and seeing my essence and those of others through this exercise.

Reflect in Your Journal:
- *When I connect with my seeds, I discover that my many seeds or essential stories all have something in common, which is...*

4

Winds

I remember having my seeds nicely organized in front of me in the form of printed stories and journals, in which I could read and see the emerging themes. The sensation was very different from the initial chaos. Instead, I was filled with feelings of surprise and awe. Being in my living room, in the excellent company of those bones – printed stories and journals – that carried my seeds, I comfortably settled in, drinking a delicious rooibos tea with almond milk (my favorite.) It was the first week of the year of my Life Re-Vision journey. Once again, I decided not to go on vacation that year. Instead, I preferred to stay at home and make sense of all the information I had uncovered.

It had taken me a full year to read my journals – wow! It was a time of reconnecting with my past, my essence, and my creative force. I took that time to remember and value my steps and saw that there was a thread connecting all those ups and downs. Even the most difficult moments had not been in vain; they taught me lessons that are still alive in me.

Having all of these stories in front of me, something clicked. I felt a huge sense of appreciation for the richness of my life. After being lost, without direction, my self-esteem in the dumps, collecting my bones (sacred artifacts) and seeds (essential stories) gave me proof of the gifts I have to offer. I remembered that I had a path I had started on earlier, a conscious search for community and creativity. I focused on understanding this path better to learn what forces and contexts had put me on it.

Some weeks later, I had the opportunity to talk to my grandmother, a woman who was still perfectly lucid at her eighty-something years of age. We started the conversation after lunch, on the way back to her house. She was driving on the streets of Miami. We had just finished talking about her retirement from the successful company she had founded with her ex-husband thirty years earlier and the challenges of handing it over to the next generation.

When we got to her house, I asked her, "Grandma, what were the big issues of your generation – the ones that propelled you and influenced you to be who you are and to value what you value?" Walking to the kitchen to get a Coca-Cola with ice, she said:

> "Well, look, in my generation, the big issue was to empower ourselves as women so that we could work. That was unthinkable for my mother, but in my generation, it started to change. I grew up in the US and in Colombia, and while in the US, women started to get good job opportunities, that was still very much looked down upon in Colombia."

She had my undivided attention and continued speaking:

> "I got a scholarship in the US. I wanted to study business administration, but my parents, with their Colombian culture, wouldn't let me. They only let me study home economics. When I came back to Colombia in the 1950s, I decided that I would work in a company no matter what. Because of this, my father stopped speaking to me for going against his rule that women in his family shouldn't work. It took some time, but eventually, I was able to reconcile with him, and he eventually respected my decision to work. It wasn't easy at all, but it was worth it. Years later, I started my own business with my ex-husband and had a very satisfying work life."

I went to pour myself some tea. Before my grandmother could lose focus (prompted by an attractive game of solitaire on her iPad), I quickly asked her, "How was your relationship with technology? It must have undergone lots of changes throughout your career." She looked up at me and said:

> "And how! I had to go from the typewriter and the telegram to the computer and then from one program to the next. I have never stopped learning something or other, although I never learned any of this in school or in college. It's been a nonstop technological change ordeal! But I'm happy about everything we can do today with technology."

Reflecting on the following generation, that of my mother, I added,

> "For my mom, things were quite different, weren't they? She was able to study business administration (which you wanted to do), and there was no stigma regarding her working. However, I understand that her working conditions weren't always easy. There was lots of machismo and mistreatment of women. In the '80s, society still hadn't completely gotten used to female empowerment, and for this, she was punished subtly and overtly. Her biggest asset was her education, and thanks to it, she had many opportunities. Because of this, the great causes that moved here were (and still are) education and women's empowerment."

Finally, I asked her, "So then, Grandma, what are my causes? What are the important causes of my generation?" She looked at me like I already knew the answer, and said anyway, "You guys have to deal with the consequences of technological progress, so much trash and pollution." She then turned back to her iPad to play solitaire. She had left me dumbfounded. My decision to study biology and work on environmental issues hadn't been an individual decision. I saw that it had to do with a logic of generational causes.

As a result of this conversation, I realized that there were bigger influences behind my personal quests. Obviously, there was a creative force (my Daemon) and essential virtues inside me, but there were also external forces that had driven me.

What are Winds?

Maby, an anthropology student who helped me organize my ideas for this book, asked me one day, "What has been the context of these stories of yours?" That same day, she showed me the biography of an important person in her field who had analyzed these contexts in his life. By "contexts," I understood that she was referring to all the familial, socioeconomic, environmental, historical, and ideological influences that had marked and directed my life.

Little by little, the response to this provocative question started to become clearer and clearer. Something bigger, outside of me, had always been propelling me. This is where the innumerable teachers, guides, books I had read, ideological and conceptual currents to which I had been exposed, and socioeconomic and historical contexts of my life came in. I understood that my personal story was framed within a much bigger story.

Christina Baldwin says that stories have three levels to them: individual, collective, and species level.[1] The individual level is seen in the seeds. The collective and species level are another level we have to get to so that we can know where we are going as a family and society (collective level) and as humanity (species level.) I started to ask myself these questions: *How have the collective and species level stories influenced me? What specific influences have marked me and why? How does this affect the direction that my life is going? What implications does this have for my next steps and future path?*

I imagined that my essence – a type of figurative DNA present in my seeds – had been blown by the winds of causes and issues that resonated with my inner values. That's where my individual nature met the prevailing culture, where this unique sensitivity of mine chose certain aspects of that culture, adopting them as my own. They are influences I voluntarily opened myself up to and let blow me in certain directions, like winds.

From the conversation with Maby and the subsequent reflections on it, the concept of "winds" was born. "Winds" are influences, trends, and contexts that surround our experiences. They blow you toward a greater purpose, to a conversation bigger than an individual one. Winds push seeds forward, they give them wings with which to fly in specific directions. They give us a sense of direction and point which way to go. Tara Mohr, author, life coach, and expert in feminine leadership, talks about how our individual purposes sometimes align with a greater force, a tendency, a current that gives them a boost.[2] This is what we call winds.

I casually found a great example of this. Sometimes in the car, my partner and I like to listen to recordings of the great Colombian historian, Diana Uribe. Listening to one of her series about the independence of the nations of the Americas, she said this, which aligns perfectly with the concept of winds:

> "Ideas are the most powerful force human beings have invented. They travel over time, enter into hearts and thoughts, inflame passions, create utopias, and cause people to give themselves over completely to causes. Behind every cause, there is an idea. The ideas of the Enlightenment are the laboratory that caused Europe to shake and birth our modern continent. And these ideas are cemented in the form of revolutions."[3]

She explained how the liberators were filled with the ideas of equality, liberty, and fraternity of the French Revolution along with the scientific thought of the Enlightenment, all of which started our Latin American countries along the path to independence. These ideas penetrated the minds and hearts of people like Simón Bolívar, José de San Martín and Marcelo Alvear, among many others. Some of these people, like Francisco de Miranda, lost their lives for their convictions, fighting for them until the end. Consciously or not, we all have ideals, movements, and forces of all kinds – "winds" – that have blown us, coming from the contexts from which we have come. Below, I will show you the winds I found in my life so that you can start thinking about your own.

My Winds

Seeing how passionate I was about environmental issues, an MBA classmate came up to me during a cocktail party and asked with genuine curiosity, "Where does your interest in environmental issues come from? What in your life drove you to care so much about this?" I had never wondered about this until that moment. This caused me to reflect back to my past and opened my mind, which later led to identifying one of my fundamental winds.

I told him that, when I was seventeen years old, in a café in Bogotá, I met Rodrigo, a mentor and very wise person. With a pair of delicious cappuccinos in hand, waiting out the typical April rain in Bogotá, we started to share ideas. He asked me what I was going to study, and I told him, "To be frank, I don't know. I'm interested in a lot of things, almost everything, but more than anything I'm interested in understanding the roots of things." I told him that philosophy captured my attention because I wanted to know how we human beings create meaning and purpose in our existence.

Rodrigo's response changed my life. He told me that as humanity, our worldview was changing, that we were in the middle of a big transition. Since the industrial age, we have valued and worshiped the logic, thinking, and efficiency of machines, believing that everything has a cause and effect, and is linear, coming out of the framework of Newtonian physics. As a collective, he said, we are starting to realize that mechanical thinking has caused most of the world's problems, so now we're starting to shift and think more in alignment with life's wisdom. This new view is coming from the framework of the life sciences, which is more in sync with the realities of humans and other species in a world of natural order.

From that conversation, I decided to study biology in college in order to understand life's wisdom. Even though I didn't have a specific career in mind, I would study and seek to understand the processes of living things. As I studied and appreciated the natural richness of this planet, an immense love grew inside of me that called me to be a guardian of our natural heritage. I worked for years on environmental issues; protecting the environment is still one of my great motivations in life. Everything came from that moment in which I connected with a wind that continues to push me. This wind represents something essential in my life quest: to promote that great paradigm change from the mechanical to the ecological.

Other ideas came and settled regarding my winds as I recalled the conversations with Rodrigo and my grandmother. These are the winds I could see and describe.

Sustainability, the cause of the 21st century. I understood that, in our generation, it's impossible not to notice the impact our Western concept of progress has had. This construct is tied to producing and acquiring more and more things, without being conscious of the environmental, social, and human impact that this implies. What my grandmother told me (dealing with the impact of technology and the resulting pollution) is very accurate. Many of us are victims of toxic environments, as well as toxic relationships and toxic organizational cultures that pollute the human soul – products of the mechanistic vision to which Rodrigo spoke.

Some years ago, I attended a workshop called "Awakening the Dreamer, Changing the Dream" offered by the Pachamama Alliance that helped me see the complete picture. The speakers at this workshop explained that our unexamined assumptions regarding progress have brought on three interrelated planetary crises: the environmental crisis, the social justice crisis and the human or spiritual crisis. All three come from human blindness, believing that we are separate and not understanding how intricately interconnected we are.

"Sustainability" can be defined as the cause that seeks to resolve these three big crises. Sustainability invites us to develop a capacity for systems thinking, which human beings are just starting to develop, as well as ecological, collective, and long-term thinking, thinking beyond individual and short-term interests. This capacity allows us to see the big picture and how everything is related in order to make wiser decisions.

Understanding our inter-relatedness and the impact that we have on ecosystems creates the imperative to protect them. As Jane Goodall said, "Only if we understand, can we care. Only if we care, will we help. Only if we help, shall we be saved."[4] Understanding this takes us to what Bernardo Toro, a wise Colombian elder, calls "the paradigm of care." This paradigm implies shifting the current mindset of competition, accumulation, and status. We elevate our consciousness to pursue the common good, brought about by taking care of ourselves and our surroundings.[5]

We are in the middle of a great transition. It has to do with the process of adopting sustainability as a key criteria for making decisions and designing our communities and operating from the paradigm of care. Every person and organization is at some point in this transition, from the most unconscious (and even sabotaging) to the most conscious who are leading this cause. We can't ignore the magnitude of this problem, which affects us all in our daily lives. As I write this book, there's great uncertainty here in Colombia about the availability of energy and water due to climatic occurrences in 2015 and 2016.

Given the dimensions of these crises, there's no other option but to think globally. Because of this, the historical invitation is to start to feel the empathy we have toward our families and loved ones at a broader level. Jeremy Rifkin, American author and activist, talks about transitioning to an "empathic civilization," where we are able to feel the pain of someone suffering at the other side of the planet, as well as the pain of nature itself. This author assures that we have the capacity to do this in our biology; our "mirror neurons" allow us to do this.[6] These are the neurons that activate when someone else is suffering. If we didn't have them, we would live in constant fear and distrust. Rifkin's invitation is that we allow these mirror neurons and our hearts to activate and propel us toward acts of solidarity with each other and with nature.[7] I have faith that that's where we're headed.

We are all change agents. I had the good fortune to attend the World Sustainable Development Summit in Johannesburg, South Africa, in 2002. In between all the forums, exhibits, demonstrations, and marches with people from all over the globe, I learned something important. We can't expect that the solution to the three crises mentioned above will come from governments or even from intergovernmental organizations like the UN. I saw how ineffective those bureaucratic apparatuses are.

I was able to see for myself how the simplest of decisions took hours to make, and that there were all types of obstructions even to take a minute step. After that, there was no guarantee or accountability for agreements to be implemented. These structures have limitations that prevent them from finding and implementing timely, long-term solutions. And we cannot expect these solutions to come from commercial or market forces who have too much interest in growth, generating profit, and continuing to extract resources, as well as a neglect of the long-term effects.

I concluded that civil society and organizations have the best possibilities for creating change. This theory predicts that real changes will come primarily from communities and social movements rather than from politicians or agreements between countries. People will experiment and find new ways of doing things. Their actions will create long-term well-being for communities so we won't have to depend on the current government systems but rather from committed leaders. Eventually, other communities, businesses, families, or individuals will hear of the new initiatives and start to replicate them. Then the change will reach the tipping point.

This approach invites continuous innovation to research, find, and replicate solutions to the current crises. It also promotes the idea of all of us bringing forth alternatives, as small as they may be, at the scale where we are able to contribute. All of us can declare ourselves change agents who can generate necessary responses at every level.

A figurative way to express this is through the *Parable of the Hummingbird*, which I heard for the first time by Wangari Maathai, an African woman and Nobel Peace Prize winner who I had the honor of meeting in Kenya in 2005. The parable goes like this:

> "The forest is burning and while all the animals are running to save their own lives, a hummingbird keeps going back to the river to fetch water in its tiny little beak to pour on the flames. 'You really think that with that small beak you're going to put this fire out?' asks a lion, surrounded by an elephant, a giraffe and a hippopotamus, who are also watching and making fun of the hummingbird. 'I know I can't do it alone,' responds the hummingbird, 'but I'm doing my part.'"

Our definition of success. Our definition of success plays a determining role in defining the direction of our lives. The ideals of Generation X are very different from those of Generation Y. My upbringing was in the transition point between the two generations. For Generation X, which has a more individualistic mindset, the important things are status, power, and money. Gen Xers try to acquire credentials and recognition and stand out in that way. Generation Y (or Millennials) tend to think more collectively, place more value in enjoying the day to day, finding pleasure in what they do, having a cause, and contributing to the betterment of society. Millennials seek to join forces with others in networks, through dynamic and changing processes, where they can have an impact and be considered equals by their peers.

I understood this phenomenon thanks to a Youtube video that my brother, Emiliano, sent me called, "What are you doing right now?" As a Gen Xer, I saw that I dedicated considerable time and energy to receiving recognition and status having completed an MBA at an elite university in the US, worked for a prestigious consulting firm and only accepted high-paying jobs. That was not who I really am or what I truly value though. Prioritizing all of this made me lose my way and forget my main purpose.

It's very easy to succumb to external influences and fall into chasing the prevailing definition of success. But there comes a time where that quest no longer fulfills us and drains us. I felt that my soul was all dried up and my energy very low. When people asked me, "What do you do?" it bothered me to have to answer them. I noticed that in order to recover my sense of direction, I needed to examine my definition of success. This confusion and breakdown contributed significantly to my resolve for undertaking my Life Re-Vision.

Redefining success was not easy at first. In my Life Re-Vision process, finding a network with which I resonated was key. This network was the beginning of what today is ImpactHub Bogotá, part of a global movement for generating community and collaborative working spaces for social innovators. Together, we wrote a collective manifesto for change and started meeting regularly for mutual support. This gave me the strength to break free of the paradigm of conventional success and start to pursue my own ideals, now that I was part of a new tribe with a common purpose.

In the Life Re-Vision workshops, I've seen people from all previous generations question their inherited notions of success they received from their parents or from society. For example, the people before Generation X (the "Baby Boomers") typically think that success is having a stable job in a large company with a distinguished title. This search for stability is almost a fantasy in the changing job market in which we live today. And if stability does happen, many restless people today find it unattractive to stay too long at the same organization. It's never too late to examine these assumptions and definitions of success and dare to declare what is really more important to you.

The feminine. As I mentioned above, one of the great causes that inspired my grandmother and then my mother is female empowerment.

My mother is a well-known feminist in Colombia and, as her daughter, I inherited some of that mindset. I feel proud to be a woman, and I give thanks for how the feminist movement opened up so many opportunities to women of my generation, which our ancestors never had. I'm surprised when I meet women that don't feel proud to be a woman, and I give infinite thanks for having a deep sense of feminine dignity instilled in me.

The way in which I live my feminism is different from that of my mother. It has to do with the search for the feminine. While in college, I read a book called *The Chalice and the Blade* by Riane Eisler. Eisler explains that, in ancient civilizations, there was a matriarchy, goddesses were worshipped, the cycles of nature were honored, and feminine virtues were cultivated: caregiving, the arts, sensitivity, tenderness, and the community.

Then this radically changed. For thousands of years, the masculine dominated (often an unhealthy kind) and considered the feminine to be inferior. The masculine is associated with meeting challenges, accomplishing things, showing force, uplifting the individual, and prioritizing autonomy above everything else. The overemphasis of these masculine values is causing our current imbalances at the family, social, and environmental levels. Eisler's book promotes an empowerment of the feminine and the rebirth of our society from a place of equal partnership between the feminine and the masculine.

Here, we are not talking about the feminine as something exclusive to women and the masculine as exclusive to men. They are principles present in all genders. Like yin and yang, these two polarities complement each other, and they are present in all of us to some degree. We all express a particular combination of feminine/masculine in our personas as a result of family and societal preferences at the time. The women from my maternal lineage, for example, tend to be strong, dominant, and results-oriented. In other words, we are very masculine.

We aren't the only ones. In order to succeed in the world at this time, many women became predominantly masculine. This means that we prioritized achievement, firmness, and independence above everything. At the same time, to some degree, we dismissed vulnerability, interdependence, tenderness, and generosity. I include myself in this group. For strong women, our journey is about rediscovering the femininity in our beings to recalibrate our inner selves and then contribute to balancing our world. This process is explained very well by Maureen Murdock in her book, *The Heroine's Journey*.

Spiritual awakening. The integration with nature, between the feminine and the masculine, and pursuing a path aligned with our souls brings us to a spiritual awakening. The winds of spirituality came into my life from my high school days by means of yoga, meditation, and of reading masters such as Aurobindo and Swami Bramdev. Today, my spiritual path is guided by Bonn Buddhism, Judaism, and the intersection of science and spirituality. There is no question for me that, by engaging in practices that bring inner peace, I am able to feel more balanced and better hear my inner guidance.

Pain and trauma of all types block this awakening and need our constant attention to heal them. Nobody will do this for us. Whatever we don't heal, we will pass on to others and to the next generations. For many of us, the specific constellation of personal and family wounds has been a constant catalyst for our personal evolution. The wisdom of the East together with new findings in neuroscience and quantum physics of the West are causing more and more of us to aspire to a higher consciousness.

Integral philosophy. In my view, spiritual awakening goes hand in hand with integral thinking. In school, they taught most of us to pay more attention to observable and quantifiable phenomena. Everything else was of less value to our teachers, including literature, the arts, and religion/spirituality. Integral philosophers like Ken Wilber taught me that this overvaluing of scientific knowledge causes us to lose contact with our inner selves and with subjective and intersubjective phenomena, which are equally important forms of knowledge. What I feel and what we all feel collectively, although it may not be measurable scientifically, creates realities that can be accessed by our inner wisdom.

If it weren't for integral thinking, I would probably not be writing this book. I wouldn't have learned to value my subjective knowledge, which brought me to create the Life Re-Vision methodology. I wouldn't have paid attention to the inner voice that guided me throughout this process, since it's not a "valid," "certified," or "credible" process. I wouldn't believe in something that hadn't been proven scientifically by means of a formal study. Today, for me, these subjective and intersubjective manifestations are just as valid or more so than any solely scientific, proven knowledge.

Integral theory also has human development models. Reading and attending workshops, I learned that our consciousness develops in stages. In the first stages, we are very centered on ourselves, in our daily difficulties, which prevents us from being available to others. We have a very low level of inner knowledge. Progressively, we start tending to our basic survival needs, security, belonging, and self-esteem, as conceived by Abraham Maslow, the 20th-century psychologist. By engaging in meditation and other contemplative practices, we begin to expand our inner peace and self-knowledge. This gives us greater capacity to listen to others and more possibilities for listening to our own inner guidance instead of following demands and standards of others.

At the same time, we begin to understand that our quality of life depends on the quality of our relationships, which at the same time depend on our ability to communicate. We start to invest more and more time and energy into having deeper connections with others. We become more synchronized with our own souls (and the divine), which nurtures our thriving. We let go of addictions, distractions, and unnecessary fears and worries. We start to increasingly enjoy the present moment, opening us to deeper fulfillment and joy. I've seen that this implies living a more integral and holistic life and taking up hobbies that generate joy within us and create true happiness. It gets to a point in which buying things and working compulsively to obtain goal after goal, or making more money, becomes less important. We start to pay attention to what is really meaningful. From my experience and understanding, these are the gems of living a spiritual life.

The Role of Winds

When I started to appreciate the winds that have "blown" me, I felt like I was a participant in major forces in society, history, and civilization. It was seeing my personal story immersed in a greater collective context, whose influences I had allowed and let in because of my own sensitivities. I felt united with others in these quests and part of a greater undertaking. I found even more direction in my life. The word "direction" connotes orientation. Seeing where these forces had taken me, I felt better situated, with a better sense of where I am currently and where I am going.

Winds put our seeds in motion. Since long ago, our seeds have taken flight, blown by the winds of our era. Our very personal stories are associated with collective forces and ideals. The winds are those positive forces and ideals, which come from our familial, social, and cultural context. These influences are like radio stations that are intercepted by our own personal receivers at a particular historic moment. They install themselves in our minds, hearts, and bodies as we are moved to explore new territories.

What do our winds teach us? We can discern which influences have informed our reasoning and our past decisions. We also receive clues about what types of influences (or radio waves) we want to keep tuning into to embolden our quests. For example, we clarify what kind of readings, programs, workshops, or trips are valuable to keep strengthening these positive winds. It's also intriguing to notice the new winds that come into our lives and to ask ourselves where they are blowing us as well as holding us.

The totality of our winds is infinite. It wouldn't be possible to capture them and count them. The key is to identify the main winds, the most substantial and persistent ones throughout our lives. These are the winds that have motivated us to do the most significant or extraordinary things. They could be great movements like sustainability or as specific as reading a single book. I know of people for whom a book, workshop, music album, or conversation changed their life.

Recognizing our winds situates us in phenomena external to us. Up until this moment, our Life Re-Vision has been centered in the individual self – our bones and seeds. Winds are of the world. They are external to us; they have moved us and will continue to move us. Being attentive to these forces and more conscious of which winds we want to catch makes us wiser.

Let's Talk about Winds

In the Life Re-Vision workshops, participants share their winds, which helps them clarify the forces that have influenced them in life. One participant, Natalia, shared her winds at the time of the workshop held in February of 2015:

> "I am driven by political issues related to a more active citizenship, social networks, protests like the Arab Spring. I am fascinated by marches and organizations committed to changing paradigms. Also, ideas that come from Pope Francisco, Barack Obama, Antanas Mockus (a distinguished former mayor of Bogotá), Michelle Bachelet, Hillary Clinton, and most recently Malala. A more inclusive feminism, where we each have our role and don't imply that one is better than the other; they complement each other. Globalization, the internet, which has brought information more quickly and a spiritual awakening along with it."

Another participant, Liliana, talked about her winds:

> "The lifestyle and culture in the city of Strasbourg, where I live now, and at the same time the land where I was born, Colombia. The immigration process. The search for happiness, the re-

turn to the sacred feminine. Seeing the connection between our health and our emotions. The separation of families (I am separated.) Very importantly, conscious maternity. I was supported by a midwife who taught me a lot about pregnancy, labor, upbringing, and being present as a mother. I went through a profound process, and I think this view of maternity is something that society is starting to adopt. Finally, the spiritual search that many people are engaged in, the wisdom of the East brings meditation and contemplative practices. Quantum physics – I've done courses with someone who does energy-based work and has exposed me to an interesting approach."

Felipe, a Colombian pianist, shared his winds:

"The idea of being 'culturally amphibious' as Antanas Mockus calls it. I lived abroad for a long time, so now I'm from here and also from there. The idea of making music as a tool for social change. New ways of listening to and understanding music, changing paradigms about my role as a musician, thinking about who we are as a Colombian and Latin American society."

There are winds that propel us and others that hold us back. These, I consider "counter-winds." An example of a counter-wind here in Latin America is the habit we have of always comparing ourselves to Europe or the United States. In musical research, we are always comparing ourselves and that needs to stop.

Winds and Counter-Winds

Felipe gave me the idea of looking more closely at those winds that don't necessarily resonate with us but at the same time influence us in ways contrary to our own nature. We will call these "counter-winds." This reminds me of Heidegger's concept of "the they," which I brought up in the introduction of this book. According to him, a human being stops being authentic when they live a life guided by what people say, by fashion or the "norm," without questioning it at all. We can easily let ourselves get swept up by the wrong winds and later end up asking ourselves, "How is it that I wound up over here if this isn't my own authentic life?"

This is very well-illustrated in the novel *The Death of Ivan Ilyich* by Tolstoy, a suggested reading in my Integral Coaching® certification program at New Ventures West. It's the story of a Russian man in imperial times, around the year 1800. He chooses a prestigious career path, has a wife and family to show off, purchases the ideal house, and is well-regarded by his entourage. Nevertheless, in spite of all this, he still feels like a failure. He becomes more and more neurotic, with constant pains and medical problems. In the middle of this crisis, he feels a profound loneliness while he is surrounded by a circle of cold aristocrats he has built for himself. His health takes a fatal turn, and on his deathbed, he does something similar to a Life Re-Vision. He realizes that his life was empty and he really doesn't know how to live. When he is capable of telling himself the truth and no longer justifying himself or claiming that his life "was good," he starts to feel at ease and dies peacefully.

This story is tragic. It was already too late, on his deathbed, to ask himself what a meaningful life is. From what I've seen and from my own experience, a life well-lived is a life in which we are in sync with our life force and creative drive, our essential qualities and the right influences (or "winds") so that we can express our own uniqueness.

Each step of Life Re-Vision invites us to define who we are and who we aren't by using discernment. There are forces in culture that are beneficial and drive us forward, while others keep us distracted and dormant, unaware of our own truth. It's important to become critical of these counter-winds so as not to end up living the wrong life. The main problem we will confront in this chapter is that we are vulnerable to external forces not in alignment with our being, which can push us in the wrong direction.

In the days in which I was writing this chapter, a colleague told me she was reading a book called *El Sinsentido Común* (*The Uncommon*

Sense.) It seemed very synchronous. I bought the e-book and started to look at the index. Effectively, the Spanish writer Borja Vilaseca does a thorough inventory of counter-winds and invites people to go through a Life Re-Vision in his own way.

The counter-winds he mentions are egocentrism, materialism, the unconscious economy, appearances, and greed, among others. In short, all of them have to do with being centered on self-interest, which leads to emptiness and meaninglessness. Borja Vilaseca invites us to change our paradigm toward the common good, and describes a paradigm as "a conjunction of beliefs, values, priorities and aspirations...Which becomes the way in which we see, understand and act in the world." Later, he illustrates this with a metaphor. "Each of us looks at and filters reality through a predetermined set of glasses, whose color has been chosen and painted by our socioeconomic surroundings in which we have developed as individuals."[8]

The antidote to counter-winds is to connect with our inner compass. This "instrument" shows us our north star and aligns us with the right winds in order to move forward. We all have a compass inside of us that detects what gives us vitality and what takes it away from us, what makes us feel coherent or incoherent, what brings us closer to our essence and what takes us away from it, what brings us meaning or what seems absurd.

To have a fulfilling life, we need to learn to constantly reinvent ourselves, based on the learning experiences of our lives. We need to know how to calibrate and attune to our inner compass, to read into what's truly life-giving in the current moment we are in. From there, we choose consciously which influences to allow in and propel us forward.

The best way I have found to explain how this inner compass works is the concept of the "felt sense" authored by Eugene Gendlin. One of Gendlin's students, Egardo Riveros, a Chilean psychologist, is a practitioner of a technique called Focusing that centers in connecting to the felt sense. Riveros defines Focusing as "the art of listening to our inner lives and dialoguing with them." In his book, *Focusing: From the Heart and to the Heart*, he describes that "The felt sense is the inner beacon that guides us in the darkness" and "a compass to connect me with my inner wisdom."9 There's something in our bodies that speaks to us, that tells us what is right for us and what resonates with our essence. Using our felt sense, we can "feel" which winds are ours to join, and from this, which direction to take.

In this process of calibrating our compass, it's possible that certain dreams start to vanish, replaced by other more authentic dreams. Sometimes, this can be frightening – bringing forward regret and hurt. I'm living this pain at this very moment as I write this. I'm thirty-nine years old, with the decision not to have children 90% made. This has been very hard on my family, especially my mother. I thought I wanted children for many years. But, upon getting to know myself better, I realized it was a borrowed dream.

A Change of Winds

People that go through deep transitions know what "a change of winds" is about. Once we are living the life we had dreamed but it isn't fulfilling, it's likely that we were following the wrong winds or that those winds lost their strength and became obsolete. Something like that happened to Catalina, a participant of a Life Re-Vision workshop. When she came to the workshop, she was still attached to her life as a public administrator. She had already analyzed her winds and counterwinds some years prior in an essay she had written and shared with me:

> "I was born on March 11, 1985, in Bogotá, in the middle of a serious economic and political conflict, in which attacks on civil society by the drug lords were daily occurrences. My education was influenced greatly by the experience my father had in his many trips to Europe, especially to France. Because of this, he did the best he could to provide my siblings and I with a Cartesian education, very methodical and rational. He found it in the French Lycée of Bogotá, in which I studied all of my primary

and secondary education without any breaks from 1989 through 2003.

"This, I believe, greatly influenced my way of thinking, perceiving, and analyzing things, along with giving me a very non-neoliberal point of view. I was given all the data and frames of mind to encourage my pathological hate for the United States and for the neoliberal model in lieu of a much more sociodemocratic model, like the one in France.

"I can't talk about my historical perspective and experience without naming globalization. Why? First, because I share my values and ideals with a much larger community. I feel I have more in common with a French or English middle-class person than with someone from my own country, like a rural person who lives 100 km away from Bogotá, or even with someone who lives in Ciudad Bolivar (the poorest district of Bogotá.)

"Clearly, my concerns and interests have everything to do with the new global connectedness, which goes beyond national interests. This interconnection gives me access to theories, information, and values I share with people, not necessarily who live in my country, but who are part of an 'imagined community' as Perry Anderson (English historian and political analyst) would say. This is a community I have never met, and with whom I communicate in non-physical spaces (the internet being the most important among these), which homogenizes space, time, and people's beliefs in different parts of the world.

"I've had to confront very difficult realities in my life, like the kidnapping of many of my family members in the Llanos by the guerillas in 1999 (eastern plains region of Colombia, bordering Venezuela), as well as the land grab and my family leaving the Llanos because of the constant threats from those armed groups. However, because of leaving the Llanos, I don't think about the armed conflict anymore, as if it had never existed, because it no longer affects me. It's not a coincidence that I'm interested in the social sciences, especially political science and history, so that I can understand the society in which I live and do something about it.

"Also, I'm framed by a middle class that grew thanks to social mobility, in turn, a result of changes in the education system and its democratization. This let my father get ahead and no longer be just another poor peasant from Caparrapi. He's now an economist working for the National Department of Statistics (DANE in Colombia.)

"Because of all this, I think I'm more of a social democrat, totally against the current social order, and even more against the stupid and inept elites that haven't been able to deliver a viable national and economic system. So then, my life's work is to bring about change, and one of my priorities was to go to a good university where, as my father said, 'you pay tuition upfront for the connections you will make.' These contacts were what would allow me later to work in the public sector, or anywhere I want to.

"All of these stories explain why I'm here and not somewhere else. They explain my way of thinking and my dream of changing things because I think they're not fair. But also, if I honestly consider the idea that we can write our own story, I can't avoid seeing that we are all up to a point determined by certain 'structures' that we reproduce daily, like poverty. I prefer to think of poverty as something structural and not individual."

In this text, we can see the winds that moved Catalina in her college years. If we were to list her winds, we could say that they are Cartesian thought, globalization, the middle class, political science, history, public sector service, and social-democratic thought. You can see the strong influence of her education and her family, especially her father.

Five years later, Catalina's winds are very different, although there is an essence that remains. After a conscious process of connecting with her own experiences and discerning the winds that are current for her now, she wrote a letter to her family, hoping to explain to them who she is becoming. We can hear a more authentic voice emerging here, one which doesn't reject her family's legacy but rather seeks to find her own way, based on her genuine sensitivity.

Spiritual awakening. A leap in the dark, this is the basis of everything. More than anything else, a spiritual awakening is a very personal experience. Everything started on the day of my twenty-fifth birthday. I had just graduated, had a job, felt beautiful, had a boyfriend...And a horrible existential emptiness. During this time, I lost all the points of reference that gave me a sense of identity: being a leader who wants to change the economic system and being Matía's girlfriend. Everything fell apart. And yet, now I feel so confident, so fulfilled, so...happy. My life has so much meaning, I can't even explain it. My fears have reduced significantly. There are moments in our lives that seem shocking, that bring us to question everything we think we know about ourselves, who we are, how we think, how we act, and how we relate to each other. I think there's a global calling to go beyond who we think we are. It's not a secret for anybody that my journey started five fantastic years ago, and now, I don't even consider starting my day without breathing and meditating.

I believe I have clarity on my life's principles which are open to further exploration: 1) SERVICE: Selflessness. How can I contribute to others' well-being knowing their elevation is tied to mine? 2) SPIRITUALITY: How can I maintain peace and spiritual practice at every waking moment? How can I calm my mind with the end goal of serving with the best efficacy? 3) NONVIOLENCE: How can I love everybody with such fervor that there's no space for bad will? How can I experience love in all my relationships? 4) COMMUNITY: I'm part of an interconnected network of life. The "I" doesn't exist independently from relationships. How can I nurture and strengthen those relationships? 5) SIMPLICITY AND REGENERATION: Sustainability is not sufficient. How can I align my thoughts, works, and actions so that I can give life back to the relationships on this earth on which I depend so much?

Intentional community. A general term that represents a broad variety of life alternatives. An intentional community is a group of people that have chosen to live or work together toward a common goal or vision. Thousands of these communities currently exist: rural or urban, communal or individualistic, spiritual or secular, large or small. They could be based around different issues such as economic cooperation, equality, environmental sustainability, education, health, participatory government, personal growth, social activism, spirituality, and voluntary minimalism.

Gift and sacred economies. When I left for France on an academic scholarship, the money I received wasn't enough to pay for my lifestyle. But in France, they gave me everything. Not only that, I was able to experience the power of being part of a solidarity-based economy. That is to say, the whole time I was there, I was taken care of by people I just met and I did the same for them. In other words, I went around for almost two years, getting everything I wanted but also giving other people what they wanted, and money was never a problem for anyone. I got everything by just asking the universe for it; it just came. It was like magic. What's more, now that I make less money, I can see that I give more.

It's impossible to count the times people opened up their houses for me, invited me along, even gave me free airplane tickets. Suddenly, my life started moving in a different way, and...It's still like that. It's impossible to tell all the stories I have of receiving people in my house, taking them on trips with me – giving, giving, giving. My last birthday, I invited my parents to a course I paid for. I feel like I can give and receive, and these "exchanges" become something sacred. As such, what

I've been doing is getting access to experiences, goods, and services – not in exchange for money or even as a barter or reciprocal arrangement but rather from a joint agreement of reciprocal donations. I give from what I know and then, from what I receive, I can then start to give.

The sharing economy, the common-good economy, and the gift economy are three tributaries that converge in a river that's becoming more and more abundant as the streams of the conventional economy start to weaken. Giving gifts creates positive relationships by directly filling a need, which at the same time creates solidarity, communication, and community. I feel like I give more, help more, and belong more.

Death in contemporary society. My relationship with death is from long ago. From suicidal thoughts and attempts from a young age, supporting Matias in grieving his father after his death, always working with issues of violence, performing rituals at different transitions of life...But what marked me the most was accompanying the agony of my Aunt Dolly in December of 2015. It was an intense time. This event impacted my life very deeply. After her death, I was invited to "accompany" the death of three other people, and it's been fascinating. On top of this, there was the deep pain of breaking up with Matias and a clear transition in my work life. Very heavy changes, all at the same time, that have brought intense grief.

Post-conflict. I'm noticing that when I support a family in the acceptance of someone's death and subsequent grieving, magic happens. If I consider that we are all one big family, I can intuit the power of giving death and pain their proper place in our planet, especially in the context of post-conflict situations. Reframing pain as a testament of the interconnectedness of our web of life, and therefore, participating in the healing of it, has become my purpose. I discovered this framing by reading Joanna Macy (philosopher, activist, and student of Buddhism) and her concept of deep ecology.

Declaring these new winds to her family required immense courage on Catalina's part. It's telling your tribe, who had another image of you, "These are the ideals and values that will be moving me from now on." Particularly, when some or all of these winds are at odds with your family's or society's worldview, which doesn't necessarily value spirituality, that hides death – that is based in an individualist model instead of a community-based one. However, she had faith, and took a leap in the dark, letting herself be blown by these new winds that filled her with inspiration.

Paradigm Shift for Catalina

Earlier Paradigm	Emergent Paradigm
Cartesian, modernist thinking, and rationality as guide	Spiritual awakening, values, and principles as guide
Middle-class social democrat thinking	Gift economy
Public service	Community and intentional community
The disciplines of political science and history, with an academic perspective	The subjective and intersubjective phenomenon of death in contemporary society and the post-conflict from an experiential perspective

Having lived a similar experience as Catalina and seen many people in transition, I highlight the importance of declaring your winds. Winds help us to perceive where we are and where we are going so that we can make sound decisions. They free us from being on automatic pilot and coming from a place of lack into being guided by inspiration. At the same time, they help us connect to other people who will strengthen our life's purpose, nurture our inner flame, and keep us in motion. When you are in a "flock" with others who are flying in the same direction, the power is immense.

Being a Source of Winds

Certain people become a source of winds in their lifetime. My friend Vivek, who is from India and with whom I connected over the internet, reminded me of the emperor Ashoka, who lived in ancient times in his country. We were talking about the Ashoka organization, which promotes social entrepreneurship, where I worked during my stay in India. He asked me, "Do you know the history of the emperor Ashoka?" I told him that I only knew that he'd been a great change agent in his time, since they had named the organization after him.

Vivek summarized the story for me. This emperor started out by murdering his father and his brother in order to take the throne. Then he violently invaded many territories neighboring his own to increase his sphere of influence. His ambition and greed knew no limits. This behavior kept on for a long time until one day, he had an existential moment. He was walking in a pool of blood after a battle, and he asked himself, "What am I doing with my life?"

After this question, he embarked on a spiritual quest culminating in his conversion to Buddhism, which had only been in India for three hundred years at that time and was still a small-scale phenomenon. Ashoka not only transformed his life with Buddhism, but he also created a kind and socially just kingdom, based on the principles of his new religion. He managed to spread Buddhism throughout all of Asia and because of this, it became a large-scale phenomenon. Vivek told me that, were it not for Ashoka, it's possible that Buddhism wouldn't have the worldwide influence that it does today.

The emperor Ashoka was the source of the wind of Buddhism in Asia. Clearly, Ashoka didn't invent Buddhism, but he was responsible for this wind influencing thousands of people. Whatever your own religion, one can appreciate the positive influence of Buddhism in bringing kindness, compassion, and peace to a kingdom. Ashoka made history because of this, and his reign is regarded with admiration.

Just as we can be receptors of winds, we can also be a source of them for our own times. Our effectiveness depends a great measure on the context. A little while ago during an interview, a wise French woman called Irene said, "We think that we invent and create things. Really what we are doing is responding to the needs of our surroundings. If we are properly synchronized, these inventions or creations gain momentum. Otherwise, they don't."

If we see things in that way, Ashoka was a channel for the transmission of a wind that his point in history needed. He was the perfect person for the perfect wind. We can ask ourselves what our role is and what our own moment in time needs. Each one of us has a particular and privileged place in life to be the source of certain winds.

The wind of reconciliation. Father Leonel Narváez, a friend and collaborator, inspires me because of his persistent spreading of the wind of reconciliation in a country like Colombia, which has been at war for several decades. Since Leonel created the Foundation for Reconciliation, it has gained incredible strength because of his clarity about the main message he wanted to spread in the world.

How did he obtain such clarity? Leonel participated in the peace talks in San Vicente del Caguán from 1998 until 2002. The organizers brought the most prestigious negotiators and applied the most advanced methods and practices of dialogue and peace-building. Despite all this, the talks failed, leaving Leonel and many others frustrated and bewildered. Leonel went to study at Harvard, motivated by two questions: "What went wrong in those dialogues?" and "What was missing in order to obtain peace?"

The answer he came to after lots of deep research, supported by a focus group that met weekly, was "forgiveness and reconciliation." Leonel was inspired by certain peace-building efforts and people that brought a spiritual element into the process, like Desmond Tutu, who emphatically affirmed, "Without forgiveness, there is no future." Desmond Tutu was one of the main figures in the truth commissions during the post-Apartheid period in South Africa. In those commissions, where peace was really forged between the victim and the perpetrator, the final thing that stopped the vicious cycle of violence and vengeance was forgiveness.

Leonel concluded from his research that you have to break these vicious cycles of recycled revenge and "replace the irrationality of violence with the irrationality of forgiveness." Leonel means that, in order to forgive, you need something more profound than common thinking, than our routine mechanisms of the ego, something on a spiritual level, an "existential leap," as he calls it, similar to the one undergone by Ashoka. We can ask ourselves the same when we are full of resentment toward someone, toward life, or toward ourselves. "Where am I going with this? What happens if I forgive myself and others?" The organization founded by Leonel in 2003 has made a massive impact, not just in Colombia but worldwide.

He has gained recognition from various organizations like the Ashoka organization, which invited him to be an "Ashoka fellow" and added him to their network of leaders in social entrepreneurship. His main method, Schools for Forgiveness and Reconciliation, are now in seventeen different countries, with networks of volunteers who spread his message in countries such as Mexico, where rates of violent crime have been growing exponentially. They see in this message a way to heal the wounds of a society that is becoming more and more fragmented. All of this came from one person who originated a powerful wind that has moved thousands; receptors whose souls were ready to move in sync with this new message. To celebrate my friend Leonel, I wrote an article in 2014 telling this story for the magazine *Innovación Social* titled "Colombia Exports Social Innovations for Peace."

The wind of eco-neighborhoods. Leonel and I met while working for an entity that was part of Bogotá's municipal government that regulates and supports the community action boards. These boards, which are government structures at the neighborhood level, promote local participation. Our boss was my mother, Isabel Londoño. I was a volunteer at that time.

It turned out that I wrote my undergraduate thesis on the theme of ecovillages and eco-neighborhoods and their viability in Bogotá. It was the model I found as a solution to the sustainability crisis we are living through in cities, with environmental, human, and social justice repercussions, which I have referred to above. Ecovillages – whose urban version I referred to as "eco-neighborhoods" in my thesis – are intentional communities of people who aspire to an overarching sustainability at the social, ecological, economic, and human/cultural levels.

Allow me to explain my personal motivation behind promoting eco-neighborhoods. Besides finding a solution to the crises, I experienced a hunger in my soul. In a city, one can grow up very lonely. This was my case; I grew up in Bogotá as an only child of divorced parents. I spent most of my after-school time playing with toys, playing video games, and doing my homework alone. I studied in a school that offered academic excellence but emotional ignorance.

I decided to study biology at a small all-women's college two hours from Boston in the US, which provided just what I was missing: a sense of community. From the moment I arrived, I felt welcomed. My differences in nationality, personality, and other markers of diversity were all celebrated. There was space for my intensity, insatiable curiosity, and contrast of being a strong and sensitive woman. It was like a rebirth. I formed deep friendships, like the one I had with Anita, a nun at that time, and Julia, a non-traditional student given her age. (She went back to school after ten years of traveling.)

With Anita, who led us on a series of spiritual retreats using symbols and objects from her trips to Africa, I discovered the power of the circle: the circle of trust, the circle of words, the ritual circle. Between the three of us, Anita, Julia, and I, we formed a little group (the "Circle of Stones") to tune into each other, create group resonance, and activate our spirits. We used music, poetry, symbols, and inner exploration to create transformative experiences.

In parallel to my spiritual explorations, I was fully living my paradigm shift toward the ecological, which Rodrigo had sown in me. I started out by visualizing Colombia as a model of sustainability, engaged in the protection of its biodiversity, pursuing a green economy, and privileging sectors such as ecotourism. Tourism would be carried out under the paradigm of care – encouraging people to care for, protect, and value that which is ours while in contact with local communities whose knowledge would be given more and more weight.

This type of local thinking brought me to ask myself how to really live sustainably from day to day. I met Steve Hall, an idealistic businessman from the BaHa'i faith, who introduced me to ecovillages. He mentored me and encouraged me to explore a model for sustainability that included the spiritual. My first direct experience was with Sirius Community, which was less than two hours away from the university. Not having access to a car, I convinced the environmental studies professor to take us there on a field trip.

Our visit to the Sirius Community ecovillage ignited something deep in me. It touched every aspect of my being as it was full of symbols and spaces that invited me to commune with others, nature, science, and spirit. Their welcoming rituals fed my emotional hunger; my scientific curiosity and connection to nature were met by way of the gardens, greenhouses and techniques for construction and regeneration of resources, to the aesthetics and beauty and charm of the living areas, made from locally sourced clay and stone.

Coincidences kept guiding me. At that time, a book had just been published about Gaviotas, an eco-settlement in the east of Colombia titled *Gaviotas: A Village to Reinvent the World* by Alan Weisman, who did a presentation at a nearby university. Tying up loose ends, I dreamed up this concept for an ecologically based settlement, both urban and rural, to become widespread in Colombia and in the world. This settlement would work as a catalyst for paradigm change, and as a solution to a system lacking in solidarity producing an inner turmoil that wasn't only mine. I saw eco-settlements as platforms for more creativity, personal growth, and community.

The conclusion of my undergraduate thesis was that, although social, economic, and environmental problems are complex, tangible solutions can be implemented at community or local levels, both in urban and rural areas (i.e., ecovillages and eco-neighborhoods.) Communities have the capacity and flexibility to work across the board and implement innovative solutions to persistent problems, using the creativity and ingenuity of its residents.

My mother helped me a lot with my thesis. One day, we were together in her car, and a light bulb went on in her head. "Now that I'm going to work for Mockus [the then mayor of Bogotá], what if I propose that we implement a version of the eco-neighborhoods in Bogotá?" The idea made both of us smile from ear to ear. For me, it meant the possibility of seeing my work manifested on a large scale and testing the viability of eco-neighborhoods in Bogotá. For her, it was the possibility of bringing a new idea to the city government, and breathing new life into the Community Action program which she had just been put in charge of.

And that's what happened. My mom and I brought the winds of eco-neighborhoods to the city of Bogotá in 2001 when she began in her position as head of Community Action. She suggested we use a pithy name, "Ecobarrios," for the initiative. This government program Ecobarrios ("barrio" means "neighborhood") was coordinated by my friend Carlos, an architect and community planner, and included hundreds of projects that were formulated by the communities themselves, all having the same four dimensions as the ecovillages (environmental, economic, social, and human) and leaving their mark on various community leaders.

Ten years later, a woman named Tatiana contacted me. She told me that she was going to do a doctorate and was interested in studying the phenomenon of Ecobarrios in Bogotá. I was surprised to discover that ten years later, community leaders were still using the same model to conceptualize their neighborhoods. At around the same time, Alberto, a great leader of ecovillages in Mexico and Latin America, asked me to write something about eco-neighborhoods in Bogotá, which had inspired eco-neighborhoods in Mexico, where the model was perfected and had a big impact. Although I was never able to publish my book about the subject and have stopped working on it, I saw that this was a wind I helped spread that kept blowing and touched other people. It was very satisfying as I understood that these winds that we originate gain force when the surrounding context calls out for them and is ready for them. Therefore, these winds will have an impact that we may never fully comprehend. Winds are given with love and will take on a life of their own life and start to move the hearts they need to move.

In conclusion, cultivating winds is an art and a science. The stories of how the wind of reconciliation emerged for Leonel and how the wind of eco-neighborhoods emerged for me evoke a slow-cooking process, which is what these endeavors require. On one hand, we need discipline to identify and recognize the winds that we have received and study them fully. On the other hand, we need to internalize these winds and then create our own blend of knowledge and messaging, using our hearts and intuition, always paying attention to what the world might need at the moment.

This description gives us a new vision of how and what to study so that periods of learning become times for contemplating existing winds and incubation of our own winds, instead of simply mechanically absorbing knowledge without any purpose or deeper meaning. We can also see that connecting to our bones and seeds can point to specific winds that are ready to carry us, supporting us in who we are becoming and who we are.

Just like Leonel found his wind of reconciliation by being inspired by his experiences in the failed peace process and how I found my wind of Ecobarrios by recalling my lonely childhood and understanding the importance of community, we can all create knowledge that has both story and soul.

Collective Winds

Just as we are able to identify and declare our individual winds, we can also do this collectively. Like Tara Mohr says, it's immensely powerful when we partner with a force greater than our own to lift our endeavors. I experienced this with two communities which I am a part of, *La Arenera* ("The Sandbox") and *Aldeafeliz* ("Happy Village".) *La Arenera* was started in 2008 by many social entrepreneurs who wanted to initiate a paradigm change. Together, we wrote a beautiful manifesto, which gathered our collective aspirations as well as the paradigm change we saw happening. Here is the gist:

Paradigm Shift

Earlier Paradigm	Emergent Paradigm
Only leaders have the answers.	We are all responsible to contribute to the answers.
Power is concentrated.	Power is distributed.
I protect myself from competition.	I participate in co-creating with others.
Values are given.	I formulate my own values.
Other people's differences threaten me.	Other people's differences nourish me.
The truth is absolute and we slowly approach it.	The truth is relative and we build it with our actions.
Linear solutions.	Systemic approaches.
Nature as a resource.	Nature as the system I am part of.

After we collectively declared this, we kept on learning how to contribute to this paradigm shift together. Part of the answer we came to was inviting others into new ways of communicating and leading. La Arenera is now part of a global network that has trained thousands of people in participatory leadership techniques using the Art of Hosting® methodology. In this approach, instead of imposing upon others, you open space for conversation and co-creation. As a result, there is a growing number of facilitators of meaningful conversations that are leading their organizations, families, and nations in new ways.

Let's consider another example of collective winds: the Aldeafeliz Ecovillage. Aldeafeliz is a collective social entrepreneurial project that we co-founded in 2006. A group of my friends and I put it into motion, led by Carlos, the architect that coordinated the Ecobarrios program, as mentioned above. After many years and inspired by La Arenera, Aldeafeliz ventured to make its own clear manifesto for change. In order to do this, we identified our collective winds by participating in a very powerful workshop called "Future Search," moderated by our great friend Alejandro and his team. On a big wall full of flip chart paper, everyone wrote their own individual winds associated with the creation of Aldeafeliz.

Carlos was the person in charge of crafting a story using all the writings on the wall. This is what he narrated:

> The founders of Aldeafeliz are the generation after the revolutions of the 1970s and 1980s. Many of us directly descended from the revolutionaries and guerillas of that era, and also from the people on the other side of the struggle (the right wing.) But these revolutions and counterattacks didn't work; they created violence and environmental and social crises. Many people were displaced, others released their armed fight and, in the end, reintegrated into society. We grew up among demobilized guerrilla members and had to bond with them

> We all were born into that complex and polarized "stew." We had lots of love crises with our partners, the world, life itself, our life goals, and sometimes we had awakenings of consciousness. We took numerous trips that brought knowledge from different places and created meeting points with other worlds.

> The creators of Aldeafeliz are a new and restless generation who traveled, studied, and wanted to experiment with new ideas.

Some of these ideas came from social and environmental summits. We discovered ecovillages in the year 2000 to create a balance between the heart and the mind (underemphasizing the mind in this ultra-rational world, but not so much heart that we would wind up in constant crisis.) Rather, we seek to find ourselves so we can grow in every dimension and generate new initiatives.

We are children of the digital age. This project was born out of people coming together over the internet. All of our communications in ten years have been digital. One of the first things we invested in when we bought this land was to install an internet connection so that we could keep working and stay connected with the whole world.

We live in the countryside. This has to do with a reverse migration since the revolutions and the violence caused a mass exodus from the cities. This new model of ecovillages is the opposite; it has to do with returning to the rural areas.

As the children of extremist movements, our purpose is to integrate the opposites. When we created the village, we went to an extreme in the amount of participation allowed in our decision making, using consensus. With this system, one has to listen to everybody all the time for every decision needed to be made. So, in that extreme we realized that consensus decision making was an inefficient and draining system. We had to come back to center and adopt sociocracy as our new decision-making framework, which is an efficient compromise between results and participation. Instead of staying at extremes, we've moved toward the integration of opposites: participation and efficiency.

Aldeafeliz comes out of all these influences like a meeting between the ancestral and the modern, generating a new way to relate to each other and our surroundings. The discussion is no longer about whether we're communists, socialists, or capitalists, but rather how we relate to each other and our surroundings. All of the emphasis is in relationships. And that's why it's called Aldeafeliz ("Happy Village"), because it's a search for happiness, for harmony with everything around us. The themes that drive us are family and healing the collective and personal.

Reading this again makes my heart beat louder. I love feeling that I'm a part of a collective with common winds; it energizes me. These collective winds have given me strength in moments when my personal life has been directionless, or when I was stuck in the middle of a relationship crisis. Getting to know our winds and collective winds with others is a way of immunizing ourselves from adverse life situations that can bring us down. These winds pick us back up again and give us strength to keep going in the right direction, even if we don't have everything clear yet.

Declare Your Winds

Once you have all your bones and seeds, you can start to see which winds are most suited to your quests – to your personal path. There are the winds that have marked you more than others, that have moved you in significant ways and are in tune with your sensitivities and your deeper needs and purpose. These are the winds that have carried your most precious seeds along.

The main premise of this chapter is that, when we identify and declare the positive influences in our lives (our winds), our confidence in our sense of direction strengthens. We identify the direction we have been pointing toward, leading us to where we are now. We can always choose which direction to follow at each new stage of our lives.

What are your winds? You probably already know what they are! This is an exciting moment because you notice that you *have* had a direction, that your winds have been blowing you along and continue to do so. We are channels for our winds, receptors, and transmitters at the same time. It's time to declare which winds are aligned with your most sincere inquiries.

Declaring your winds has a very important implication. You are no longer at the mercy of the random winds of your era. "The they" from Heidegger (or the "shoulds") have less power over you because you declare which messages and paradigms are yours. Without a clear guide, we let ourselves be moved around by whatever is around us, which is sometimes good but not always. Push away those influences that you no longer want to move you. Sometimes winds can be contradictory. Exercise your right to decide what moves you and what doesn't. Use your freedom of discernment toward all the winds you are exposed to.

You will begin to recalibrate your inner compass so as to direct yourself more deliberately in directions that have real meaning for you. Activate the felt sense of your gut as a way of navigating through life. Follow the instinct of your Daemon. This is an act of trust. When you identify a wind that is pulling you – sometimes in a completely new direction in your life (as happened to Catalina) – it can be challenging. But the fact that you declare it as a wind allows you to let yourself, little by little, be guided by this new force, which, if aligned with your essence, will lead you to a good place. Like the wise poet Rumi said, "Let yourself be silently drawn by the stronger pull of what you truly love. It will not lead you astray."

Let's get to work then. A general principle regarding winds is that they are collective in nature. They aren't personal stories or particular people, unless they are myths or heroes for many. One thing is a wind and another is its channel. For example, I received the ecological-thinking wind from Rodrigo. Rodrigo was the channel.

So that you can get better oriented, there are different types of winds. Although they are not confined to this list, these categories are a good start with their respective examples.

Conceptual: Currents of thought that are used as filters to interpret reality. Examples: Cartesian thought, integral philosophy.

Political: Movements with ideologies that define the way we should organize ourselves collectively to resolve our needs. Examples: the sociodemocratic current, ecologism, the "Indignados movement" (2011, Spain.)

Historical: Moments we live in that motivate us to learn more and possibly participate in what is happening. Examples: peace processes, post-conflict, post-apartheid.

Religious, Spiritual: Systems of values and practices that influence the way we live and answer existential and moral questions. Examples: Buddhism, Catholicism.

Academic: Disciplines that guide our interpretation of reality, as well as the ways in which we exercise our professions. Examples: economics, political science, history.

Cultural: Ideological currents that influence a group of people in their ways of thinking, living and creating. Examples: impressionism, baby boomers, generation X, millennials.

Personalities and Guides: People of great influence whose ideology offers life alternatives for a number of people. Examples: Gandhi, Mandela, Malala.

Reflect in Your Journal:

To identify your winds, you can use these questions:

- *What currents of thought were present as you were growing up or in your education that influenced and defined who you are today?*
- *What books have you read that marked you the most? What workshops have you attended instilled powerful ideas in you? What are your greatest interests?*
- *Who have been your heroes/heroines or role models? What's your idea of success and where did it come from?*
- *How would you characterize the people you like to have around you? What kind of conversations do you like to have?*
- *What are your political preferences and why? What values are behind those preferences?*
- *What stories have you been told that have stayed in your memory and keep inspiring you?*
- *What kind of music do you like to listen to and what does that say about your ideologies? What other cultural currents have captivated and influenced you?*
- *What historical or social phenomena happened in your lifetime and moved you in a certain direction?*

VISUALIZATION

Consult with Your Daemon

If you have forgotten any of your winds, this is the time to reclaim them again from the desert of neglect. Go back to the scene of the campsite with the bonfire, your bones in front of you. These bones show you what is important to you. Observe them. With your song and the heat of the fire, these bones assemble together to form a being: your Daemon.

Now you have your Daemon in front of you. In the fur of your Daemon, there are seeds embedded, your essential stories. Visualize again how you put the colored seeds on a fabric, on the stand so that you can admire them. Then, see how these seeds take flight as winds elevate and blow them to new worlds.

Ask your Daemon what these winds are. They are the values, ideas, and most important contexts that have moved you, that make you resonate and align with others. Ask your Daemon to remind you of these wind – in particular, those that are most relevant now. When you receive a response, thank it for its wisdom and let it run free again.

For someone to be a source of winds, they first have to acknowledge the winds they have received and been blown by. In the following lists, start with recognizing the winds that moved you, which came from other channels. Then, if it is the case, harvest the winds that originated from you and influenced others in the context in which you find yourself. Take note of how harvesting these winds makes you feel. Let yourself feel connected to something bigger than yourself, the forces of culture and civilization for which you are the antenna and transmitter.

Reflect in Your Journal:
- *What are the main winds that have moved you?*
- *What winds coming from you have moved others?*

Giving Life to Your Winds

Just as we learned to give life to our seeds, we will talk about how to give life to your winds. The writer Christina Baldwin says that in the first years of writing journals, she focused only on her own story. But as her writing matured, she started to include more and more of "the world's story," as she tells it. Today, she continues to interweave her personal story with the greater story, which helps her feel like part of a collective process.[10]

To give life to your winds, the invitation is to constantly identify the external influences and contexts that are moving you in the right direction. In this way, we allow these winds to strengthen and move us. This makes us feel alive and like participants in something bigger than ourselves. You can do this in many ways, including

Your recommended reading list: Make a list of the books that have influenced you the most that you would recommend to others. This is something I learned in my coaching school, New Ventures West. When I was training as a coach and then as a Master Coach, they gave us a reading list of forty books. I read them with dedication and then wrote summaries of them. This exercise gave me the conceptual base with which to work as a coach. I still use these books all the time when I design coaching programs and make recommendations to my students. All of these books are well-organized on a bookshelf in my office, always within reach.

Daily reading: Reading consistently to feed our interests helps keep us alive and current. Taking time out to read in these times is not easy. There are so many distractions and the volume of virtual information that we receive every day is overwhelming. For this reason, deliberately taking time to read is important. Just like we discipline ourselves to work out, we can do the same to dedicate some time every week for reading. What works for me is to read after lunch for thirty minutes when my concentration is too low for other tasks. This could also work right before bed. I also make a list of books that I want to read and try to read one at a time so I don't wind up scattered or lose the thread of what's going on in the book.

Go over the news: Making clippings (or saving the links) of important news that moves you to take action can be powerful. Christina Baldwin recommends that you have a special place in your journal, notebook, or photo album for external phenomena.[11] This way you can keep yourself informed about broader themes happening around you. For example, I've been monitoring the news on the peace process in Colombia. I've been surprised how many people don't trust this process and have learned that the only way to influence people to believe is with information. I try to highlight news items that give solidity and veracity to the process and share them with others. Also, the positive news gives me hope that we are on the right path as a nation.

Attending events: Go to forums, conferences, and seminars to deepen your knowledge and get more in tune with your winds. I remember how important my experiences at the World Sustainable Development Summit and the World Social Forum were. They opened up a world of ideas and contacts for me and helped me gain clarity to focus on social innovation within the enormous world of sustainability. Becoming better informed will help you fine-tune your focus within your winds.

Participate in conversations: Participating in conversations on issues that interest you is one way of staying on top of trends. It also guarantees that you are personally relating to the knowledge on the subject. Many times, although they are very enriching from a conceptual point of view, conferences aren't very interactive. They are structured so that the participants are simply passive receptors of information. Try to find spaces where you can really have dialogue about what you are learning and how this knowledge and these trends impact you and how you relate to them. Personalize your relationship with your winds.

Write: Writing blog articles on new trends helps you internalize your winds even more and share them with a wider public. You will become a broadcaster of winds who contributes positively to your environment. In 2014, I wrote an article about a new framework for decision-making we are using in Aldeafeliz called sociocracy. This article has been well-read. Many ecovillages are now transitioning to use this framework. Although I'm not an expert in sociocracy, I wrote this article from my own personal and community experience and this is what people liked the most. It was also an excellent way to get myself out there more and to better understand what collective winds are moving many of us in the world of ecovillages. I also like to write microblogs about winds on social media to encourage other people to read and learn about issues. Spread your winds!

Learning communities: Creating learning communities with other people is an excellent way to be successful in many of the strategies mentioned above. A learning community is a group of people interested in a set of winds that they wish to understand better and put into practice. Although there can be people with more experience than others, in learning communities, everybody teaches and everybody learns. I've already mentioned La Arenera, in which we formulated a manifesto for change and trained many in participatory leadership. Another example of a learning community is the Society for Organizational Learning (SoL). SoL is a global network with chapters in more than twenty countries (including Colombia). Its purpose is "to discover, integrate, and implement theories and practices of organizational learning for systemic change and progress toward the vision of a living system, in order to co-create a sustainable world."

I co-led SoL Colombia for eight years. Every month, we offered a learning circle on an issue (wind) that we thought was aligned with our purpose and relevant to our context at the time. We usually invited someone with expertise that made us think and then put that thinking into practice. Later, we all reflected on what we had learned. This was a very rich space for us to enhance our winds, build trust around issues that interest us, and invite others into dialogue. We had a running list of recommended books and events organized to involve participants in a conversation and some kind of practice to make sure that real learning happened.

The exercise of running a learning community influenced me so much that I try to create a similar dynamic in all the communities in which I participate. In Aldeafeliz, for example, with the help of expert, Camila Reyes, we created a learning community around non-violent communication based on the book of the same title by Marshall Rosenberg. We got together every month, read a chapter of the book, and put into practice the exercises in the manual. As a result, we started to see a significant change in the way we communicated. This is something you can promote in the communities you are a part of – turn them into learning communities.

Closing of Winds

The key ideas of this chapter are the following: We are vulnerable to external forces not aligned with our beings that can push us in the wrong direction. To have a meaningful life, we must learn to sense the winds, which will provide the space for us to reinvent ourselves constantly, and connect with ourselves and our collective communities.

Developing an inner compass provides the guidance and illumination of our core purpose and possibilities of who we are and what is ours to be and do. Our felt sense and our Daemon's guidance prepare us to see the full context of our lives and discern which forces are life-giving. Upon identifying the positive influences in our lives, our confidence in our own sense of direction strengthens.

This can be a good moment to leave the wrong influences behind, adding them to your completion list. You could write a letter declaring that you are no longer guided by the counter-winds. Go out for a walk and reflect on what has moved you in your life. I invite you to consciously take a series of steps, one for each wind you wish to blow you from now on, which leads you to make coherent decisions with your essence. Go back home and write your reflections in your journal.

Reflect in Your Journal:

- *What forces, trends, and contexts have formed you and directed your actions?*

Keep reflecting on this as your self-knowledge increases. For now, we're going to do a provisional closing of this exploration. Write a few lines in your journal answering the following:

- *When I connect with my winds, I discover or reinforce that the following things move/motivate me...*

Declaration for Closing Winds
When you are ready, declare the following:

I'm now in contact with my winds, with the direction my story has taken, and with the influences I have received. I now become a transmitter of my own winds and those of others that inspire me; I commit to letting go of the winds that no longer align with my being and don't honor my essence.

5

Territories

In April of 2006, a pioneer group of idealists started to look for a piece of land to make their ecovillage dream come true. Each person had their own story, full of bones and seeds that inspired and directed them to live a healthy and ecology-focused community life. Each was moved by a set of common winds shared among them. In many get-togethers, they sat in a circle around a fire to share their stories. In the figurative sense, they put their bones on the table.

One architect had done work on Gaviotas, a community in the eastern plains of Colombia that promoted sustainability. He had already built many blueprints and eco-houses and had experience in community planning. A psychologist shared her research on happiness and human development. Another psychologist shared books and artifacts from her collection during years of living a spiritual life. A biologist had written her thesis on ecovillages because she saw it as a solution for the social, environmental, and spiritual tragedies that we are living through.

During these conversations (which went late into the night). people shared their worries about the planet's current situation. Many of them had participated in eco-neighborhood-related activities already because of their interest in alternative ways of living. Their common winds were the search for sustainability and an ecological life, building communities, and aspiring for an individual and collective transformation. Starting with these purposes, they started to visualize the land on which they would sow their dreams.

Their guide was a drawing that they co-created in one of their get-togethers, a canvas reflecting the attributes they imagined their utopia would have. There would be a round kiosk for community meetings, spaces surrounded by trees for building eco-houses, many natural nooks and crannies to recharge their spirit, a place to swim, a river for con-templation, and places to grow food, among other spaces.

The group went looking all over the department (state) of Cundina-marca, Colombia with the drawing in hand. It seemed like an impos-sible task. They kept searching until they finally came to the promised land: a property near the town of San Francisco, a green paradise with a river, a lake, open spaces for crops, and even the kiosk they had dreamed of. The group was happy and decided to purchase the land.

This piece of land was the perfect, fertile place to sow their aspi-rations that they had been cultivating for months collectively and for years as individuals. Many group members resonated with the winds of ecovillages as an alternative lifestyle that was sustainable and com-munity-based. They had decided that ecovillages were the solution to the great ecological and social crises the planet was going through, as well as the loneliness and hopelessness of the spirit. Many in the group had had community-based experiences already, proving that a collective dream of this nature could indeed be created in the middle of an indi-vidual and consumerist world.

Without a doubt, the world needs not just one ecovillage, but thou-sands of them; we had to start with something concrete. The group needed to offer society a demonstrative example of the new world that's being born; a world of solidarity, ecology, with abundance for every-body (from a perspective of simplicity) that fills the spirit with happi-ness. Once we proved that it worked, the model inspired many others, also hungry for a different mode of living – one that resonates with their spirits and with the needs of our planet. Creating an ecovillage needed all the attention of the group for many years, as if it were a baby.

They couldn't divide their forces among many pieces of land; one was sufficient.

Nobody in the group was a farmer or had any farming experience. All of them had grown up in cities, yet the countryside was calling them. The following years involved a huge transition to a new lifestyle, one where there was harmony between people, with nature, and inside each person. Incredible learning took place. They got to know and take care of the land, exploring, cleaning, sowing seeds, and creating the conditions for a robust ecovillage to take shape.

This required consulting lots of people who had the wisdom to guide this collective toward its vision of harmony and mutual support. Step by step, they started to acquire physical and psychological tools to overcome obstacles and realize their own intentions and purposes. The group began to change. Some left, some stayed, some lived on the land, others lived in the city most of the time, but everyone contributed to the journey of building this dream of community in their own unique way.

This story is not yet over. It's just a little part of the story of the Aldeafeliz ecovillage, whose heart is still strongly beating and has been since 2006 and whose members live in "common-unity" (community), guided by a clear purpose, calling out to those who want to participate in its experiences, and offering its eco-products to the world. The lessons on how to live together are ongoing as well as those on how to properly tend to our land. These days, a shared happiness brightens our lives, which comes from knowing that we have touched many lives already, inspiring and building capacities we consider essential for the new world that is emerging.

What Is a Territory?

The story of finding the land for Aldeafeliz is a metaphor of the encounter we can have with the territory where we sow our dreams. There comes a time, after being blown around by many winds, in which we find the environment we want to plant ourselves in and contribute to:

the right place, with the right people, inspiring us to commit whole-heartedly. If we never settle down, we are like a seed in the wind, going from one place to another without any roots or possibilities to bloom.

At Aldeafeliz, we have been caring for a particular piece of land for more than a decade, and it has taken us a long time to learn how to live on it and be guardians of it. Over time, we see the delicious and healthy fruits of our labor: the warmth of our relationships, organic coffee, eco-buildings, and educational events that positively impact others. This happens when we find fertile territory and dedicate ourselves to fully living in it.

What is a territory? Let's first review our steps in this Life Re-Vision process. Our **bones** sparked the fire of life force and creativity. Our **seeds** took flight with the help of **winds** that took us to different worlds. After exploring oceans, forests, plains. and deserts, each seed lands on a particular **territory**. It's the appropriate and fertile ground for that seed to germinate. It's the territory that will host and allow the seed to manifest all of its potential. It's where our story can continue to develop, with new and exciting events.

Territories are worlds where we foster and contribute our gifts. The philosopher Heidegger says that worlds are "the unified and coherent whole that structures our relationship to people and things around us, and guides our activities."[1] Territories are more than just academic disciplines, like political science. A territory isn't theoretical; it's something living that exists as a network of conversations and actions. Each territory has a *modus operandi*, a way we live in it, that includes how we approach the people and the tools of this particular world.

Existing territories are numerous and varied. Some examples are the territory of politics, business, technology, family, gastronomy, journalism, law, social innovation, sustainability, personal development, agriculture, health, or marketing. Each of these has its own language, points of reference, practices, institutions, and its own way of doing things. Some of these can be learned from books, but their respective essences can only be truly understood when we inhabit them in the flesh. We learn who is who and what works and doesn't work in this world as well as how to communicate effectively.

Every territory has its characteristics, rules of the game, references, jargon, and practices. Inhabiting a territory means understanding and being immersed in all of this. Let's consider this analogy: living in a territory is like being a farmer who lives in a certain geographical area and has grown vegetables for many, many years. This farmer understands the climate, the cycles of the seasons, the needs of the land, the animals and the microorganisms that exist there, and his neighbors from the next farms. His vegetables are delicious, and he shares them with many people.

Territories are different from winds in that they fulfill a different role. Winds move us, but they don't always determine where we ultimately plant ourselves. A wind can take us to a territory where we will put down roots. In this case, we start to inhabit that territory. For example, we could have received winds from a political movement that will push us to study, travel, and relate to certain people, and eventually we decide to inhabit the territory of politics. In another case, the person might not choose to inhabit the territory of politics but rather relate to those influences as winds.

For me, biology was a wind for a time, one that pushed me to study, travel, and make certain decisions, but I didn't end up rooting myself in the territory of biology, the world of scientific research, or the conservation of endangered species. To get to our territories, we need to explore many winds. We are visiting territories all the time, but we don't always consciously and fully inhabit them.

Territories will be the areas and the world in which we leave our legacy. Identifying our territories helps us to be more focused and visualize what we want to offer. Territories show us where we want to spend our energy to reap the best fruits of our labor. Because of this, we should stay focused on just a few territories (a maximum of five) so that our energy can be channeled properly to benefit others.

Ecosystems Within Territories

Within every territory, there are several ecosystems. In this model, I define an ecosystem as "a group of people engaged in direct exchange." For example, Aldeafeliz is an ecosystem, a company is an ecosystem, a family is an ecosystem. A network who shares a common interest and groups several people together is an ecosystem. Down below, we categorize the different ecosystems we have seen. Every ecosystem is part of a greater territory. Aldeafeliz is in the territory of social innovation and sustainability since this is the greater purpose of ecovillages (sustainability at the ecological, social, economic, and spiritual or human levels). At the same time, the sustainability territory harbors many more ecosystems.

Recently, my friend Sofía was telling me about her trip to Guatemala. Although she went alone, she came back with lots of new friends. She wound up celebrating her birthday at a restaurant near a volcano and going to a Mayan solstice ceremony with perfect strangers. How did she do it? She is part of a network called "CouchSurfing." When she travels, she stays with local members of that network, who open the doors of their homes, and in some cases show them around. This network is an ecosystem. The people in this ecosystem have a common purpose of meeting fellow travelers, traveling, and experiencing their destinations through locals. That ecosystem lies in the territory of tourism. The magic that happens between these people is possible because of the clarity of their collective mission.

It's helpful to identify the ecosystems we are a part of, and from there, we can figure out which territories they belong to. A. J. Robinson, a North American strategic planning consultant, has identified the following categories of ecosystems.[2]

Organizational: When we work for an organization with explicit contractual bonds, we start to inhabit an organizational ecosystem. Some examples of this are government entities, companies, or NGOs. Specific examples are Ashoka (the nonprofit organization), Interface (the carpet company), and the Washington City government. Every organization inhabits a territory. For example, Ashoka is in the social innovation territory. A telephone company is in the communications territory.

Geographic: These ecosystems have to do with specific geographic locations, like the pacific coast of Colombia or the Middle East. There are people who dedicate their lives to studying and absorbing the characteristics of a geographical area, especially geographers and tour guides. Others tend to connect to this geographic dimension from time to time when we visit a place conceptually and physically.

Political: These ecosystems host the political dynamics of our communities, towns, cities, countries, and planet. People who exercise a political role or aspire to do so, or who dedicate their lives to studying and taking part in political decisions, are clearly inhabiting these ecosystems. The rest of us visit them when it's time for us to participate as citizens, by voting and informing ourselves about what's going on by consulting the media. Here we can find ecosystems as broad as international or national politics or as specific as environmental politics.

Social: People are inhabiting a social ecosystem when they are in long-term relationships with others, structured by a series of dynamics between them, including practices, language, role models, and rules of the game. Here we find ecosystems such as associations, social media, groups of friends, and learning communities. For example, a network of alumni of a college is a social ecosystem. Some social ecosystems are in a particular territory, others are not. A network of alums of a business school is in that particular territory (business). A diverse group of friends is probably not in a particular territory. If there is no common purpose, one isn't inhabiting any particular territory. Those are floating ecosystems.

Sectoral/Industrial: When you participate in a professional network or association, you start to inhabit a sectoral ecosystem. This allows you to be up to date on the trends of your sector, create alliances, and participate in events. Doing this will increase your knowledge, understanding, and interconnectedness inside a territory. Some people have a job but never ask themselves what territory it is part of. Participating in a sectoral ecosystem will enhance this aspect of our collective identity.

I would also add the following:

Educational: When you're in a school or university, be it formal or informal, you are inhabiting an educational ecosystem. These ecosystems have their own rules and codes, and they invite us to see the world in a particular way. These educational entities have their mission and structured ways for interaction. New Ventures West, the coaching school where I trained – and still teach – fosters a lifelong commitment to being part of this community and continuing to learn and grow together.

Avocational: These are ecosystems we inhabit to cultivate a hobby, although at a significant level of engagement and commitment. The people who inhabit these ecosystems are looking to achieve a level of competence in their hobby, connect with others who regularly practice, participate in events, and share their achievements or contributions with others. Here you can find groups that focus on all kinds of hobbies such as gardening, sports, amateur music, stamp collecting, and blogging, among others.

Family: Beyond the social, there are family ties. We all are born in some sort of a home ecosystem and stay there for varying periods of time, sometimes until adulthood, sometimes for our entire lifetime. When we get married or move in with a partner, we make up another home ecosystem. These homes lie within a broad territory that we can call "family." The family territory can be characterized as the primary territory, the first one we inhabit. This territory goes beyond genetics; an adopted person is still within the territory of their adoptive family. Everyone decides how to inhabit this family territory, and even if and when to completely abandon it. There are ecosystems for our immediate family as well as our extended family, and their existence depends on how alive the relationships between these people are and whether an active dynamic exists between the members or not.

Let's Talk about Territories

Just as the wrong winds can drag us somewhere, we can easily wind up in the wrong territory or ecosystem. When she understood the concept of a territory, Catalina, a participant in a Life Re-Vision workshop, exclaimed:

> "I'm a papaya and I need a tropical climate, and I was planted in a seasonal climate. I was never going to grow there!"

She had just come back to her birth country, Colombia, from France after having lived there for several years. In her birth country, she was finding the land with the climate and nutrients necessary to develop her "papaya" nature. When she came back to Colombia, she started to explore a change of territory to one where she felt more comfortable. When we are in the wrong territory, we feel hungry and even wasted because we are not receiving or giving what we need from our surroundings to develop.

Many people come to the Life Re-Vision workshops with the restless feeling of wanting to get out of a territory. There are times when we are so bored with what we are doing that we can't take even another day. Later on in the same workshop, Catalina exclaimed with sincerity:

> "I'm part of the territory of politics, but I'm tired of it! And I don't know how to get out of there. Everything takes me back there."

I tuned into this feeling of frustration, which I understand very well, and responded to her:

"First, we need to know if it's the role or the ecosystem that needs to change, or if you really need to get out of that territory. What role have you had and which ecosystems have you been inhabiting?"

Catalina answered:

"My role has been as a public administrator, and the ecosystems I have been inhabiting are public entities or political parties. I can't take those environments anymore. They aren't bad in and of themselves, but they're just not for me." She repeated her metaphor: "I'm a papaya and this is not my climate."

I thought about what to say to Catalina. Sometimes a change of role or ecosystem will help, but in her case, I saw that she needed something totally different; she needed a new territory. So I told her,

"I understand. I have also felt the frustration of being in the wrong place, and my Daemon felt like it was dying. It sounds like you need to explore other territories. What do you like right now?" I asked her. "What other territories are grabbing your attention?"

"To tell the truth, I don't know," Catalina answered.

It's understandable that being in the wrong territory or ecosystem can consume so much energy that we don't have the strength to look outward and see what other spaces are calling us. A participant, Elizabeth, contributed:

"One good way to explore territories is by working in consulting. One does different kinds of projects and sees which territories she likes the most."

I agreed. In my time as a consultant, I explored a great many territories and ecosystems, which gave me clarity. It was a time of valuable transition where I was able to explore many different things and get paid for it. Lola, a participant in the workshop, said,

> "I think that what you may be interested in, Catalina, could be related to social innovation. You should explore that."

Recognizing these contributions, I added,

> "If you want to explore the social innovation territory, you could come to 'La Pola Social,' an event that brings social innovators together every month so they can network and promote their projects. This is a space that could help you figure out if this is the right environment for you."

Catalina considered these options and thanked the group. Being in conversation about territories is the most valuable thing we can do because people around us may have a piece of our map. Among the different fragments, we can start to reconstruct the complete map of our territories.

As a result of this conversation, Catalina started visiting the social innovation territory by going to "La Pola Social." We will see later how Catalina started to gain more clarity regarding territories. This isn't something that happens overnight. It takes time and is a conscious process of exploration, visiting many territories of interest.

For people who are bored with their territory, I invite you to have patience. Leaving one territory and entering another is a whole process. Maybe we aren't able to get out as fast as we'd like because there are things we need to finish first. When we are ready, we will make the leap.

Sometimes, what we need is to be clear about our territories. Susana, another participant, came to the workshop bored with her professional life:

"I know I need to change my job. Susana said. But I like being in my field; it's knowledge management. I believe in it, and I think that it's fundamentally necessary for organizations. But there's something missing..."

I noted,

"Susana, I intuit that you need to clarify your territory first. You had formulated two territories, knowledge management and support networks. But these aren't an end in themselves; they're a means to an end. From what I've seen of your winds, to help the planet and take care of others. What if we looked at sustainability as one of your territories?"

"Yes, sounds great!" said Susana.

I kept explaining:

"Thinking of yourself as an inhabitant of that territory gives meaning to the work you do. You're no longer just giving your fruits to an organization; you are contributing to a cause that resonates with you and to which you put yourself at its service, which is sustainability."

Susana exclaimed,

"Ah! Now I understand what a territory is for. It gives meaning to what you do, it gives you a sense of belonging to something bigger."

"Exactly," I affirmed.

In another Life Re-Vision workshop, we had a clarifying conversation about what a territory is and isn't. It came from a comment by a participant, Zulema, who had been working for years as a translator but wanted to explore a new territory. She started by announcing that she wanted to belong to the "material well-being" territory. I oriented her:

> "Zulema, that's a very good start. It sounds like the theme of material well-being interests you right now. Tell me more about your interest, and let's see if you really want to live there and what that territory is really called. Since territories are collective, they aren't our creations. Part of what we are doing is recognizing that we are part of territories that already exist. What could be the name that we have collectively designated for this theme?"

Zulma reflected and then said,

> "I'm part of a group of people who have had problems in making a living, in being productive. This is one of my purposes now. I think we could call it 'financial independence.'"

I clarified,

> "Very good, I do recognize this territory, although I've heard of it under the name of 'personal finance.' Financial independence is a goal within the theme of personal finance."

I consulted with the other participants of the workshop to verify that they also recognize this territory, and I see that they do, that the name "personal finance" is overarching and familiar. I continued,

> "The other thing you have to keep in mind is that the territory is where you are going to plant yourself, where you want to contribute and to be an active participant in the purpose of

this territory (personal finance). You can have the goal of financial independence, which is timely and transitory. But this doesn't mean you are wanting to commit to this and permanently plant yourself in this territory as your main pursuit. It could be that you are visiting the territory of personal finance so that you can become more wealthy, obtain the tools you are looking for, and that's it. Your real territories could be elsewhere. Or, do you see yourself becoming a personal finance advisor?"

She shook her head no.

Territories are where we plant ourselves and where we make our greatest contributions. We can easily confuse them with other areas of our lives. Everybody needs a number of elements to have a balanced life, for example, money, work, spirituality, family, friends, hobbies and interests, health and well-being, social contribution, etc. We all have some sort of a relationship with the majority of these areas and if not, our lives may be out of balance.

Territories are those environments in which we provide a sustained contribution over time. At the metaphorical level, we produce fruit in these territories, which are shared. Conversely, the life areas are meeting our own individual needs, but we are not contributing directly to others in these areas. For example, in the area of money; I could have various practices to keep my personal finances healthy, but I don't systematically share these practices with others (meaning I don't produce any "fruit" to society in this area). This means that I don't inhabit the personal finance territory. Another example: Many people travel when they are on vacation, but that doesn't mean that they are rooted in the tourism territory, like people who make a living from tourism or organize trips for others.

We can compare this concept with the "core business" of an enterprise, that is, its main activity. Many businesses have an IT department, but that doesn't mean they are IT businesses. For example, I remember when I was working at Ashoka. They had a whole group of people working in IT. However, the mission of Ashoka is "to build an 'everyone is a changemaker' world" in the social innovation territory. They use technology as a tool to perform their main activity. In the same way, Zulema used her personal finances as a way to sustain herself in a relevant territory with her bones, seeds, and winds. Personal finance would be a territory for her to increase her personal stability and well-being.

Coming back to the workshop, and in order to explain what is and isn't a territory, I added a little bit of my history:

> "I visited various territories from the time I was twenty until I was thirty. I didn't know where I was going to wind up permanently. I studied biology, worked on environmental issues, and worked as a management and environmental consultant. Although I didn't stay in any of the territories associated with these activities, these explorations were important. I acquired a great deal of knowledge, tools, and winds from there. Subsequently, from my thirties on, I became aware of what my real territories are: personal development, social innovation, and music."

Zulema paused and then said,

> "It's true. I need to identify the territories where I really want to be planted. Although I do need financial independence, it's not what I want to dedicate my life to. I'm more interested in inner growth, with the body and everything that has to do with that. My other interest is the meaning in life, something called 'logotherapy,' and that's specifically focused on the search for meaning."

I elaborated on this:

> "Zulema, the territory associated with everything you've just mentioned seems to be personal development. If we look on

Wikipedia, we can see that this includes a whole bunch of areas, including personal finance, which you mentioned before. It also includes logotherapy and body-related themes (often referred to as 'somatic')."

I continued to explain:

"All of these sub-areas (logotherapy, personal finance, and the somatic) are within the territory of personal development. Every sub-area can take you to a specific ecosystem you can inhabit. You could, for example, participate in the sectoral ecosystem of logotherapy while exploring educational ecosystems dedicated to personal finance and somatic coaching. Getting inside these ecosystems will help you start to fully inhabit the personal development territory. You can also explore other related territories like humanistic psychology, of which logotherapy is a part. It all depends on what resonates the most with you."

Zulema responded,

"I agree with personal development. It seems more broad than humanistic psychology and encompasses everything I'm passionate about right now. And these ideas of ecosystems are excellent for me to explore."

That is how Zulema figured out which territories she was going to explore – by means of some of its ecosystems. We can imagine that Zulema will end up finding the appropriate ecosystems to participate and interact with others in. In this way, she will establish her presence in this territory and make a valuable contribution to it.

In the Re-Vision workshops, the participants gradually start to grasp what is and what isn't a territory. Roberto, an agriculture teacher, was exploring the teaching territory. I told him that being a teacher is a role not a territory. You can play a role in an infinite number of territories, depending on what subjects you teach. If you dedicate yourself entirely to teaching, you probably are inhabiting the education territory, which was not his case. Roberto discovered that he inhabits the agriculture territory, and that teaching is a role of his within that territory. In Chapter 6, we will explore more about the roles within territories.

Carolina came to the Life Re-Vision workshop motivated by the idea of starting a project and announced that her territory would be an eco-hotel. I cleared things up by saying that she's in the process of creating an ecosystem (the eco-hotel) within the territory of tourism. Projects don't always turn into ecosystems. Some transitory projects don't take permanent root in territories. But if we are creating something more permanent, then they do become ecosystems. These are projects or organizations, like an eco-hotel, that are within a bigger territory, tourism.

Diana desired to create a sewing circle and named it as a territory. I reminded her that a network or a circle is not a territory. It could be a social or vocational ecosystem within a bigger territory. In this case, the territory could be crafts or textiles, although the territory could be something totally different. Sewing could be a vehicle for achieving a purpose beyond arts and crafts such as doing community service, like my mother-in-law whom I admire a lot. She leads a social ecosystem called *El Costurero* (the Seamstress) that gathers women of all ages together every week to sew. Last year they made one hundred baby jackets, which they donated to hospitals in the poorest areas of Bogotá. I consider *El Costurero* to be in the social responsibility territory.

María Teresa was worried because she only had one territory, sustainability. She had worked in that field for her whole career very successfully and had made all her friendships there. Her Daemon looks like a land-based jellyfish with huge eyes that stir up everything they see. María Teresa sees herself as a change agent for promoting ecology, bringing practical solutions to the table that rocks, the boat of the status quo. When the workshop was over, she felt the impulse to formulate an initiative that compiles tools and instruments to protect forests.

Although she is fulfilled in her territory, her Daemon asked for other spaces to express all of its energy. I helped her see that she was starting to inhabit her family ecosystem. In fact, she'd just bought some land so that she could be closer to her family, showing her commitment to that ecosystem. She's now helping others with their family issues because she thinks that family is fundamental to our well-being, which proves she is now inhabiting the greater family territory. She agreed and said,

> "In fact, since I came back to Colombia, I'm much more involved in family matters and have been focused on promoting family unity."

As she took notice of this, her eyes began to shine. A set of actions she had taken related to family that didn't seem to have any particular purpose was now starting to blossom. By attuning to her winds and the calling of plant roots, she discovered her territory. María Teresa doesn't just dedicate time to her family by accident; she has a clear intention and commitment to do so. This clarity gives direction to her life (family unity) and helps her make decisions, like the painful but necessary decision to break up with her boyfriend because she wasn't willing to move to another country far from her family.

> "When we close a door, another one opens," I told her. "You're now opening the door of inhabiting your family ecosystem and the broader territory of the family with more conviction, allowing you to benefit many people."

Bernardo Toro, a Colombian philosopher and educator, says that the paradigm of care is what should direct us at every level.[3] Because of this, when we choose our territories, the question could be "Which territories do I want to take care of?" And this paradigm widens the notion of territory beyond what the current economy dictates, which is solely based on money.

"Taking care of" is related to attending to fundamental needs. In

2013, I went to a training called Ecovillage Design Education (EDE), which was divided into four modules: ecological, economic, social, and worldview. In the economic module, we studied Manfred Max-Neef, a Chilean economist and winner of the Right Livelihood Award (considered an alternative Nobel prize).

Max-Neef believes that the economy is a means of exchange to satisfy our human needs. Some of these needs are subsistence, protection, affection, understanding, participation, creation, recreation or leisure, identity, freedom, and transcendence. The conventional economy doesn't necessarily contribute to the satisfaction of these human needs but rather often ends up in unhappiness, resulting in loneliness and alienation.

Any effort that contributes to the satisfaction of these human needs, remunerated or not, should be taken into account and considered a legitimate ecosystem, often part of a territory. Small and passionate efforts are valid and important, such as *El Costurero* which my mother-in-law leads. Therefore, territories are realms that meet particular needs beyond making money or being professionally recognized.

I think Max-Neef would celebrate the strength of winds and the life force of the Daemon that takes us to territories so we can genuinely contribute to the needs of others. Because of its instinctive nature, the Daemon forces us to be honest with ourselves and to answer these questions: With my work, how much am I satisfying my real needs and those of others? How much am I using my talents to do it? How in tune am I with my life force? Am I letting it flow and putting it in service to others? You can feel into the answers to these questions; you don't have to think about them much.

Territories as Habitats for the Daemon

Territories allow us to use our talents and put them in service. I remember a metaphor that my friend Carlos, collaborator of Ecobarrios and co-founder of Aldeafeliz, used to describe the lack of territories. At a specific time, he was living as a nomadic student, absorbing massive quantities of information (being exposed to many winds), without the possibility of putting things into practice. He felt like the seed of a giant oak tree planted in a tiny, little pot. This image evokes limitation – no room to grow and expand.

Carlos didn't have adequate space for his seeds to germinate into their full splendor. "What we have now is a tiny little bonsai!" he expressed with frustration, referring to all the gifts he had to give but not finding the space to do it. This changed once Carlos came back to Colombia and planted himself in the proper territories for his talents: architecture and sustainability.

In essence, territories and their ecosystems are nurturing habitats for our Daemon. Remember our initial encounter with the Daemon in Chapter 2: Bones? The Daemon is the guardian of talents, our wild and creative force. The Daemon is frequently represented by an animal or combination of animals and, like any living being, needs its habitat.

In ecology, the habitat is "the array of resources, physical and biotic factors that are present in an area, such as to support the survival and reproduction of a particular species." If you take a spacies out of its habitat, it probably won't survive. Species depend on their habitat. Our Daemon requires the same thing: a favorable environment where it has the necessary nourishment and space to emerge and unfold. Conversely, if we enclose our Daemon in the wrong territory, it will have negative repercussions for its development and, consequently, for our own vitality.

In order to choose our territories, we should keep in mind the talents and needs of our Daemon. This, although it sounds easy, is a challenge for many. The problem is that we are constantly co-opted to adopt other people's maps for our own lives, which causes us to live in territories not suited for our talents. For example, this looks like adopting our father's concern about losing "that stable job and paycheck" or our mother's conviction that "we are really good at what we do" even if we are miserable.

Society and its values have too much influence on us, and we don't always know how to challenge it. We adapt and end up sacrificing our essence because we are afraid of going against this social influence. But believe me, living a life in the wrong territory is an even greater risk. We end up alienating ourselves and can lose our life force and even our desire to live.

We should be brave and find the appropriate territories for our Daemon. When we are planted in the proper territories and are committed to fully inhabiting them, we find real fulfillment. We also feel a deeper sense of belonging, which allows for a more inspiring and long-term vision. We bloom naturally. We become caretakers of our own surroundings, leaders, and change agents. This starts when we freely choose our territories, take root, and start to bear fruit.

In order to start identifying your territories, it's a good idea first to be clear about your talents, since your Daemon is their custodian. Human beings are multi-talented, which is why most of us need more than one territory to give what we came into the world to give. More and more, we are seeing doctors who recognize and exercise their talent for music, lawyers who start businesses, engineers who get serious about their love for cooking. Or, without even going that far, everyone who has a professional career and is also a parent.

Bones and seeds are important guides. They indicate our possible talents we may have expressed from a young age or more recently. Review which talents you have been expressing at different moments in your life. Widening the vision we have of ourselves, beyond what we have formally studied or what we do for a living – seeing ourselves as integrated human beings with many talents – helps us take care of our Daemon's real needs.

Every territory is a necessary habitat for your Daemon. You are going to have a meeting with your Daemon so that it can tell you about your talents, needs, and the type of territories that it needs to be happy.

VISUALIZATION

Consulting Your Talents with Your Daemon

Imagine that you have a meeting with your Daemon. Your Daemon shows up for the meeting, and you see it in front of you in all its splendor. You connect with its force, its particular drive to create and contribute to this world. You can see that this Daemon desires to go out into the world and use its gifts. You recognize this in your Daemon. "Dear Daemon, I thank you for your motivation and for giving me the strength to express my potential." See how your Daemon responds to your acknowledgment. It's pleased, conscious of its unique and fundamental role in your life.

Some moments later, you tell it, "Daemon, I have a question for you today. Since you're the guardian of my talents, I need you to show me what they are because I want to help you to strengthen and manifest these talents. I want to support your work as their guardian. Please show me what they are." After formulating your question, let your Daemon send images to your mind showing you your gifts. Your Daemon is very sure of your core talents and is also aware of new talents that are emerging but need more development because they are also part of your essence.

Give it some time for images of activities and abilities of yours to come flashing across your mind. You will start to imagine yourself taking part in these activities and using your abilities. You are enjoying them and feeling in flow. These activities and abilities call forth every part of you. You are fully present and you feel whole. Now you have a good number of images representative of your main talents.

Thank your Daemon again, "Daemon, thanks for showing me what my most important talents are – those that I need to care for, develop, and manifest. I am your ally. I commit to support you in being the guardians of my own talents. Thanks for performing your function so well."

Reflect in Your Journal:
* *Once you finish this visualization, seize the moment to list in your journal your most important talents. What are they?*

Recommendations for Finding Your Territories

A territory is a fertile place to plant your seeds and manifest your talents. You just clarified what they are and promised your Daemon that you would take care of them as its ally. Now, we are going to reflect on your particular territories, such that you can find nourishment there and contribute more powerfully to the world.

Many of us study a particular subject, but when we understand the territory associated with that field, we realize that "this isn't for me." When I studied biology, I explored the possibility of working in biotech because there could be innovative solutions for some of our social problems. But in my labs, I saw that I didn't enjoy that kind of work. I got bored spending many hours conducting similar experiments and then documenting them by myself on a computer.

It also happens that some territories have greater status, and because of this, some of us went and got stuck there. There are people who study something not connected to their Daemon but associated with social prestige. They then start working in that field and can't wait to quit, or try to get out and don't succeed. Finally, they retire, and that's when they really start living.

Let's talk about family now. The importance each of us gives to the area of family varies. For some of us, family is a territory in which we are rooted in addition to our professional territories. People take on a specific role such as "spouse," "mother," "father," or "aunt" that requires significant dedication. But for others, the nuclear or extended family is not where they focus their talents and energy.

I propose that we refrain from judging ourselves or others for their family situation. Let's respect their decision to have a partner or not, to have children or not, to root themselves in a family territory (temporarily or permanently) or not, depending on whether or not it nurtures them or goes with the essence of their Daemon. This includes respect for the way in which each person decides to live their sexuality or express their gender identity.

Choosing territories should be an act of freedom. I repeat, an act of *freedom*. It should be a conscious decision that we as adults make to declare the spaces that enrich our Daemon. This happens by way of self-knowledge and as a result of exploring various territories so that we can finally recognize the right place for us. If you didn't enter into your territories consciously, it's never too late. Allow yourself the right to do so now.

During the period of experimentation, when we don't really know where we are going to plant ourselves, we are in territories of transition. We can stay there for some time, exploring them and receiving their benefits, while unsure whether we are going to stay. Current trends point to a longer exploration prior to committing to a territory. People are taking more time for studying and experimenting before getting married and putting down roots. Also, there are many transitions in life (separations, personal or professional stumbling blocks, illnesses, etc.) that invite us to open ourselves up to new ways of living.

I remember when they fired me from my management consulting position; I had no idea what to do. I accepted a job in the territory of international development to see if it was for me. This was a territory of transition. From the beginning, I wasn't sure. Yet I needed the income and appreciated the learning experience offered to me. Effectively, international development ended up not being my territory. I have had many friends who worked as servers in restaurants to make a living. None of them had the intention of planting themselves in this territory, but they were there for a certain period of time while they met their financial needs. This is the equivalent of a staycation in a country where we know we aren't going to stay long-term. This is another way of inhabiting a territory of transition.

There are also territories of enrichment. These are territories that we visit frequently but don't inhabit. For example, Natalia is passionate about the personal development territory. She was very consciously engaged in a coaching process with me. She participated in the Life Re-Vision workshop and the "Introduction to Coaching" workshop that I teach. She also attended a number of other workshops in order to deepen her knowledge and experience in the personal development field. She is consistently visiting the personal development territory as a territory of enrichment for herself. She may or may not decide to fully inhabit this territory one day; for now she visits to learn.

However, spending too much time in a territory without planting ourselves can generate a feeling of drifting, of being rootless. It's as if your seeds are stuck in the air, being blown around all over the place by winds. Decide for yourself when it's a good time to explore territories of transition and enrichment. Then, afterwards, opt for choosing where you want to settle down.

It's never too late to enter into a territory that's good for your Daemon. One way to enter into a territory is to go back to school and get a degree. Here you will instantly meet fellow students and mentors and receive tools and information relevant to the territory. When I did my MBA, many of my fellow students were there to change territories. For example, to go from being engineers to becoming business managers, or moving from finance to marketing, or switching from the private sector to NGOs. They used the MBA as a platform from which to make that leap.

Entering or leaving a territory takes time to adapt. One example is a change of sector, like my change from management and environmental consultant to coach. These are transitions that imply an inner transformation, overcoming fears, and often grieving the loss of what we leave behind. Realizing that changing territories isn't an easy process can help us to be patient and compassionate with ourselves, because the adaptation doesn't happen overnight. We can ask for support to work these difficulties out, including attending workshops and seeing how most people are fearful of any change or crisis in their territories. Life-Revision workshops aspire to be one of these growth and support spaces.

As I said above, changes of territories can happen at any point in our lives. I'm proud of the story of how my father entered a new territory, one that filled him with passion. He always had an artist's soul; in college, people told him he was an excellent photographer. However, after graduating, the demands of family life took him in other directions. He didn't cultivate his artistic side until he was fifty-four years old when he decided to go back to school to study art history. He had been working in e-commerce and real estate all that time. He invested in various properties, and as he began his new career, he decided to use part of a commercial space to open an art gallery. While he was studying, he started to inhabit the territory of art as a gallerist. He kept studying, traveling to see other galleries and art-related projects, and immersing himself in the world of art. He joined study and discussion groups on art theory in order to refine his discourse. He took up the daily habit of reading about the history and philosophy of art in order to become a legitimate voice in this territory.

This process required a great deal of dedication...and he achieved it! Today, he's a dynamic actor on the contemporary art scene, producing exhibits at various art fairs in the Americas and leading events, such as the Gallery Night in Bogotá, which mobilizes dozens of galleries and individuals to appreciate and invest in art. In October of 2016, right in the middle of Colombia's peace process, my dad was invited by President Juan Manuel Santos to inaugurate the Dove of Peace by Botero (a famous Colombian artist) in the Casa de Nariño (Colombia's White House) together with three other important actors in the art territory in Colombia. This represents a recognition of his commitment to the territory of art.

My dad didn't leave his other territories behind. His real estate business that functions through e-commerce sustains him economically. Family is another important territory for him. We can inhabit certain territories pragmatically to sustain us economically. That doesn't have to be in a soulless way. The important thing is for territories to connect to our Daemon, our seeds, and winds in some way.

One day, I asked my dad, "What connects you to the real estate business?" He responded,

"From my dad, who died when I was young, I learned the importance of being an entrepreneur and investing in order to sustain my family, which is my priority. He started with nothing, as a traveling merchant in the coffee region, and he built his fortune by himself through investing and growing those investments. He left us several properties that I have learned how to manage, and that's where the interest came from. Managing those properties was like taking care of my family's legacy. Also, those investments have given me stability, and I like to share that stability with others. Nowadays, I dedicate myself more to renting out 'fincas' or country homes, because the happiest moments I lived in my childhood with my family were in fincas, surrounded by animals and nature."

Territories in Correspondence with Everything

In my father's example, I could see that even in the most pragmatic territories, like real estate, where one might assume there is no soul, actually there is one. The capacity to inhabit a territory fully has to do with the connections and consistencies, or "correspondences," we find between our bones, seeds, winds, and territories. Charles Baudelaire, the French poet, evokes that connection, in his poem "Correspondences." I'll include a fragment here translated by William Aggeler.[4]

> Like prolonged echoes mingling in the distance
> In a deep and tenebrous unity,
> Vast as the dark of night and as the light of day,
> Perfumes, sounds, and colors correspond.

This idea that "perfumes, sounds, and colors correspond" is what we are looking for among our bones, seeds, winds, and territories. There's unity and a conversation between them. We don't find ourselves in any specific territory "just because." Rather, there's a poetic logic to the choices we make in life.

Lulú, a participant in the Life Re-Vision workshop, understood very well that territories fit perfectly with bones, seeds, and winds. In our workshops, participants write their bones, seeds, and winds down on index cards. After contemplating their cards for a while, they speak to us and point to the territories that fit with our other Life Re-Vision elements. When we put them together, we form our Life Matrix. For Lulú, it was obvious, as can be seen in this matrix.

Lulú's Territories:

BONES	SEEDS	WINDS	TERRITORIES
- Wedding album	- The story of my wedding: a white picnic	- Family values: the family as the nucleus of society - Counter-wind: crisis of values	Family
- Pictures and a table designed for my mother with love	- In Switzerland, I discovered my love for my country and my culture	-Muisca culture, community service	Crafts
- My diplomas	- Crying in my first elevator pitch	- Education as a pillar	Education and human development
- My handmade products	- Our marathon day in a festival	- Collaborative economy, agile, innovation	Entrepreneurship

The territory of family, which she is very committed to inhabiting and considers to be the nucleus of society, is associated with the wedding album (bone) with the story (seed) of her wedding (a picnic where everybody wore white) and the counter-wind of the crisis of values that made her a great defender of family values.

The territory of crafts is associated with her paintings (bones), which she had been making since she was little, to the history of how she learned to value the aesthetics and culture of her country (seed) and the winds of the Muisca culture (the aboriginals from her hometown) and the value of community service where she was committed to contributing to vulnerable communities through her professional work.

The territory of education and human development is associated with her commitment to her own education and that of others. This is manifested in the various diplomas she earned (bones), in the story of how she cried in her first "elevator pitch," where she saw the need to create spaces for training to strengthen her abilities (seed), and the winds of education as a pillar of society. Today she works at a university and continually contributes from there.

Finally, the territory of entrepreneurship is associated with her company, where she has created various products like alpargatas (traditional shoes used in Colombia by natives, similar to moccasins) of her own unique designs, to the story of her marathon day in an arts and crafts festival (seed) and the influences of innovation, the collaborative economy, and agile, a framework for iterative design and innovation popular in other fields because of its effectiveness (winds).

In Lulú's example, we see how all the elements of Life Re-Vision are assembled to create a coherent and harmonious life-design – with a "deep tenebrous unity" as Beaudelaire would say.

The immediacy of clarity that Lulú found in the workshop doesn't happen for everyone. For most of us, it's a longer, multi-step process, throughout which one sails on uncertain waters until things click. Let's look at the example of Catalina again. As we have already said, Catalina came back to Colombia after having lived abroad for years where she felt like a "papaya planted in the wrong soil." She was withering. Upon coming back, she began exploring her true territories. At thirty years of age, in what she called a time of crisis and re-invention, she took some time off in her life to clarify where she came from and where she was going.

The Life Re-Vision workshop was a starting point for her. In this workshop, she saw that the winds that blew her in her university days were different from the winds blowing her now. Cartesian thought, globalization, the middle class, political science, history, public sector service, and sociodemocratic thought were no longer at the forefront. She was identifying new winds which were taking her to new territories yet to be discovered. These new winds were spiritual awakening, intentional communities, gift economies, death, and the post-conflict.

In the workshop, Catalina concluded that she wanted to leave the politics territory and started inquiring about other territories she could be called to inhabit. Her companions in the workshop suggested that she explore social innovation. She felt a little bit lost at first but trusted that she had the tools to get to an answer.

After the workshop, she strengthened her relationship with her Daemon. In a dream, her Daemon appeared to her as an owl. She painted it, hung the painting up in the center of her study, and started to listen to sounds of owls in order to get more familiar with their energy. The owl she painted had a skull, which symbolizes the capacity of this animal to be with the darkness, the shadows, with death. She saw that her interest in death comes from something very deep inside of her.

She went over her bones. She had lots of family photos and written texts and videos of her telling important stories of her life, which were seeds at the same time. Many of these stories were of traveling, in which she came to important conclusions about her life as well as her relationships, also a source of rich learning. She extracted the lessons from all her stories, which led to formulating her new winds.

These winds made her question her territories, which is not an easy process. At first, she thought she needed to leave the territory of politics. She felt that this territory was not fulfilling and her Daemon was not expressing its talents. The owl helped her go through the mourning process of letting go of the way she was living in this territory. She made an altar to honor her bones, seeds, and winds that brought her to be a public administrator. She included her undergraduate, graduate, and professional work, her diplomas, the experiences lived, and the subjects that she had come across and studied.

The most difficult thing was confronting her emotions. On this altar, she put some stones that represented her guilt and disempowerment. She felt guilty for achieving visions from recent years – now obsolete – and for the discontent that her transition brought to her family, who had paid for her education and admired her work as a public administrator. She also felt tired of living in a territory where she felt dissatisfied and all the negative effects of that, such as being fired from jobs and feeling lost and devoid of passion.

After allowing herself to confront and feel these emotions, the moment came to let them go. Catalina went to a mountain, chose some stones, took them in her hands, and felt them. She walked with them for a little while until she started to really feel their weight. When she felt heaviness, she decided that it was time to let them go. She went to a river and threw the stones as a symbol of shedding her past, which now felt like a burden. During this grieving process, Catalina was supported by meditation, fostering a connection with her soul. She attended meetings offered by a spiritual group that gave her strength. She wanted to fully inhabit this world of spirituality, to help others live through difficult transitions like the one she had just lived, and therefore, declared that one of her territories is spirituality.

Around this time, a determining event occurred in Catalina's life. Her aunt, whom she considered her second mother, fell gravely ill, and Catalina felt called to accompany her in her last days. This experience of being beside someone as they were dying marked her. She discovered a talent she had for being there and contributing intelligently in very delicate and painful moments, giving emotional and spiritual support to the family. It was so powerful that the experience became a seed.

We can recognize that a story is a seed when someone's eyes begin to shine when they tell it. Catalina came to a coaching session enthusiastic about telling her experience with her aunt. She looked radiant. In the air, there was a force, a magic, that seemed to surround and inspire her.

With this energy, there was a sensation that everything was possible. It was inevitable to see that in this story or seed, there was something very important for Catalina, a life force.

"My aunt asked me to accompany her in her last days. At first, I didn't know what to do," said Catalina. "But something was guiding me. It was as if I was born for this." During that time, she had dreams where her guides told her, "You know how to do this," which made her feel more sure of herself as she was supporting her aunt. Her Daemon started to talk to her more clearly and told her, "You are the shaman of death." From a deep well inside of her came the answer to what she should do every step of the way until her aunt passed.

"And it was incredible," she said with a big smile. "My aunt died in peace." This illuminated a new territory for her to inhabit. It still didn't have a name but she knew it had to do with caring for people in their end of life. At first, she called this new territory "the transformation of being." I reminded her that we don't name our territories, they already exist and have a name. Catalina started researching end-of-life care to learn more.

In an individual coaching session, she declared, "The closest thing to what I want to do is called palliative care." When she looked for other projects and people dedicated to this, we found that they were all associated with the healthcare territory. At first, she was a bit resistant to declaring that her territory was healthcare. She knew what she was doing was different from conventional medicine, more spiritual in nature. But she saw that spirituality could be another one of her territories, which would inform how to inhabit the healthcare territory.

With time, Catalina saw the benefit of placing herself in an existing territory. She no longer had to see herself as a solitary idealist in the middle of an inhospitable world. Now she was an actor with an important role in the territory of healthcare with a unique and different focus. She also understood that she needed to create a network with other actors in the field of health and wellness, and that once she did this, she'd fulfill her role as the "shaman of death." She felt a strong drive from her Daemon to plant herself there and contribute, by giving new meaning to death and accompanying those who were undergoing that transition.

At the same time this was happening, she visited the social innovation territory to enrich herself. She regularly attended meetings put on by social innovators and started to see their logic. In social innovation, one finds a problem in an area that nobody is taking care of. One finds an innovative solution within people's reach and that promotes a balance between the economic, the social, the ecological and the human components. Catalina realized the Colombian healthcare system was lacking in the type of palliative care that she wanted to give. She also realized that, in order to go forward with her social innovation initiative, she needed financial, administrative, and logistical support.

In order to find this support, she got involved with a foundation that defended people's right to die with dignity. She felt at home in the foundation and was invited to contribute. From very early on, she organized a series of conversations about death-related topics and accompanying patients, family members, and friends in their end of life. She started to build a network of people involved in palliative care. Upon getting involved with this foundation, she started to inhabit a new ecosystem within the territory of healthcare.

Although she learned a lot from the territory of social innovation and considered it to be an "enrichment territory," she didn't plant herself there. She realized that while she was creating her holistic palliative care business, she needed to generate income. Using her degree in political science, she found an interesting job at a university focused on peace-building, and outside the world of public administration. She saw that she had always been committed to peace issues, and it was connected to her spiritual work. Her volunteering in prisons, her work with the families of those who are dying, her work to promote reconciliation in families at those times of death, everything pointed to peace. This gave a different orientation to her professional background, with which she reconciled. She declared that her second territory was peace.

In short, Catalina discovered that her territories were spirituality, healthcare, and peace. After all this sincere soul-searching, she saw that there was common ground among her territories, her bones, her seeds, and her winds. She found the coherence and the new life map that she had been looking for. This declaration brought her to acceptance of her new life and led to a radical transformation of her habits, her social circles, and even in her language. Effectively, she's living in a new world.

Catalina's New Life Matrix:

BONES	SEEDS	WINDS	TERRITORIES
- Videos of her learning experiences - Journals of her mourning experiences - A book of her family's history	- Stories of her trips and internal transformations	- Spiritual awakening	Spirituality
- Painting of an owl with a skull (Daemon)	- Stories of accompanying people as they are dying	- Death and palliative care	Healthcare
- Photos of her volunteer work in prisons - A play she wrote - Prose, poetry	- Stories of living in community - Stories of teaching inmates	- Intentional communities - The post-conflict	Peace

Signs You Should Change Territories

To know whether we are in the right territories or not, we need to be in close contact with our Daemon. The Daemon will tell us in its own way what is needed. It's just a matter of connecting with that gut wisdom to see whether we are in the right or wrong place.

This happened to me when I was working in a consulting firm after having completed my MBA. I decided that I wanted to have some experience in the corporate world in order to take those tools to the social sector. I also wanted to save up some money after three years of being a student with no income.

I knew I wasn't passionate about my work, but I wasn't aware how much bitterness I had inside. I was part of a project in a bank where I proposed new corporate banking products. Once, I was putting together presentations at the last minute without an ounce of inspiration. Feeling exhausted and wanting to escape, I compensated for the lack of energy in two ways. First, I ate all day to try to inject some energy into my system. (I gained a lot of weight because of this.) Second, I literally escaped! I told my colleagues I was going to the bathroom where I brought along my self-help book (*We: Understanding the Psychology of Romantic Love* by Robert A. Johnson). I stayed in there for thirty minutes while I recharged my batteries reading about conscious relationships, meditating, and secretly longing for a partner. (I was single at the time.) The team asked me what happened and I responded falsely, "Everything's fine," because I wasn't ready to confront the root cause of my distress: I was in the wrong territory.

Things were not working out. I didn't put enough energy or focus into my work, and the end result was that I was dismissed from that firm. It was hard, but when I understood that this was not my territory, I was able to let go of my attachment to the prestige attached to that position. I saw that it wasn't for me. There's no seed, wind, or territory of mine related to that line of work. My Daemon wasn't connected to that world. That experience taught me a lot: how to learn to let go of roles that may be prestigious and comfortable but not right for me.

I eventually found a partner, the love of my life. Carlos, my husband, had a similar experience when he started to feel that he was in the wrong territory. He was a jeweler for ten years, and it was a very gratifying occupation in many ways. But he also began to see signs that he needed to get out of that territory. When he got to work, he felt low energy. The subject of jewelry in and of itself wasn't his natural focus. For example, he would go to the movies and his sister would say to him, "Did you see those beautiful jewels that the protagonist had on?" and he hadn't even noticed. Instead, his attention had been completely on the psychological dynamic between the characters. When he gave classes on jewelry, the thing that interested him most was the conversations he had with his students about their lives. All of this started convincing him that his Daemon needed to be in another territory, that of personal development.

Over time, I understood that there are signs that tell us we need to get out of the territory we are currently in. Some of these are: lack of energy, passion, commitment, or starting to make mistakes as acts of self-sabotage. There are people that can stand situations like that for a long time, but the consequences can be dire – from losing valuable relationships to even getting sick. Therefore, we should be attentive to messages from our Daemon. We can ask our Daemon, "Are you really happy in this territory?"

The author Marci Alboher, a specialist in work-related topics and in changing careers, says that a few decades ago, a career change was cataclysmic.[5] Now, that is not the case. Actually, it's standard for us to do that three or more times throughout our lives. The territories we leave behind, the professions or occupations, leave us an important legacy of information, contacts, and learning experiences we can value, but we don't have to stay tied to something that no longer nurtures us. Understanding this gives us the impetus to take the next step.

We can formulate our requirements for our territories. The bones, seeds, and winds give us clues. For Catalina, the winds changed and made her look in new directions. At this stage, we need to slow ourselves down in order to listen to ourselves internally.

Listen to your intuition, your emotions, and your dreams. Something that shed light on my own requirements was a recurring dream I had. I constantly dreamt that I went back to school or to college. I was excited to be in a learning environment surrounded by many people in a community. I also felt challenged because there were exams and projects to be handed in with the purpose of advancing and deepening my knowledge. All of this had a lot of meaning for me, and I always woke up feeling content.

The author Danielle Laporte talks about our "core desired feelings" in her book *The Desire Map*. She invites us to identify the experiences and emotions we wish to have on a continual basis.[6] My Daemon in essence looks for vitality, expression, connection and discovery. This helped me understand what to look for in my territories.

After reflecting on my life's experiences and the recurring dream, reading Danielle's book, and opening my intuition, I identified that my territories had these requirements:

-Feeling a part of a community
-Constant learning
-A creative and authentic environment
-A high level of humanity and deep personal development
-A high-energy and "alive" environment with lots of movement
-Economic independence
-Recognition

Reflect in Your Journal:
Now, it's your turn to answer these questions:

- *What are the requirements for your territories?*
- *What are the central experiences or sentiments that you wish to have constantly?*

There are territories that don't fulfill any requirement for you. Those are the ones you should get out of. But let's be realistic: one single territory will probably not fulfill all of your requirements. This is why many people have more than one territory, where we are nourished and make our contributions. I have four territories. There are people who have more; others have less. I would recommend not having more than five territories because we can spread ourselves too thin.

Having more than one territory is aligned with our need to be integral human beings. Before, the only option was to choose a field and specialize as much as you could within it. Now, besides that option, which is still valid, composite careers are now valued, along with the synergy they create between the various fields.

In the book *One Person/Multiple Careers: The Original Guide to the Slash Career*, Marci Alboher offers various principles for combining occupations effectively. There are requirements for income, stability, flexibility, and creativity that can be satisfied by a mix of territories. In her book, she offers various examples of people who have done it, like a psychologist that also makes clavichords, an actor that sells objects on eBay, and an artist that sells real estate. She observes that people with more than one territory feel more satisfied because they have more spaces in which to express their talents and satisfy their needs.[7]

We need to be very realistic and grounded when we choose our territories. Each territory demands an enormous commitment if one wants to really inhabit it. It's not possible to be in too many places at once and still make quality contributions. This is why there is so much emphasis these days on finding a balance between personal and professional lives – on so many people trying to live in more than one territory in a balanced way. Sometimes the best thing to do is to let go of roles to give us greater peace of mind.

Most people go through a stage in which they commit to too many things. They become agitated and have the feeling of not doing anything well. One aspect of maturing is related to understanding our real capacity and what it means to inhabit each territory. Then, after a healthy exploration and getting to know the territories more deeply, we can make decisions about where we want to be and have the capacity to sow our precious seeds there.

Declaring Your Territories

You are now ready to define your territories. You now understand better what a territory is and isn't and the dedication required. It's like a large garden you choose to take care of, plant, prune, and water. You know that if you don't care for this garden, it will hurt your heart. You will feel like you are betraying yourself. Choosing our territories is a conscious decision; inhabiting a territory means contributing to it so that it can develop as well. Even if you're not exactly sure how you're going to inhabit your territories, you commit to doing so, and life itself will eventually tell you how. You know that it's the home of your talents, of your essence.

Reflect in Your Journal:
Write down the names of your territories, each one on a separate card. Put a star beside a territory you want to enter but aren't there yet. For example, you know you want to have a family and dedicate yourself to it, but you don't have a significant other yet, write:
Family*
Same thing for territories you want to enter, for example, if you want to be a movie director, you would write:
Cinema*
We don't invent the name of each territory. It already exists. Other people will also recognize that they belong to this territory and take part in its practices, conversations, and tools. So, reflect on what other people call this territory and the people with whom you interact when you go there. Let's get to work!
What are your territories?

My Territories

At the beginning of my exploration, I had three territories. Now I have four (since I got married, I entered into a new territory – that of family). But when I did this exercise for the first time, I had a sign in a dream that there were three.

In the dream, I had gone to a soul doctor. He saw my spiritual state of health in a giant crystal ball. At first, there was a huge mixture of colors, smoke, textures, and shapes. It looked "muddy." This doctor put his hands on the crystal ball and started to clean up the impurities. The forms began to take shape. Finally, inside the crystal ball, you could see three different colors of butterflies: yellow, blue, and red.

"Doctor," I interjected, "isn't it necessary to unify the three butterflies into one single color?" With authority, the doctor responded, "No. Some people have more than one color, and you have three."

At that moment, I woke up and I understood. My creative energy has three different modes that would become clearer as I kept advancing on my Life Re-Vision process. My Daemon needed three different habitats in order to fully develop its potential. These territories are social innovation, personal development, and music.

Below you can see my Life Matrix, where I've made note of my bones, seeds, winds, and territories (with associated ecosystems).

My Life Matrix:

BONES	SEEDS	WINDS	TERRITORIES
- My thesis on ecovillages - Reports I did for Ashoka - Written articles	- Ecobarrios take over Bogotá - My first daughter, Aldeafeliz	- Sustainability, the cause of the century - We are all change agents - Ecovillages, eco-neighborhoods	**SOCIAL IN-NOVATION** Ecosystems: Aldeafeliz Fundación para la Reconciliación
- Journals - Notebooks - Written Stories	- Punching Malden - Circle of Stones - The spiritual pilgrimage to India - My Life Re-Vision	- Spiritual Awakening - New definitions of success - Integral philosophy	**HUMAN AND ORGANIZA-TIONAL DE-VELOPMENT** Ecosystems: Re-Vision Academy New Ventures West SweetRush

- My repertoire of music - Programs from plays - My songs, my CD	- My debut as a school diva - The beautiful face of Colombia - Absence & Light story	- Popular music, Classical music, Jazz, and improv - Russian discipline - Theater and musical theater	**MUSIC** Ecosystems: Noche musical ImprovCreative Anbridge
- Family photos - Jewish objects - Genealogy books	- I meet the love of my life - A co-created wedding - The first decision of my life - Reconciliation at teatime	- Genealogy - Forgiveness - Family constellations - New masculine/new feminine - Rituals	**FAMILY** Ecosystems: Carlos and Ana's home The Londoño family The Aristazábal Leost family

My Experience in the Social Innovation Territory

At the beginning of this chapter, I told the story of Aldeafeliz, about how we found the land for the ecovillage. It's a description of the process of finding a piece of land. A similar process of exploration in tune with my bones, seeds, and winds led me to the social innovation territory.

When I was eighteen, I decided to study biology. I was inspired by the words of a wise man, Rodrigo, as I have mentioned, who brought me a decisive wind: a big paradigm change from the industrial era to the sustainable era, from a mechanical way of thinking to an organic and eco-centric one. However, that did not lead right away to my real territory. It was the beginning of a long period of exploration. During this exploration, another mentor changed my life.

As a biology student, I quickly saw that I didn't want to spend my life in a lab, nor did I want to do field work. I decided to train in a tool very much in vogue in the environmental sector, Geographic Information Systems (GIS), and to work as an environmental consultant. I found a well-paid internship focused on this area, which was perfect. After two months of doing this work, I noticed I was bored. I was making good money, my colleagues were nice, and the schedule was reasonable; yet every day, I counted the hours I worked and did the bare minimum in order to fulfill my functions – with zero inspiration.

One day, for a change of routine, I asked for an interview with Sam Mygatt (RIP), the late owner of the company where I had done my internship. This man, who showed up to work in a multi-colored bowtie every day, seemed to be passionate about his job; maybe he could give me some direction. I wanted to know more about his reasons for working in the environmental sector and what perspectives he had about the future. He was a perceptive man, and after answering several of my questions about his career, he changed the dynamic and started interviewing me.

"What interests you, really?" he boldly asked me. I told him that I liked a combination of environmental issues with social and human ones. I told him about my thesis on ecovillages (a bone), that grounded my interest for more sustainable living models at every level. I wasn't sure that technical, political, or scientific aspects of sustainability were for me, and so I wasn't sure if the environmental or sustainability sectors were where I wanted to be.

"And where does this interest for environmental and social issues come from?" he asked me. I told him an important fact about me (my seed):

"I was born in a huge city, Bogotá, in a bubble of privilege, far away from social and environmental problems. My French education, although rigorous, was individualistic and hyper-rational. Everyone was focused on good grades in order to be successful. I did well academically, but I felt very lonely. I was longing for community and contact with nature. I wanted a more collaborative and creative space where I could feel that we were experiencing new things and contributing to society. That's why ecovillages (a wind) interested me."

I then added an important context that had also influenced me (another wind):

"I come from a country plagued by violence and poverty but with lots of potential. I've always imagined our environmental patrimony as an asset that could help us get out of the darkness and make us feel proud about our country and create abundance from there. This love for the natural world could be the base to unify us as a society and learn to protect our resources, reaching our potential in a sustainable manner."

Sam thought for a long time after hearing this. I felt like I was sitting before an oracle who was about to give me the answer to all my confusion. After a silence that filled me with hope, he told me:

"You should explore social innovation. Twenty-five years ago, a friend of mine, Bill Drayton, created an organization called Ashoka, which is dedicated to promoting social entrepreneurs who try to resolve social and environmental problems in the world in creative ways. It seems to me that this organization and this world could be interesting to you."

This advice had a ground-breaking effect in my life. Sam had no idea how big of a door he opened for me to the social innovation territory.

From that conversation forward, I learned about the Ashoka organization and worked there for many years. I worked on challenging projects that stimulated my continued growth. The purpose, focus, and aspirations of Ashoka continue to be a big influence on me many years later.

At Ashoka, I learned that social innovation is a way of addressing society's problems. This organization subdivides problems by topic: health and wellness, sustainability, education, civics, economic development, and human rights, among others. However, social problems often fall into more than one category, and it's necessary to work on them in a unified manner. My experience was in sustainability, so when I went into the social innovation territory, I opened my perspective to many other issues because that's the way in which social innovation operates: it's interdisciplinary.

Thanks to this experience, I started participating in organizations with similar purposes to Ashoka in Colombia and abroad. These organizations are based on the idea that we can all be change agents, more so than governments or large companies. This wind sustains that change will come from individuals or brave communities that present innovative solutions to environmental and social problems and that solutions will replicate themselves on a large scale.

In the World Summit on Sustainable Development that took place in South Africa in 2002, I saw the magnitude of the impact that a social innovation initiative can have when it replicates and goes massive, to the point where it changes the system. This was the case of the Green Belt Movement started by Wangari Maathai. This African woman (RIP) and her brightly colored dresses created an initiative that mobilized thousands of women in Kenya to create greenhouses and plant trees. At the same time, this offered new ways of generating income for these communities. Together, they were able to plant thirty million trees all over the country, which went a long way toward solving the energy crisis, reversing deforestation and helping combat climate change. For this project, she won the Nobel Peace Prize in 2005. Getting to meet her and visiting this project is one of my most prized seeds.

I've been close to another social innovator, Leonel Narváez, who I have mentioned already. He invited me to be part of the board for his Fundación para la Reconciliación (Foundation for Reconciliation). Leonel is an example for me of how to inhabit the social innovation territory. When I went to the board meetings, I was surprised by how systematic they had been in joining forces with other stakeholders, to offer their services and to expand their presence in the political arena and in the media. The foundation's programs are now in twenty-two different countries.

With Leonel, I've been able to see the different stages a social entrepreneur goes through as he develops. Ashoka has identified three stages:

1. The formulation of an original idea that changes a paradigm. In the case of Leonel, "forgiveness and reconciliation as a pillar for building community and society."
2. The creation of an effective model and strategy to bring about that paradigm change. For Leonel, these are the EsPeRe (Schools of Forgiveness and Reconciliation) workshops where people receive support in making the leap from resentment or resignation to forgiveness and reconciliation.
3. Creating a theory of change at the macro level that seeks to influence the broader system. For Leonel, it was "the political culture of forgiveness and reconciliation," a book and theory he formulated.

Until then, I had been enriching myself in this territory. I began to inhabit it and become a social innovator one day when I said yes to an invitation.

I was in the US, doing my master's in environmental management (MEM) and business (MBA) in 2006, when I got an email from my great friend Carlos with the subject, "Should we create an ecovillage?" This email was an inspiring invitation to crystalize a dream we had for many years. Without a doubt, my response was positive. At that point, the creation of a new ecosystem in the social innovation territory began: Aldeafeliz. Many years later, Aldeafeliz has grown and become an actor that trains leaders and communities in social technologies. With its events, workshops, and learning spaces for students and volunteers, it has generated a rich network centered around its aspirations in social innovation, sustainability, and personal development.

When I came back to Colombia after graduate school, I knew intuitively that I had to seek out other people in the social innovation territory. I found a new group of friends, who brought the concept of ImpactHub to Colombia, and got involved in that network. As its name indicates, it's a hub designed to bring social innovators to work and learn together in a physical space for collaborative work. There is a global network of these spaces that promote strengthening the field of social innovation. Initially, we didn't have a physical space, so we met in different spaces. The emphasis was on community, which we called "La Arenera" (The Sandbox).

Besides providing a physical gathering space (the "hardware"), the ImpactHub functions with a social technology called the "art of hosting" (the "software"). "Art of hosting" is the art and practice of meaningful conversations and co-creative processes that lead to participatory leadership. A host is a person who facilitates, designs, and holds space for relevant conversations where people open up authentically and co-create new solutions for current issues – a process that is conducive to social innovation. The spaces facilitated and cared for by these hosts nurture diversity and are considered essential for any high-impact, innovative processes.

Eventually, the Arenera Collective found the funds to set up a physical location in Bogotá. ImpactHub Bogotá was consolidated by three organizations: La Arenera, Somos Más, and Fábricca. Eventually, it was bought by one entrepreneur. Today, it's a dynamic ecosystem within the social innovation territory. This ecosystem hosts various social enterprises and social entrepreneurs in a coworking format. New relationships have been formed among the members and the greater social innovation community. Many other initiatives from the greater ecosystem, such as SoL Colombia (the Colombian chapter of the Society for

Organizational Learning, which I co-led for many years), benefitted from the ImpactHub Bogotá's efforts.

Through graduate school, I connected with other social innovation ecosystems in the USA: Byron Fellows and Dalai Lama Fellows (DLF). These are both scholarship programs for social innovators where they receive a week of training on their leadership skills. DLF trains younger leaders – mostly in college – and Byron Fellows trains young people who are completing their graduate degrees. I've participated as a leadership trainer for these fellows, designing curricula and facilitating spaces of co-creation with them.

All of these organizations and networks – Ashoka, Fundación para la Reconciliación (Foundation for Reconciliation), Aldeafeliz, ImpactHub, Byron, and DLF – are ecosystems that have allowed me to inhabit the social innovation territory. Over time, I have seen that, without a doubt, social innovation is a fertile territory for me, a place where I want to stay planted. It inspires me as a context for learning and contributing. I came to this conclusion when I started to know and dwell in this territory, in Heidegger's sense of this word. This implies getting inside the territory, learning its theories, its actors, participating in its practices, and contributing to leave a legacy.

Social innovation was the first territory in which I planted myself after a long period of exploration. Life brought me to three other territories that were necessary for my Daemon to fulfill itself (personal development, music, and family). The story of my experience in these territories is on my website (www.anamariaristizabal.com/EN) where I share more information about my own Life Re-Vision.

Giving Life to Your Territories

One way of giving life to your territories is to tell the story of each one from the moment you entered into it. This is what I did above for one of my territories (social innovation). I invite you to do the exercise of narrating the events, people, and circumstances that took you to each territory, and then describe what happened within them. When you do this, you can start to identify some of the bones, seeds, winds, and ecosystems of the territory, thereby deepening your Life Re-Vision.

Here is another example. Natalia's territory is politics. She tells us how she came into that territory, which includes seeds from her parents and winds that came from her college years:

> "I was looking for the reason why I gravitated to the field of politics. The first image that came to mind was seeing my parents as public servants working for the coroner's office and the ombudsman's office, respectively. Even though the provinces where they worked didn't have much of a budget, my parents always performed their duties with dedication and strong ethics. Seeing them work with such diligence inspired me to work in that sector as well.

> "Discussing their work with my parents, I began to consider studying the social sciences. First, I had been inclined to study social communication, but then, at a career fair at school, I stopped at a stand of a university that offered a degree in political science. In looking over the curriculum, it seemed super complete to me. It included the branches of the social sciences that I liked and required a lot of reading and writing, abilities I knew I had. Because of this, I decided to pursue this major. When I found that another university had the same program but with an emphasis on governmental studies, I knew I wanted to go there. There, I gained valuable tools that equipped me to perform well professionally in the public sector.

> "In 2003, I landed an internship with the Ministry of the Interior and Justice, working as a legislative assistant in the Office of Political and Electoral Issues. It was a very positive experience; I helped coordinate the legislative agenda by compiling the information required for the establishment of the Legislative Support Plan. I had the opportunity to sit in on the debates of the

(Colombian) Congress with the task of following up on issues of interest for the national government. Then I monitored the performance of regional elections and the referendum of October 2003. This gave me a good perspective on how Congress works and issues of national interest.

"In 2010, while I was earning my master's degree, my thesis tutor included me in an interesting project. I was a member of the Colombian research team for the project titled, "Quality and professionalization of politics in Latin America" led by two universities, one in Colombia and the other one in Spain. The experience I gained in the Colombian Congress in my previous internship allowed me to survey more than one hundred congresspeople.

"In September of 2012, I applied for a position with the (Colombian) attorney general's office and was hired in November as an analyst in the National Office of Analysis and Contexts. I worked on the design and implementation of research methodologies in the social sciences and the selection of analysis variables. This work supported prosecutors in criminal cases as we built a framework of criminal macro-contexts and an analysis of crime-related phenomena.

"This job reinforced the importance of working on a team and with people from different disciplines, since we all had interesting and complementary points of view. I am now a researcher for the public sector. This is a new era for me – I'm learning new things in my role as a public servant."

We can see how Natalia planted herself firmly in this territory of politics. She reflects in the above text on how she entered into the territory and what her experiences have been upon inhabiting it.

Reflect in Your Journal:
I now invite you to reflect on your territories.

- *How did you enter into them?*
- *After having entered, how have you developed in them?*
- *What have been the milestones (seeds) of your participation in this territory?*
- *Who have been your mentors, those who directed you to new places within the territory (winds)?*
- *What ecosystems have you gotten involved in?*
- *What bones have come out of it?*

Write this story down in your journal or computer for each territory, and you will see how enriching this exercise is. What do you notice? When I did this, I noticed that I had already gone on a significant journey inside that territory, which I began to value. You might feel the same way. It's also possible that you start to feel that your life isn't that chaotic; it's more harmonious than you had previously thought. There's a certain order, even an aesthetic, when you visualize a specific number of territories. You're not as lost as you thought you were. And if you want to leave your current territory and enter another, you know now that it's never too late, that other people, like my father, have done it in the second half of their lives.

When you finish your territory stories, how do you feel? What did you discover? It's a moment to celebrate your progress and trust your path. Your Daemon has been guiding you to explore territories: to enter into some, to leave others behind, and to see where there is fertile ground to plant yourself. This exploration, which never ends, is part of life's trajectory, which we can learn to navigate more fluidly.

Closing of Territories

This is the main message of this chapter: We are constantly co-opted into adopting other people's maps for our lives and living in mistaken territories for our talents. We must root ourselves in the right territories for our flourishing. Knowing yourself and knowing your territories will help you create a new map for your life. When we plant ourselves in our own territories and commit to fully inhabiting them, we experience a deeper feeling of belonging and contribution.

Go out for a walk and reflect on your territories. Add the territories you want to exit into your completion list. Maybe you want to perform some sort of a ritual or write a letter that makes the act of leaving one territory and entering another official.

Declaration for Closing Territories
When you are ready, declare the following:
I am now in contact with my territories, with those spaces in which I freely choose to plant myself in order to belong and contribute from there. I aspire to become a guardian of my territory. I commit to honor my history in each territory, constantly gathering and dignifying my contributions within it.

Reflect in Your Journal:
Now that you have an idea what your talents and territories are,

- *How have you been inhabiting these territories, and how do you want to inhabit them now?*

6

⚬⚬⚬

Ecology

When I got involved in the territory of social innovation, I realized it was essential to engage in constant learning. Even just the name of the territory – "innovation" – appeals to learning and unlearning things constantly. And so, I entered into an ecosystem called SoL (Society for Organizational Learning) and co-founded the Colombian chapter of this global network, SoL Colombia.

With my friends at SoL Colombia – a learning community that tackles issues of sustainability and social innovation – we asked ourselves the following: "How can we make our food healthier and at the same time contribute to the sustainability of the region?" We were planning a learning circle on this topic but didn't want to leave it as just a theoretical exploration. We wanted to start putting this concept into practice in real life. Everybody shared ideas, and mine was, "I'd like to be able to get locally-sourced food when I'm in Aldeafeliz. Even though the food I buy in the markets in the nearest town, San Francisco, a rural area full of possibilities, it comes from Bogotá!"

The next time I stayed at the Aldeafeliz ecovillage, I gave myself the task of finding organic, local food. Carlos, my husband, supported me in this. I called a neighbor, Alex. His WhatsApp message to me said, "In this area it's hard to get organic vegetables, but you can get eggs and fruit." He sent me the contact info of a man named Don Victor and said, "I recommend his 'blue' eggs; they're delicious."

"Blue eggs?" I wondered with curiosity. Excited, I called Don Victor. He invited us to pass by his farm to pick up the eggs. His farm was about three kilometers away from Aldeafeliz, on the road to the village of Supatá. We wrote down the directions and hopped in the car.

We had no idea how interesting the visit was going to be. When we got there, he had the eggs ready for us. I opened the bag delicately. The eggs were huge, and half of them had a blue tint. I was so excited to try this new type of egg.

"Come in for a moment!" Don Victor said to us. His mother was there and surprised us with some corn *envueltos* (similar to tamales but sweeter) and a cup of *aguapanela* (raw cane sugar boiled with water). I felt a warmth in my heart from the hospitality we received. "These are the kind of neighbors you dream about!" I thought. We sat down to enjoy the food and started to talk.

"It's been very dry lately, no?" I asked.

Don Victor nodded his head. "Climate change has hit us hard. The dry seasons are much more pronounced."

"When are the wet and dry seasons?" I asked him. After ten years of coming and going to Aldeafeliz, I still wasn't clear about when they were. "The dry seasons are July and August and December and January, and the rainy seasons are March–April and October–November. Also, the drought conditions are due to chemicals that stay in the soil and make it more arid. That's why I use cow patties as fertilizer so that the soil gets richer. He went and got us a t-shirt that said: "Con agua y mierda, no hay cosecha que se pierda – www.mierdadevaca.com" (With water and shit, no crops will be lost.)

"How nice!" I told him. "And how important it is that you are restoring the soil and fertilizing the land with...Ehhh...Manure."

"With shit!" Don Victor corrected me. "Learn how to say it shamelessly."

"Hahahaha, OK, with shit," I said. "And what grows well in this area? What's the vocation of this territory? What's the agricultural potential here? I know that there are lots of chicken farms around here that are polluting the river, and there are lots of mono-crop coffee plantations."

"Originally, they grew sugar cane here. The structure you see over there was a cane press," he said, pointing to what is now a warehouse.

Later, the region became a coffee and fruit-bearing region. But you have to plant coffee together with other fruit and medicinal species. The problem is that many orchards, like the plantain orchard, now only lasts for two or three years. Before, they used to last for at least ten years. The soil is a living thing, the organic layer starts to deplete, which is the main source of food for the plants. One has to restore the soil and also maintain the biodiversity which helps birds, insects, and other animals come and help in their own way.

At that same moment, Carlos pointed out a blue bird with yellow wings. "Look at that beauty! I've never seen a bird like that! I can see you are doing something special here to attract that kind of exotic bird. What happens is that there are very specific conditions here because this is a microclimate with all the different crops we have sown. This attracts birds and other fauna."

We finished our snack, and Don Victor invited us to take a complete tour of his farm to illustrate what he was talking about. We went to the main entrance of the fields where there's a sign saying "Miraflores Eco-Farm."

"This is where the fields start," said Don Victor. "An eco-farm isn't necessarily aesthetically pleasing; it looks more like the wild."

"The wild is beautiful," I said, remembering my training in "art of hosting" where one tries to find a balance between order and chaos: the "chaordic," where there is a minimum of order, a minimum necessary structure, that favors creativity.

"If you look closely," Don Victor added, "you can see the basic structure of this field. There are some rows of coffee, and between them, several other crops that I will be showing you. For example, here are the hot peppers. I'm a big fan of eating spicy food; there's nothing like some beans with hot peppers. The hot pepper plants attract certain pollinators and also protect the coffee. Here we can see what we call allelopathy. Plagues can make a home in the coffee plants, but if there is a hot pepper plant or other different aromas near them, the plagues don't stay. That's why we don't promote mono-crops. Our coffee plants are all of different species. This is 'borbon,' this is 'tipica,' this is 'castillo,' and this is a Colombian variety."

"Is there any special reason why you have different types of coffee plants?" I ask.

He responded, "Each kind of plant has a different aroma. So this way, the animals that come to wreck the plants get confused and don't attack all of the plants."

As we were walking, I recalled that years ago, I attended a talk on permaculture, where the speaker, Albert Bates, shared the principles of this discipline, such as multifunctionality, where everything has at least three uses. At that time, they used chickens as an example. Hens lay eggs, the way they scratch the ground to find food aerates the soil, and their excrement is used as fertilizer. The fact that the hot pepper plants also have three functions (they protect the coffee, flavor the beans, and attract pollinators) means that the system is more optimized and everything works better: plants, people, and animals.

"The advantage of this ecological process is that one finds a bunch of nests when one goes to harvest the coffee beans. And therefore, there are many different species of birds here," Don Victor told us as he showed us a small nest.

"This plant," he told us, pointing to some tabby-colored plants growing vertically, "is a cure for herpes or the famous 'shingles.' They call it *la espada de Bolivar* (Bolivar's sword). Others call it *Lengua de Suegra* (mother in law's tongue)."

"It's very long, no?" I said, jokingly. "I want one of these for my garden. It's better to have your mother in law's tongue working on your side. How does one take care of this plant?"

"It doesn't need very much water or light. It grows very well in this area. I planted one, and now there's a bunch of them. It's a super 'grateful' plant."

"Just like my own mother-in-law. Really, I get along very well with her," I said, turning to Carlos to see the look on his face. He laughed.

"You have to ask the plant's permission to take it," Don Victor recommended. He said a quick prayer under his breath and carefully pulled the plant out. This communication and level of respect for living beings moved me.

Full of gratitude, I told him, "Don Victor, thanks for all of this. If it weren't for neighbors like you, one would never get to know the area."

Don Victor blushed a little and changed the subject quickly. "Can you see those bees there? They're pollinating," he added, making sure we understood the connection between plants and insects and the effect that a plant has to create more diversity.

He then showed us another one of his treasures. "These are our local raspberries. They're ripe." With a shining expression, he offered each of us a raspberry to try. Don Victor was really excited to offer us this treat; I tried to enjoy it as much as possible. The fruit slowly melted in my mouth, leaving a combination of sweet and sour. At that moment, I reflected on the pleasure of sharing fruit from a garden with others, as it is the product of effort and dedication and a profound conviction of the goodness of this offering.

Afterward, he pointed to a brown mountain. "Here is where we process the shit. We make a mixture. We have shit from chickens, hens, quails, and pigs as well as coal and husks."

"Let's take a picture of all this shit! How beautiful!" I said, learning to use the word more and more freely. I thought at that moment that this "shit," although not as appetizing as the raspberry, is equally an offering and a "fruit" of his labor that originates in a deep knowledge of the ecology of the area. After that, Don Victor kept taking us all around the fields, which were relatively small (about three hectares) but very productive. He showed us several ornamentals, food-bearing, and medicinal plants that lived on his property.

"I'm worried about the issue of the chicken coops. What can be done? The pollution they generate bothers me," I said.

"They're already changing. They're starting to implement more eco-friendly methods; their own customers are demanding it. We all have the ability to move things in the right direction."

I was surprised at how peacefully he answered me. Some people would see these agroindustrial complexes as the enemy. Don Victor sees them as part of a greater process of change where everybody does their part.

"Don Victor, the time has come for your hug." We looked each other in the eye. I intuited that on this day, a friendship had been formed that would last for many years.

I left this visit with my hands and heart full. I saw in Don Victor an example of generosity, deep knowledge about the region, productivity, and a collaborative attitude with the surrounding processes. In fact, he himself incarnates other principles of permaculture: converting problems into opportunities, cooperation between species, and harmony without so much effort.

I went to buy eggs and I found a wise mentor, a farmer who really knew and took care of his territory. Besides being passionate about what he does (a very awake Daemon!), it seemed to me that Don Victor is deeply connected with the ecology of his territory. With his inspiration, a new door opened up for me to inhabit that region in a new way, with more ecological awareness. This awareness makes me feel more rooted in the territory and to have more respect for what is there. This consciousness of territory in itself merits attention. Here, a new element of the territories opens up: their ecology. We obtain this understanding by means of the Wise Council, which we will address below.

What Is Ecology?

Every territory has its ecology, its biodiversity, and its cycles. Summarizing and interpreting Wikipedia's definition,

> *Ecology is the science that studies the interrelation between living beings and its surroundings. It studies how these interactions affect factors such as distribution or abundance of species (biodiversity). It studies the cycles, such as the nutrient cycle, and the various activities that build the habitat and regulate the nutrient flow. These processes*

are carried out by a variety of organisms, which make up its biodiversity. Ecology seeks to explain:

- *Life processes, interactions, and adaptations*
- *The movement of materials and energy through living communities*
- *The successional development of ecosystems*
- *The abundance and distribution of organisms and biodiversity in the context of the environment*

When I talk about the ecology of territories, it goes beyond what we call "nature." Let's see how these attributes of ecology can apply to any territory. What we are doing is bringing an ecological perspective, that of life itself, to the thematic realms (territories) which we inhabit. It's also a systemic perspective, which is interested in the actors, the structures, the interrelation between the actors (organisms), and their processes or cycles.

Two Ecologies: Inner and Outer

Most people who come to a Life Re-Vision do so because they lack a clear purpose. They feel disconnected from themselves and from others and don't feel they are making the impact that they could. They often lack a passion to propel them or bring out the best in them. A life of purpose has clarity of vision and mission, which implies constantly listening into the inner and outer ecologies. We can do this through the following steps.

We've already seen how, when we gather our bones, we start to rekindle our creative potential, represented by the Daemon. At the same time, the Daemon awakens our energy, vitality, and passion. We see how when we tell our essential stories, or seeds, we become conscious of our virtues. When we tune into our winds, we remember what we value and what moves us. We choose our territories, keeping in mind that they are our Daemon's habitat and our Daemon is the guardian of our talents and gifts. Our vitality, our virtues, our values, and our talents are all elements of our inner ecology. Our new map, the product of this Life Re-Vision, should take all of that into account to cultivate the relationships between those aspects of ourselves to create a healthy, robust, and resilient inner ecosystem.

A Life Re-Vision starts with our inner ecology; however, this process doesn't just incorporate our inner ecology. We start here because any living being needs to be internally strong to survive in any ecosystem. Although it's an essential dimension for a life well-lived, we must also turn our attention to include the ecology of territories, or the "outer ecology." For this, we will bring in a new "trusted source," a word used by the renowned purpose coach Tim Kelley, which will guide us to skillfully inhabit our territories with the Wisdom Council.

The Wisdom Council: Three Perspectives

At the beginning of this chapter, I shared the story of how I met Don Victor. People don't always operate with the kind of wisdom we see in him. Instead, we often see a Daemon overrun with greed and ambition. Some years ago, a group of technocrats came to the territory of Aldeafeliz and declared that this land would be an agroindustrial zone. This incentivized several investors to create large-scale chicken coops and pigpens, taking advantage of the rich water sources in the area, but this affected the pure water quality of the rivers. Do you think that these technocrats tuned into the vocation of this region? Could it be possible that some people's ambition causes them to overlook the wisdom of the local people?

Yes, in fact, this happens all the time. Often, very well-organized actors with interests alien to the territory want to extract and exploit instead of care for and value what exists. But local wisdom is waking up and starting to protect its resources. At the time this book was written, seven municipalities in Colombia had referendums where people voted against large hydrocarbon or mineral extraction projects in their territories. There were forty-two more municipalities in line to revoke big extractive projects. The Aldeafeliz community is already participating politically in advocating for an eco-tourism vocation for our region.

Our Daemon calls us to our territories. This life force has an impulse, a positive energy that infuses life within us within our territories. The Daemon is trustworthy because it connects us with our vitality, our instincts, our talents, and our creative force. These faculties are essential to live a full life. However, sometimes our instinctive drive runs wild and doesn't take into account our surroundings. The Daemon needs perspective.

The Wisdom Council is the symbol that represents the wisdom of the territories, one that offers a wider perspective to our Daemon. It's a council because understanding the ecology of a territory needs the point of view of many sages, not just one. Similar to what Don Victor told us about the biodiversity of the coffee farm making it healthier, diversity of wisdom in a territory helps us have a holistic perspective on what the system needs to thrive. Having this diverse perspective keeps us from invading a territory with what we think is best for it, like an exotic weed that takes over and causes problems.

The Wisdom Council invites us to listen to many sources of wisdom and enter into territories with humility, being aware of their processes and their real needs. This humility opens up our sense of curiosity about what has already been done there. It also opens us up to the history and the learning that has taken place (so we don't repeat past mistakes) as well as the current and future possibilities of the territory (pointing to a common good). It's a gesture of respect and care to consult the Wisdom Council in order to harmonize our contributions with what is already in existence there.

The Wisdom Council reminds us that we need to pay attention and see the big picture. When we enter a territory, we look around and notice that there is already a process in motion there. This process has its actors, structures, knowledge, conversations, property, history, practices, tools, and reference points – a whole ecology. This ecology, which has its own characteristics and cycles, determines what's good and what's not good to "plant" there. Also, there are several needs the territory has because of its particular history and dynamics.

For many people, Don Victor is one of these sages within the geographical area of Aldeafeliz, in that particular rural area of San Francisco, Cundinamarca, in the heart of Colombia. The conversation with Don Victor allowed me to understand its ecology better, identifying some of its species, the relationship between them, their processes, and the potential of this region. This conversation also motivated me to seek out other sages to enrich my understanding of this territory. Inasmuch as we inhabit our territories, we will continue to engage with sages. Their knowledge, along with our curiosity, will open our hearts as well as our minds to know, understand and contribute with positive impact as we will know the territories more holistically.

The Ancestral or Historical Voice

One dimension of the wisdom of territories to get to know is their past, their ancestry, their history, and the perspective of those there who have more experience. This doesn't always happen; many times we ignore this perspective. The emphasis the Western culture has on novelty often discounts the historical perspective. Hence, we leap forward and only see a future, looking ahead without understanding the history. Like my husband Carlos says, "We quickly jump to what needs to change without even knowing what is."

I have seen this attitude in myself. Not only have I ignored the ancestral point of view, but I have also rebelled and rejected hierarchies, and older people in general. The root of this stance is: I have judged the previous generations harshly for their mistakes and the undesirable results we see today (crisis on every level). My instinct (coming from my impetuous Daemon) is to raze it all to the ground and start again. After having matured a bit (and with therapy!), I've been able to gain some perspective and start to be thankful. I can now value the fact that, without the support of my ancestors and the base they have left for us, we wouldn't have the civic rights, quality of life, and therefore, the perspective we have today.

What is maturing inside of me is also maturing around me. The peace process underway in Colombia (at the time of writing this book) emphasizes an acknowledgment of the historical memory in order to heal as a society and to protect our cultural heritage. I see all over the Americas a resurgence of respect for indigenous cultures that lived in these territories before us. It's a movement that seeks to recognize and honor the origins of our culture, which was based on a reverence for the earth.

This movement seeks to value the traditional and the local. Although it isn't closed to the new, it tries to preserve the knowledge of our historical and cultural origins. For example, here in the Andean plateau of Colombia, people are growing quinoa, balu, and cubios again, foods of our ancestors. Also, I can see how the symbolic value of tobacco, coca, cocoa, and chicha has been restored, and a number of malokas ("houses of wisdom," round structures with tent-like thatched roofs) are being constructed for carrying out indigenous ceremonies.

At Aldeafeliz, one can see the reconnection with the ancestral wisdom. We have gotten advice from another wise person of the territory, Antonio, who we call "Jate" (pronounced HA-tey). Jate has made a great effort to walk the ancestral path, learning the culture and cosmology of the central Andean region, listening to "the grandfathers," or the elders of these traditions. His guidance inspired us, among other things, to build a maloka of the Muisca tradition on our land, called the Cusmuy to honor the tradition of the area and the ceremonial practices of its inhabitants. This maloka was built using traditional methods and has been an anchor for our spirituality and our health at every level.

Other ancient cultures, such as Judaism, have their own ways of honoring their ancestry. All year long, parts of the Torah are read to remind us of the perspective of the patriarchs and matriarchs of this tradition. Every year, ritual dinners are celebrated that remind us of significant chapters of Jewish history. For example, one such ritual dinner (my favorite) is Passover, when we remember the exodus of the Jewish people from Egypt under the guidance of Moses. This ritual highlights the pain of slavery but also the possibility of freeing ourselves, which is always available to us with divine help and that of the community.

In Judaism, this search for freedom and dignity, represented in the story of the Exodus, is fundamental. Without understanding this aspect of their past, it's difficult to understand Judaism. To me it's impressive how this religion keeps their ancestral legacy alive, and from this, an exemplary strength, unity, and sense of community emerges.

In professional territories, it's also essential to know the history. That's how you understand the roots of an academic or professional endeavor. In my biology studies, I remember a class on Darwin – his life and how he contributed to the field of ecology with his theory of evolution. Something that marked me in that class was seeing Darwin's notebooks where he wrote with great detail what he saw in the natural world. In these notebooks, he started to make connections between one species and another, creating the basis of his theory of evolution. Darwin's practice of being an attentive observer of his surroundings, and his habit of recording it in a notebook, became ingrained in me.

The American educator Parker Palmer, in his book *The Courage to Teach* offers a fascinating historical perspective of science. These ideas resonate with the changes I'm seeing in many fields right now. Parker cites Ian Barbour, who describes three stages of science. In medieval times, the basis of reality was mysterious "substances." Then, in the Newtonian Age, our focus changed to separate particles and atoms, which behave according to the laws of Newtonian physics.[1]

According to Barbour, science is now entering into a new paradigm. In the current age, we are starting to see the basis of reality not as separate entities but as communities. "In this era, nature is understood to be relational, ecological and interdependent. Reality is constituted by events and relationships rather than separate substances or separate particles."[2] Barbour invites us to understand the phenomena from a quantum perspective, as "a historical community of interdependent beings."

This new vision of science, which highlights interdependence, is very much in line with what spiritual guides have been proclaiming for centuries. The other day, Santiago, the leader of my Sangha (a Tibetan Buddhist group to which I belong) said, "Tibetan monks have known for centuries what quantum physics is just now discovering." We can see how the historical perspective is manifested in other fields. Exploring the territory of personal development (one of my territories), we get to the history of philosophy. Steve March, a colleague of my coaching school New Ventures West, sums it up by delineating three stages: premodern, modern, and postmodern.

In the premodern stage, everything was explained from a religious perspective: the purpose of human beings was to live according to the will of God. The only source of authority was the church.

The modern stage corresponds with the advent of Cartesian thought, of Descartes' "I think, therefore I am." Authority passed from religion to science and to rational thought. The purpose of human beings was to become rational, objective, and independent. Although this was progress compared to the dogmatism of the premodern age, we are starting to notice that science and objectivity have their blind spots.

In the postmodern stage, we start to validate other forms of knowledge beyond science and the rational, like phenomenology and ontology, which explore direct experience with the senses and the exploration of the self. This postmodern era has two tracks: 1) that of extreme relativism, where "nothing is true; everything is permitted," and 2) moderate relativism.

Some philosophers like Ken Wilber call the second track the Integral Era.[3] In this new era, the purpose of human beings is to develop integrally and start to elevate their level of consciousness. Elevated levels of consciousness allow the inclusion and valuing of all dimensions of being: body, mind, emotions, and spirit. Instead of focusing on independence, one looks for interdependence and a transpersonal consciousness (beyond self-interest), to include all of humanity, the planet, and the cosmos in our circle of concern. This view resonates with the new paradigm of science, which resembles what spirituality has been teaching us for centuries.

It's worth reflecting on the historical or ancestral perspective in any territory. Let's look at an example from the territory of family. Listening to the perspective of sages in family territories is very healing. Family constellations have helped many people to "hear" the voice of their ancestors and to heal their intergenerational wounds. It's very helpful to understand the history of previous generations to transform negative patterns and free oneself from burdens. Personally, this process has helped me a lot. When I recognized my ancestral past, a space for powerful action opened up in front of me.

What I'm about to tell you is something I share in my *Ausencia & Luz* (Absence & Light) concerts, where I use music to draw a parallel between my songs and the poems of my great-grandmother. Here is the story.

Some time ago, I went to Barranquilla to facilitate a workshop. When I was there, I felt an inexplicable sadness. I asked my mother, "What happened here in Barranquilla?"

She told me, "It was there that your great-grandmother Mina had to deal with the death of her mother, Ana Marina Lopez-Penha, when she was just five years old. It was there that your great-great-grandfather, Jacobo Senior, Ana Marina's widowed husband, lost his head after that death and also lost all of his fortune." After further investigation, I learned that he eventually died in emotional and financial ruin. Very likely, he lost his own faith, because he didn't pass on his Jewish faith to his daughters.

And so I went to visit Jacobo's grave in the Jewish cemetery of Barranquilla. I was able to go near the source of that sadness, which was so deep that I got a sense of the origin of the great absence or inner void that came from the sudden death of a mother and a spouse-triggered grief that was never fully metabolized or healed. This unresolved grief was passed on from generation to generation and caused disorder in my whole family system. Even though my grandmother, my mother, and I all had mothers, there was still an enormous sense of abandonment, like that of being orphaned. My mother discovered from Marianela, her family constellation therapist, that she "decided" to become an orphan (with her mother still alive) in solidarity with Mina, her grandmother. It seems that many children do this as a form of distorted "love."

By recognizing this inherited pain, I now have the opportunity to heal it and make peace with my feminine lineage. Because I received the creative force of my great-grandmother, my grandmother, and my mother, I was empowered to become a singer, seeing that Mina had a strong inheritance as an artist. As a poet, she was able to express her sentiments in a variety of inspiring verses. I decided that in all my Absence & Light concerts, I would share these verses right next to my songs, to show the parallels, shedding light on the healing needed in our family system. Honoring these poems from my great-grandmother helped me honor my own creative process. Everything flowed easily. I feel that this musical project has Mina's support and that of my ancestors – may they rest in peace.

Collective Intelligence

Territories have a great variety of actors and views. Learning how to recognize this multiplicity and appreciate its richness connects us to the wisdom of our territories.

Recently, I received a newsletter from an organization of friends of mine called *Somos Mas* (We Are More) which, in its own words, is dedicated to "activating collective intelligence in social ecosystems." In the newsletter, there was a video of its executive director at the time, Ximena Lara, who said,

> "In our culture, everybody wants to act individually, without taking into account what others are doing. If we want our business and our initiatives to get ahead, or to achieve the goals we have as a society of eliminating poverty, protecting the environment, taking care of the needs of our children, our seniors, and other vulnerable groups of people, we need to act collectively. This implies connecting ourselves to what's happening, mapping actors

and understanding what our role is within the ecosystem in order to activate collective intelligence."

What a synchronicity to receive this message while writing this
chapter. I had been thinking about the mapping I had to do in my work
as an environmental consultant and what I had discovered. For example, in 2003, when I worked for the Ministry of Environment in Colombia, I had the task of mapping the activities carried out on behalf of
protecting biodiversity, reducing climate change and combating deser-
tification – three very urgent environmental issues. In all three cases, I
found that there were many actors and many actions, but they were all
disconnected. Because of this, they didn't have the positive impact that
they could have. We often ignore and waste our collective intelligence.

In 2004, I performed a similar study in the Andean region for
Ashoka's Environmental Innovations Initiative. One of the results of
the study was that the actors in the environmental sector operate in isolation. They have difficulty communicating among themselves and with
other areas, and therefore, the collaborations and alliances needed for
creating systemic change weren't happening. What environmental innovators were urgently asking for was collaboration.

Unfortunately, things haven't significantly changed since then. I recently ran into Lili, a classmate from my graduate studies in environmental management. Coincidentally, she was mapping climate change
initiatives in Colombia, and reported a similar landscape. In this country, there are a lot of actions aimed at stopping climate change, but
many times they don't know about each other. In many cases, actions
are replicated but there's no coordination.

This happens in many territories. Some time ago, I clipped an article
from the *Semana* magazine, in which Rosario Córdoba, a Colombian
opinion leader, said emphatically on the issue of innovation, "Without
coordination, we aren't doing anything."[4] I have seen this need in all of
the territories I have been in: the need to engage in collective action to
increase positive impact.

The wisdom of territories that highlights their ecology isn't only concentrated in a few people, "the experts." It can be within common people, in the community. Jess Rimington, a talented social innovator from a network in which I take part, wrote an email at that time sharing her "Unpack Impact" initiative. She showed that the majority of social sector organizations and the government don't involve their beneficiaries in the planning of their projects. They deliver a service without even knowing if that's what people really want or need. This leads to undesired results, and once again, less impact.

In Rimington's promotional video, she shows an example in the Philippines, where the community organization Multiversity suffers from this phenomenon. In 2009, in the wake of the typhoon Ondoy, an area was declared a danger zone and the government ordered 24,000 people living there to evacuate – without consulting them. The people resisted and created their own local plan to mitigate the risks. In that case, it was the inhabitants who had been there for decades – people wise about their own territory – who really knew the habitability of that area and how to adapt to the dangers. They stayed in their territory, waiting for the government to validate their plan and recognize their wisdom.

We are in a moment in which technology favors these exchanges of knowledge about territories. We can conclude that it's essential to listen to the wisdom of the territory, to know its ecology, and to inhabit the territory in a conscious and responsible manner. Collective wisdom or intelligence should be consulted when designing any project or initiative, whether it be at the individual, organizational, governmental, or global level.

Accessing collective intelligence requires us to be intentional. We can foster diversity in the events and projects we organize to harvest perspectives beyond the ones with which we are already familiar. Additionally, we can talk to people who inhabit our territory and understand it in a different way. By reading magazines and attending events like conferences, forums, and seminars, where many types of knowledge are brought together, we can expand our grasp of the relevant issues of the territory – what's going on and what needs to happen.

What makes this so difficult if it seems so obvious? It's surprising how little we tap the collective wisdom, but at the same time, it is consistent with the individualistic and colonizing mentality of the West. As a Western culture, we tend to promote an impetuous Daemon that has not developed the ability to listen to sages in the territories where we enter.

One emblematic case in the history of this lack of connection with the wisdom of the territory and its collective intelligence was the conquest of the Americas. The Colombian film *Embrace of the Serpent*, which came out in 2015, shows how horrifying the conquistadors and missionaries were in colonizing our territory without respecting or learning about the culture beforehand. It was the inculcation of a cultural, economic, and religious model that happened very violently, leaving deep intergenerational wounds.

This same film shows what could have happened with a higher level of consciousness. Through a harmonious relationship between a European and an indigenous man, a different scenario is depicted, where there is a respectful entrance into the territory that doesn't interrupt nor affect its magic, where people listen and learn from its dynamics, where a dialogue of worldviews takes place, opening to deeper understanding on each side, taking advantage of the virtues of both perspectives. Maybe we could have taken advantage of the Daemon of the conquistadors, its impetus and sense of adventure, if it were in service of the common good, keeping in mind the wisdom of the territory and its sages. I believe we are slowly but surely raising our level of consciousness, taking steps to get there, healing wounds, and opening up to the dialogue that needs to take place.

This brutal example of conquest happens on a smaller scale all the time. We unconsciously colonize territories, without making any maps, without tuning into the collective intelligence, its wisdom, its ecology, and its real needs. This often happens with the "best intentions." Like literary critic Maria Popova says in her newsletter "Brain Pickings," we live surrounded by information, but there's a deficit of wisdom that could direct our actions to be more in tune with their surroundings and create well-being for everybody.[5]

The Emerging Future[6]

The wisdom needed for inhabiting a territory consciously goes beyond understanding its present condition and protecting its stability. There are moments in which ancestral wisdom and the common sense of collective intelligence fall short. Sometimes the majority is wrong; they can be full of fear and can't see "what the world wants from us." The media is good at playing with the public's emotions and shifting their opinions in support of questionable interests that don't protect the common good. Because of this, we will appeal to a particular group of sages who I will describe below.

There are certain sages who, because of their finely-tuned connection with spirit, can see beyond fear, beyond any type of confusion and manipulation. They are people with a heightened level of consciousness, who are attuned to the desired future to emerge in the territories and the crops that should be planted. Otto Scharmer, a professor at MIT, explains this in his book, *Leading from the Emerging Future*.

These sages have an ability to perceive beyond their egos, to see what a historical moment needs. They are people who can enter into very deep levels of communication and perception, who can tune in precisely to contexts. Scharmer says that we all have this ability, but it's something we have to develop. Generally, we are operating at a very superficial level of perception, lost in a cacophony of opinions and information. We can learn to hear the wiser voices talking to us above the rest, discerning what future wants to emerge, despite our individual egos.

When I started working at Ashoka, they told me that the average age of the leaders or social entrepreneurs they support ("the Fellows") was around forty (naturally, there are exceptions). They told me it's because there's a stage of exploration of their issues and what the world is currently offering, for example on the subjects of education, health, the environment, etc. Many long interviews are carried out in order to make sure the leaders have reached a certain maturity in their proposed solutions. This means the leaders thoroughly understand the existing approaches, the actors in their territories, the problems, and their root causes, before formulating their own "theory of change."

A theory of change is a clear vision of what is needed in the territory we inhabit. Sages have invested considerable time and energy in reflecting on their territories, in mapping out actors and processes. From these reflections, they make a prediction of which factors are the most promising to achieve systemic change for the territory and for the overall common good.

This process of inquiring into a territory and formulating a theory of change assures that what is proposed isn't disconnected from what exists. It also makes sure the plan will be truly transformative and meet the needs of the territory. When this level of maturity is absent from the reflection, there's no clear theory of change; it's not easy to obtain a lasting impact over time, nor a timely contribution.

Something powerful happens when individuals get together who have dedicated a great deal of time and energy into understanding their territories; they are like Wisdom Councils in action. Otto Scharmer says that the most important challenge of the twenty-first century is the creation of platforms for collaboration between change agents from different parts of the world that allow them to connect and exchange perspectives so that they can understand the whole system together. In this way, they will be able to act from impulses that come from this shared consciousness.

The idea of the Wisdom Council is not an elitist concept. We can all be sages in our own territories. But this starts with the humility of acknowledging those who have already walked a certain path. It's a fact that there are people who have dedicated considerable time getting to know their territories, listening attentively, and tuning into what needs to happen there. In this way, they become guardians of the territory. They've also dedicated time to working on themselves internally so that they can listen more deeply and moderate their individualistic impulses. In this way, they really become defenders of the common good. We can all aspire to this – and achieve it! This book gives you some recommendations. The first step is to recognize and listen to those who have already fulfilled the role of wise person.

When We Listen to Sages

What happens when we listen to the sages of a territory? Let's look at a case where the wisdom of a territory and its ancestral knowledge, collective intelligence, and the emerging future were in fact listened to. In 1995, an American couple, Bill and Lynn Twist, arrived in the lands of the Achuar, the indigenous people of the Ecuadorian Amazon region. The Achuar were concerned about big plans from companies that wanted to exploit local resources and possibly destroy the habitats of their communities. Bill and Lynn wanted to help. After many meetings with the shamans and elders of this community (the Wisdom Council), they co-created a strategy to empower people through monitoring and protecting their territories.

Bill and Lynn founded an organization, *Pachamama Alliance*, to respond to these needs. They raised the necessary funds and gave the community tools to defend the integrity of their territory and their culture. This first intervention included self-governance strategies, mapping territories, getting clear titles to their land, and sustainable economic development.

Pachamama Alliance supported the Achuar for many years. The organization maintained close contact with the Wisdom Council. Bill, Lynn, and their collaborators made an effort to continue listening attentively to the messages from the community elders. Suddenly, one day the Wisdom Council changed their view. In a meeting, one of the medicine men announced, "Thank you for your invaluable support. But we don't need those types of tools anymore. Now, the task is different. We have to go to the root of this problem." He added with solemnity, "We ask you to go back to your country and change the dream of the modern world."

The members of *Pachamama Alliance* were perplexed by this request. Change the dream of the modern world? Was that even possible? For the next year, they kept asking more and more questions, until one day they decided to take action. Without knowing exactly how they were going to do it, a team of committed people decided to try. They performed several small experiments that culminated in a four-hour symposium called "Awakening the Dreamer, Changing the Dream."

From that first symposium, they created a series of educational programs called "Up to Us." This curriculum has the goal of examining the paradigms of the modern world that have us in the middle of an environmental, social, and spiritual crisis. It invites us to a new paradigm of interconnection where sustainability, social justice, and spiritual fulfillment are possible and to take action to put this into practice.

The first time I went to one of the symposiums of the *Pachamama Alliance*, I was surprised how, in less than four hours, they were able to communicate so effectively the urgent need for change, and at the same time empower people to take action. At that moment, I remembered everything I had learned in my undergraduate in biology and my graduate work in environmental management. I was impressed at how well it was summarized and portrayed in such a compelling way. I recalled the endless conversations I had with people who didn't feel the same urgency and what it cost me to try to transmit the message effectively. In the *Pachamama Alliance* symposium, I saw people all around me changing their opinions and becoming citizen activists in a "blessed unrest" as the symposium invites us to be. I immediately wanted to become a facilitator of this experience, which I managed to do a year later.

Pachamama's symposiums and programs are in a simple format that makes their facilitation within reach. Facilitators of the symposium create a space for numerous people to question and change their paradigms, which is very satisfying. Because it has been so effective, the "Awakening the Dreamer, Changing the Dream" symposium has generated worldwide interest and created a network of more than 4,000 facilitators from more than seventy countries.

Today, the mission of the *Pachamama Alliance* is to be a bridge be-

tween two different worlds, as they say, "Our programs integrate Indigenous wisdom with modern knowledge to support personal and
collective transformation that is the catalyst to bring forth an environmentally sustainable, spiritually fulfilling, socially just human presence
on this planet." Their purpose is really relevant today; it has great depth
and offers hope, mainly because they consciously intended to listen to
the wisdom of their territories and adapt as a result.

Turning to the Wisdom Council is powerful. It leads to conceiving
initiatives like that of the *Pachamama Alliance*, which responds to what
the world really needs. As a result of the work of this organization, I've
seen the creation of a citizens' movement that seeks to raise awareness
about what's happening and empower others to bring solutions to the
table. I think the world won't change without a critical mass of people
who awaken and start actively generating alternatives to current problems. This initiative is aimed at exactly that, which fills me with hope.

The Vision: Attuning to the Outer Ecology in Three Steps

In a life full of purpose, there is clarity of vision and mission. In the
previous example of *Pachamama Alliance*, we saw what happens when
we listen to the wisdom of the territory and formulate a clear mission
that responds to what the world needs. The result is an extraordinarily
positive impact on society. This fills us with hope and the desire to contribute.

Let's start now by working on our vision, a vision that responds to
the following questions: What is the ecology of this territory? What
needs to happen here? What fruits need to be planted and harvested?
What fruits is this territory ready for right now?

As we can see, vision is related to the outer ecology. Attuning to the
outer ecology has three steps: mapping the territory, connecting with
sages, and formulating your vision.

Step 1: Map the Territory

Mapping a territory is similar to doing the market research that businesspeople do before they roll out a product or service, but it's not exactly the same thing. Both involve a process of getting to know and investigating a niche by means of interviews, field visits, focus groups, and other methods. Both allow us to identify opportunities. But their intentions are different.

By definition, market research is focused on market opportunities, whereas mapping a territory focuses on improving the ecology of the territory, which involves a wise perspective, not just an opportunistic one. Mapping aims to create an ideal future situation that promotes the common good, apart from any particular commercial interest.

Consultant Dr. Alonford J. Robinson is dedicated to mapping ecosystems and territories with his firm, Symphonic Strategies. In a presentation for the Center of Excellence in Public Leadership of George Washington University, he indicated that in order to make these maps, we need to think holistically, embrace complexity, see beyond the silos, understand long-term trends, anticipate problems, and integrate different sources of information. His analysis of the healthcare territory gives us clues for how to map other territories and ecosystems.[7]

In his analysis, Robinson contrasts the healthcare ecosystem as it is right now ("the current state") with how it will be in its more evolved version (in the "emerging future"). First, he maps out the relevant players: patients, doctors, government agencies, public hospitals, health departments, community centers, and private hospitals. In the current state, technology, institutions, and providers are at the center. There's an emphasis on the commercial aspect of health. Relationships between these actors are distant, and there is fragmentation of effort because each entity is looking out for its own interests. Its processes lead to rising costs, chronic illness, and people being left behind.

In the emerging future, the health system puts patients at the center. The system focuses on a wiser goal: the well-being of the patients. Different stakeholders enter into collaborative relationships in order to take care of the patients' needs. The most important processes are schemes of prevention, a holistic approach, innovation, and healthy competition encouraging new ways of providing healthcare services and allowing new players to come in and compete.

Mapping Scheme of the Emerging Healthcare Territory

Actors	Emerging structures/ relationships	Emerging processes
– Patients, doctors, government agencies, public hospitals, health departments, community centers and private hospitals, and new actors coming in	– Needs of the patient are at the center – Collaborative relationships between actors around these needs – Public policy maintains accessible costs	– Prevention schemes – Holistic approaches – Innovation and healthy competition

A preliminary mapping such as this helps us to orient ourselves, explore what our role is, and join efforts with other players. It's recommended to map your territory with other people so that they benefit. David Peter Stroh, the author of the book *Systems Thinking for Social Change*, says mapping helps to stimulate conversations that lead to discoveries and coordinated action with others.[8] We can imagine how this could activate collective intelligence.

For Stroh, mapping offers a wise perspective and should involve the spirit. He considers that the mapping process (or systems thinking) is spiritual because everything is connected and, at the same time, everybody can play a role to connect that which needs to be even more connected and get rid of dysfunctional connections. For him, good connections are those that are oriented toward improving life for everybody in the long-term, not only to benefit themselves. For Stroh, the wise point of view asks, "What does the world want from us?" instead of "What do I want?" which leads to an ego-centric attitude.

I shared the mapping schemes of the healthcare industry with Catalina, the participant in the Life Re-Vision workshop mentioned in the last chapter. She found this vision to be very useful, as health is one of her territories. I gave her the task of mapping her very specific sub-territory, end of life or palliative care. It's helpful to study one's territory at the scale that makes the most sense for your purpose.

Catalina had already started to create a network within her new territory as part of her exploration. She was already a volunteer at the "Fundación Derecho a Morir Dignamente" (Foundation for the Right to Die with Dignity) in Colombia. In this endeavor, she started to meet many of the players in her territory. She started to make a database. She made the most of the meetings at the foundation to start asking about the trends in this territory and its emerging future. People started informing her about the structures and processes of this territory.

Catalina perceived that the current paradigm is trying to maintain life at any cost and that the doctor is the primary decision maker. Many times, doctors have been co-opted by pharmaceuticals and their economic interests. For her, most doctors aren't prepared to understand and address the emotional complexity of palliative care, nor its spiritual dimensions. The sages of the territory helped Catalina to see the emerging paradigm. In the new map, just like in the example I shared with her, actors collaborate to meet the patient's needs. Instead of maintaining life at any cost, the right for a patient to die with dignity is respected.

Some other aspects of the emerging future of Catalina's territory became clear. Personalized attention would be provided at the end of life. This support would seek to understand and honor the spiritual aspiration of the patient regarding death. In parallel, support would be provided to the family in the process of accepting and preparing for the death of the loved one. This includes fostering forgiveness and reconciliation within the family group and thereby creating the conditions for a peaceful death at both levels, individual and family.

Mapping Scheme of the Emerging End of Life Territory

Actors	Emerging structures/ relationships	Emerging processes
- End of life patients - Palliative doctors - Funeral homes - Pharmaceuticals - Government entities (i.e. the Ministry of Health) - Spiritual and religious leaders	- The needs of the patient must be at the center. - Multidisciplinary teams are needed to take care of the patient's needs. - Specialized end-of-life centers need to be created. - Public policy supporting the right to die with dignity is needed.	- Personalized care - Involving the family - Spiritual processes - Individual or family psychological help - Forgiveness and reconciliation

This mapping of the territory gave Catalina enormous clarity. I reminded her that this was a very preliminary map, that many methodologies exist for a map like this, but that this start would help her understand the bigger picture of her new territory. I told her about a virtual course I took called "Systems Mapping" where I learned techniques for doing more rigorous mapping processes. Everybody can find their own tools and ways of mapping.

After this analysis, Catalina asked herself a series of questions that we will look at later, related to the mission, including, "What is my role in all this?"

Step 2: Connect with Sages

Moving along, we become more familiar with the ecology of the territory, what's happening, and what needs to happen. We start to identify the relevant people in our territories. We read books, watch videos, do interviews, have conversations, go to conferences, take classes, and visit places. This exploration strengthens our self-determination and capacity to untangle ourselves from "The They." Heidegger indicates that the best way to rise above conventional thinking is to identify our "heroes" or "sages" as they are called in this book, separate from the celebrities and politicians shown by the media – who are very rarely sages.[9]

Natalia – who we met earlier when I discussed her territory of politics – declared in an individual session we had that her sages that represent for her three different perspectives are the following:

Historical perspective. Visionary leaders who have wholly committed to what their historical moment required: Gandhi, Martin Luther King, Obama.

Collective intelligence. Collective processes that have relevant results in their countries: Iceland and its constitution reform efforts through the involvement of citizens, the Peace Negotiations in Colombia, as a collective that achieved the signature of a peace agreement with the FARC guerrillas: the student movement after the referendum in Colombia that mobilized in favor of the peace agreement, and many others.

Emerging future. Current female leaders who are values-lead and serve in the sociopolitical arena: Malala; the governess of Putumayo (a region in Colombia); Claudia López (current Mayor of Bogotá).

Catherine, a woman working on her doctorate in the US, who did the Life Re-Vision process virtually with me, did a thorough exercise to list her sages. In one of her sessions, she declared that in her territory of agro-ecology, her sages are:

Historical Perspective: A researcher connected with indigenous and ancestral wisdom (Robin Wall Kimmerer)

Collective Intelligence: A man who, through his model of edible forests, connects people to nature (Dave Jacke), a farmer in Honduras who loves to show what he has learned from the earth (Don Julio Sarmiento).

Emerging Future: A designer who includes ecological considerations in her design, beyond the aesthetic (Joan Iverson Nassauer), a researcher of systems thinking and interdisciplinary studies that has created a model of sustainable and resilient communities, especially in regards to climate change, using different forms of capital beyond money (Cornelia Flora), and a technology maven, capable of putting tech in service of noble causes.

Just like Natalia and Catherine, you can design your ideal Wisdom Council by listing people you admire and who represent each of these three perspectives. In order to define this Wisdom Council, you have to invest some time in getting to know your territory with the goal of identifying its wise people's voices. It's not necessary to be in personal contact with the members of your Wisdom Council; it's enough to have access to their wisdom by some means (books, videos, etc.) and this wisdom will light your way as to what needs to happen in your territory.

> **Reflect in your Journal**
> - *Take some time at this moment to define who your wise people are for now. Make a preliminary list in your journal.*

Step 3: Formulate Your Vision

After some time of study and reflection in which you are able to connect with your wise people, something magical occurs. These wise people's voices start to internalize. What does this mean? It means that you are now a carrier or channel of this wisdom. You are becoming a wise inhabitant of your territory, a guardian of its ecology. You are no longer functioning in an impulsive manner. These wise people now speak to you without even being present with you, a channel opens up to receive their wisdom and moderate the sometimes careless actions of your Daemon. This doesn't mean you don't need to keep listening to wise people, but rather that you now have a channel open to their wisdom. These wise people speak to and through you.

For Natalia, her wise people communicated to her the vision for the territory of politics (in Colombia):

> "A society where its political actors have a historical perspective so that we can lay out a chronology of the Colombian conflict that helps us understand why armed groups acted the way they did. We develop a systemic vision of politics, a broader one, beyond the electoral, one that values citizens' movements, and creates interventions and dialogues. We awaken collective intelligence to identify the abilities of every member of our teams so that we can work together optimally. We seize the current historic moment in Colombia to make the necessary changes."

The following vision came to Catherine, whose wise people we got to know above.

> "A society where people are inspired regularly to act as guardians of the earth. Everybody understands that when they do this, they are taking care of themselves and of all of humanity."

As we can see, the wise people don't speak to us personally but to the whole territory. Their focus is on the common good not on your personal well-being. Their tendency is to talk from the "us" point of view.

Another marker is that they address the needs of the territory, what needs to happen. They see the big picture.

Taking some time to be alone – in the shower, in nature, walking or sitting with something hot to drink – allows these wise voices to talk to us. As we are at peace, in a dream-like state, aware of the possibility of these voices, suddenly we are connected with something larger than us, an extraordinary clarity comes of a clear future for a territory or with the next step to be taken. Download this critical information! It's as if you are connected to an information channel. What it takes to get there is not necessarily easy, but it is possible.

When these wise voices are activated inside of us, it's just a matter of listening. We are already ready to formulate the vision we have for each territory, or, as an alternative, a global vision for all the territories we inhabit. The vision doesn't come only from our desires, or from a whim; it comes from the ecology of the territory (or territories), which we have internalized by mapping the system and connecting with wise people.

When you communicate with the Wisdom Council and open a channel to the field, you become a visionary. You now know how to imagine a new future and translate it into a story that you can tell others. It's like what Gandhi did in the territory of Indian politics. He saw that it was fertile and ready for planting the fruit of independence from Britain. He knew how to read signals around him at many levels, like a gardener would: the weather, the soil quality, the microorganisms, and knew that the ground was ready for an important planting.

A visionary has the humility to be very attentive to his or her context. They don't see themselves as the only "savior" who will fix every problem with an act of heroism. That's naive. Every contribution we offer is increasingly joined with what exists and is currently being co-created. Learning how to consult the Wisdom Council is putting this humility into practice.

Being a visionary implies widening one's vision. In the book *Systems Thinking for Social Change*, author David Peter Stroh recommends, "Listen to the course of being in the world...and bring it to reality as it desires."[10] Deep down, we all want to transcend our limited means of perception. Parker Palmer says that we all long to be introduced to a bigger world than that of our egos and our direct experiences – a world that expands our personal limits and enlarges our sense of community.[11] When we do this, we satisfy a spiritual need for contribution and meaning. In our heart of hearts, we know that our identity goes beyond "me" and includes a community of souls ("we") that vibrates with love and has the potential to enable everyone's flourishing.

That's how we could possibly inhabit our territories – with this level of connection and attention. Like the gardener who has seeds to sow but at the same time makes sure to put his hand in the soil first to see what the conditions of the soil are that day. How's the humidity and texture of the soil? Is it the right time to plant this crop? What does the earth need? What's the weather like? What other spaces are there around here? Maybe what is needed is to till the soil, fertilize it, water it. Maybe it's not the right time for planting. This requires patience. We have a clear vision of what we are going to plant. But this parcel of land might need some rest and renovation to be ready.

Although this connection happens many times spontaneously, we're going to do a visualization that seeks the guidance of our Wisdom Council.

VISUALIZATION

The Guidance of the Wisdom Council

Imagine that you have just finished the harvest feast as we saw in the last visualization. You still feel the happiness of celebrating and having shared your harvest with so many loved ones at this cycle's end. You feel a sense of abundance in your chest, of having enjoyed the fruits of the harvest with many people you love. You feel a vibration of fullness throughout your whole body.

You are in the company of your guide and your Daemon, and both of them invite you to take a well-earned rest. It's time to stop and renew energies before starting a new cycle. Breathe deeply, connect with the stillness of your body, with the silence of your mind, with the deepest tranquility. It's as if you are going into hibernation, and days or weeks will pass while you are completely still, submerged in the deepest sleep.

When you wake up, your Daemon is beside you. It motions for you to follow it. It takes you to a beautiful natural well. Your Daemon immerses itself in the water and signals you to do the same. You bravely jump into the well, immersing yourself completely in that refreshing and renewing water. You swim and play in the water with your Daemon for a while. When you come out of the water, you notice that you feel full of energy.

You're now ready! It's time to start the new growing cycle. Before you start to plan, you know that you need to consult your Wisdom Council. These sages can help orient you in what's good to plant at this time in the territory because its circumstances are always changing. This Council represents the wisdom of your territory, a trusted source of knowledge you can refer to in order to be more in tune with life.

Your guide helps you identify sages and bring them together. Your Wisdom Council receives the invitation and gets together in a circle in the middle of the woods. The sages arrive, one by one, and take their seats in the circle. You observe each of them. Some of them may not even be humans. You connect with them visually as they come into the circle. It could be that new people or entities come who were not part of your original plan. Let them come in and greet them warmly. When everybody has settled, you can pose these types of questions:

What is good to plant in this territory at this moment? What wants to emerge in this territory? What ancestral or historical circumstances should we keep in mind now? What new points of view, actors, and trends should we consider and include? What is needed at this moment?

Let every member of your Council express themselves and respond to the questions you ask them. Maybe the most important question is, "What is needed at this moment in my territory?" Make sure you get an answer for this question. When you have received enough answers, thank them for having given you this great amount of wisdom. Say goodbye cordially to each sage individually and go back to your guide and your Daemon to thank them for their company and to get ready, with this amazing team, for a new planting cycle.

When you finish this visualization, take note of everything you saw and heard. These are elements of your vision. Don't be too worried about writing them down perfectly. For now, just take note of all the rough ideas, even if they seem separate. You will begin to see later how they are connected.

You now have elements for your vision. You probably have a list of loose phrases, so you can start to organize this list by themes. Subsequently, you can formulate a short paragraph that captures the main ideas. Don't make things too complicated; this is only the beginning. You're now ready to start sharing your vision and to be guided by it. Let yourself be pulled by it. Write down elements of your vision in your journal.

The Daemon: Three Perspectives

A life of purpose has clarity of vision and mission, which implies constantly listening to the inner and outer ecology, which fills us with strength and wisdom and moves us forward with conviction. We've already seen how we can listen and attune to the outer ecology by consulting the Wisdom Council. With this approach, we now have a first draft of our vision. Now we are going to focus on our inner ecology, represented by the Daemon.

A life where we are disconnected from our Daemon is an inauthentic life, as it's only guided by external pressures and ideals. In an era like ours in which there are so many demands, stimuli, and needs in the world, we can forget about ourselves. We need to find that balance between the two ecologies, learning to also perceive what's happening inside of us. One of the many ways of doing this is to get to know and honor the particularities of our Daemon – "imperfect" and wild as it is. We can attune to our Daemon by opening up to three perspectives: vital energy, talents, and virtues.

Vital Energy

Let's go back to what the Daemon is, in essence. As we saw in the "Bones" chapter, when we honor our creations and give them their rightful place, something amazing happens. A vital energy starts to awaken again that seems to say "YES! What I do is worth it!" It's as if something in us has been brought back to life, a part of us that was shut away and put to sleep. Metaphorically, the bones reconstitute the body of the Daemon, and we begin to give it space and permission to exist, move, and create, to express its nature.

The Daemon represents your vital and creative forces. It's like a river that needs to flow, to be in motion. It's a wild energy, that's why it's often represented as an animal or a combination of animals. The animal is instinctive; it moves by its sense of smell. It doesn't need any explanations to be; it simply is. If you observe any animal, it never has doubts or philosophies. What it has is a mandate to express its nature, period.

Western culture has been hard on our animal natures, which have been labeled as the enemy of our rationality and spirituality. Anything impulsive, eccentric, different is rejected because it doesn't fit in with the "shoulds" of our societies. In the book *Women Who Run with the Wolves*, Clarissa Pinkola Estés says that we have excessively tamed the human being (especially women), and as a consequence, we've stripped ourselves of the force of our wild nature.[12] This has all been done in the name of creating a civilized culture, which is fine, but maybe it went too far and cost us our spontaneity.

What would it be like to go back to enjoying the spontaneity and sensuality of life, activating your senses to be more alive and passionate about what you do? We need to recover the wild part of ourselves. There's a great reserve of energy concentrated there that pushes us forward. It's connected with our passion and our instincts, as well as the drive to self-actualize. When we open to them, we get impulses from the Daemon that indicate where we truly want to go – inexplicable longings that move us to act, manifest, create, be.

The Daemon is an energy that seems to say "Yes!" to life, to ourselves, to that which calls us. As it is called, the Daemon responds. Imagine a wolf who gets a call from its pack to help protect it. Do you think he's going to think twice about it? It simply goes; it says "Yes!" to the call. In the same way, this part of you has the ability to sense what's calling you and respond without hesitation.

The book *The Gifted Adult* by Mary-Elaine Jacobsen, associates the Daemon with intensity, complexity, and drive. Intensity is an enthusiasm for being alive; it's the result of a nervous, sensory, and emotional system that is receptive and has the ability to respond. Complexity is a proliferation of sensations, emotions, and thought (sometimes contradictory). Drive is a sense of ambition, of setting a goal and doing everything possible to achieve it, wanting to get to the bottom of things or to go further, with higher standards, because of an intrinsic and unstoppable motivation.[13]

Chinese philosophy talks about an "animal soul" alongside our "spiritual soul." The book *The Web That Has No Weaver*, by Ted Kaptchuk, describes our animal soul as the irrational and uninhibited passion that propels life. It has the ability to react instantly when faced with something unjust or wrong. Our animal soul also has the ability to connect with the perfection of an instant and receive the perfect impulse to act from its instinct.[14]

Most of the personal growth literature in existence is centered on our spirit, our "highest" dimensions. It often leaves out this wild and unrefined but powerful aspect of us. This book aims to give a voice and dignity to that part.

What can we do to recover our animal soul? Ancestral cultures in the Americas appeal to the strength and intelligence of animals to awaken our power and our full potential. In the documentary *Humano*, a young person from Argentina who had lost the ability to smile goes to the Peruvian Andes in search of an answer and meets a shaman who guides him in rituals to reconnect himself with life.

One of the rituals has to do with imitating a puma and moving around the mountains like the feline. With this exercise, we remember that, besides having a mind, we also have instincts and life force. In that cosmology, three essential animals are talked about that we need to awaken within ourselves: the puma, the condor and the serpent. Other cosmologies focus on other animals, and from my perspective, any animal or combination of animals can connect us to our animal soul.

And how can we do this? The first thing to do is to activate the imagination. The metaphor of the Daemon helps us to imagine this instinctive part of us as a magical and wild being who enlivens us and to whom we need to pay attention and care for. Many books and movies explore this metaphor which comes from ancient Greece. *The Golden Compass* is a film based on the novel *Northern Lights* by Philip Pullman. Every character has a Daemon that accompanies them wherever they go. In childhood and adolescence, the Daemon can change; sometimes it's one animal, sometimes another. By adulthood, it has become a fixed Daemon.[15] We could interpret this as along the way while we get to know ourselves, we're not really sure what type of "animal" we really are. But then we start to get to an animal or pair of animals that really represents that side of our nature.

We can activate our imagination with visualizations. This is a very powerful tool to develop our ability to imagine things, which we often don't use enough. We've already done several visualizations that connect us with the Daemon. Here's another one. I remember some time ago, on a trip to Turkey with a group of wild women, one of them guided me in a visualization to find my "totem animal," as she called it. The visualization was something like this:

VISUALIZATION

Connecting with Your Totem Animal

Close your eyes. Imagine that you are on a journey in search of your totem animal (your Daemon).

Your voyage takes you through different types of landscapes as you look for your animal. Wherever you go, you look around and see the animals there, trying to find it. You pass through forests, mountains, valleys, rivers, seas, deserts, and plains. You go to every continent, all over the Americas, Africa, Europe, Asia, Oceania, the Poles.

You look at animals of every kind: reptiles, amphibians, mammals, birds...When you feel a strong connection with an animal, you stop. You look it in the eye, receive its energy and declare, "For now, you will be my totem animal, my Daemon!"

Once we awaken the Daemon in our imagination, the second thing we can do is to follow its instructions. He will give you impulses of what to do. They are subtle signals, but if we are attentive, they are very clear. Listen to it. Does it need you to bring it to life through theater? Does it need you to go out for some fresh air? Does it need to shout at the top of its lungs in the middle of the woods? Does it need an extended hug from various people from your tribe? Does it need to be in the water?

My Daemon spoke clearly to me, and this is what happened. After my Life Re-Vision, in which I gathered my bones, one of these being some songs, I followed the instructions to take these songs and record an album. This album was stored for a while, with no other instructions about it. A year later, my Daemon told me, "Now you have to release your album publicly." I followed its instructions again, found a way to make it happen, and everything conspired in my favor. Doing this made me tremendously happy. The fact that this direction came a year later showed me that this was the exact moment in which the Daemon was energetically ready for this. The Daemon knows.

The third thing we can do is adjust our lives to give more space to our Daemon. For example, in my case, the Daemon was not satisfied with just releasing the music. Two months later, he told me, "I want you to have a band and to rehearse regularly." This made perfect sense because, seeing how much vitality, happiness, and contentment music brings me, this had to be part of my weekly routine. So, I got together a group of committed people and adapted my house to be able to rehearse there. I created a new ecosystem (a band) for my Daemon where he is nurtured and then nurtures me, and I'm charged with energy for the rest of the week.

When you do your Life Re-Vision, gather your bones, and connect with your own creative forces, you will see how this unfolds in your life. The proof that you are connecting with your Daemon is that you start to feel more energy, life force, passion, and freedom. It's as if something primitive in you is waking up. Pay attention to your desires to start painting again, walk in the hills, cook, teach, ride a bicycle – whatever your Daemon asks you to do. Follow its instructions. One thing you can continually ask is, "What makes me feel alive?" Listen to the response and take bold action on it.

Some precautions regarding your Daemon: At first it can be overwhelming. Remember that this energy can be wasted if it's improperly channeled – for example, through inappropriate sexuality, substance abuse, relationship drama, etc. Don't be confused. The emphasis here is in learning to properly channel the energy of your Daemon to activate your life force and your creativity. Everything else that's not in service of your authentic and healthy expression needs to be worked on and healed.

Like any wild animal, the Daemon can be a victim of its own instincts. In order to make the most of the Daemon's force without falling to excesses, we appeal to consciousness and spirituality. Remember the guide that helped us find our way in the desert at the beginning of this book? That guide represents your connection to the divine, the highest part of you. Your guide also shows you how to be a master of your Daemon and how to tune into the Wisdom Council. Appeal to your guide for help in appropriately channeling your Daemon's energy.

The Daemon has its shadow as well as its light as strengths. We need to learn how to train our Daemon without subduing it. This could be enough matter for a whole new book, which I would love to write. We are people in constant refinement of our instincts. Refining my Daemon has been (and will continue to be) a whole process deserving of another entire book. But for now, we will focus on the positive elements of the Daemon and how important it is to activate its energy in order to live a passionate existence.

Talents

Remember that the Daemon is the guardian of your talents and will not rest until you have expressed them. A talent is an aptitude, an ability which you have available. The Latin word *talenta* refers to an inclination, a longing, a desire. According to Michael Meade, American author, mythologist, and storyteller, talents indicate the particular way in which our souls are inclined toward life and how we channel our vitality and creativity.[16] An innate talent shows us particular values and the unique ways in which each person contributes to the symphony of existence. My grandmother, for example, has a talent for beautifying spaces. Every time that I have moved houses, I've called on her to bring her special touch. She likes to do this, and it's a joy for the rest of us to have her help.

In the "Territories" chapter, you had a meeting with your Daemon where it told you what some of your talents are. This information was necessary because territories are the habitat of your Daemon and, at the same time, the ideal place to manifest your talents. Now we are going to add to this intuitive information with some tools.

Michael Meade equates talents with elements on a periodic table. Each talent has its form and weight.[17] I like this metaphor because it evokes the idea of becoming a scientist to understand the particular combination of talents we each have. From here, we can take charge of them and cultivate them. In order to properly take charge of a talent, the first thing is to identify it.

We can identify our talents intuitively. Some are very obvious and appeared when we were children. My aunt Ana María played "teacher" with her little siblings from a very young age. Her talent for teaching expressed itself since she was very young. Other less obvious talents could require tools to identify them. The book *Now, Discover your Strengths* by Marcus Buckingham and Donald O. Clifton helps people identify their five main strengths by using a tool they call the "StrengthsFinder." The authors affirm that we don't have one but rather several talents to explore. Every person is a unique constellation of talents. Knowing what your talents are is only the start. The real tragedy, they claim, isn't the lack of talents, it's not being able to use the ones you have. Therefore, the authors think it's essential that everybody identifies and connects with their talents and strengths, that they use them and keep developing them.[18]

In the Life Re-Vision workshops, I use a simple tool I will share with you. Some years ago, I was given a set of "calling cards." These cards come from the occupational model designed by John Holland, an academic and a pioneer in complex systems, the father of the genetic algorithm. Each card has a verb or function that we are familiar with (for example, dialoging, teaching, connecting ideas, selling, doing the numbers, etc.) that fit into the following six categories: Realistic (Doers), Investigative (Thinkers), Artistic (Creators), Social (Helpers), Enterprising (Persuaders), and Conventional (Organizers).

The big question of the game is "What do I truly enjoy contributing?" As we keep going in the game, you have to ask yourself, "Do I consistently enjoy doing this?" and then "Is this what I most enjoy doing?" Talents are verbs, they are about doing. Asking these questions helps us get to the most preferred verb. That's how we start to discover or clear up our most important callings in a playful way. Playing this game is a great way to start to identify the verbs that resonate most with our Daemon.

Catherine, who I have mentioned before, was determined to discover her talents. She employed that scientific approach to get to know herself more deeply and take charge of her talents. She used all the tools I gave her to identify them. First, she played with the calling cards. She shared the the most important cards for her with an explanation of why they appeal to her:

Seeing the big picture: She noticed that although she studied biology, her biggest strength was ecology. She doesn't really enjoy the details of each species in particular but rather the relationships between species.

Making connections: Catherine is passionate about understanding things and making connections to generate solutions.

Creating things: Catherine has a series of bones related to jewelry which she stopped making, but it's an activity she enjoys and does well.

Facilitating change: Related to the seeds, she enjoys overcoming challenges and affecting internal and external changes for a better relationship with nature.

Fixing things: Since she was little, Catherine has liked to fix things and reuse them as a way of living more simply and sustainably.

Catherine remembered she had taken the StrengthsFinder test some time ago and pulled her results for us to see. StrengthsFinder combines both talents and virtues. We compared her results with the calling cards she chose. According to this test, her five main strengths are:

Intellection: Relates closely to "see the big picture" and "making connections" as well as figuring out solutions to fixing things. She knows this about herself.

Adaptability: This is a virtue she was not surprised to see, as it is part of being able to facilitate change.

Input: Catherine is inquisitive by nature and enjoys collecting information, which helped draw her to research for a dissertation. This also shows up in her appreciation of collecting objects, which was apparent in her bones – quote collections, artifacts from travels, and making jewelry and showing it. This is a variation of creating and fixing things with different components, promoting aesthetics and a good use of our resources. It makes sense.

Restoration: This is very similar to "Fixing things." Being restorative in action translates to a propensity for identifying problems and solving them as well as bringing things back to life.

Empathy: This is a virtue she had not yet seen in herself at this point. This result had her reflect on her capacity to connect with others and to support and facilitate change.

We can already start to see Catherine's talent categories. Similar elements start to appear again and again. Then, Catherine went a step further. She sent an email to her family and close friends to get their perspective on her gifts. She asked them what were the best strengths they saw in her without sharing her previous work so they could think about it freshly. Here were their responses:

Seeing the big picture: No doubt about this one. It has come up again and again.

Desire and ability to understand everything completely: A recurrent theme we see in "making connections" and "intellection."

Caring, empathetic: This is a virtue instead of a talent. Again, this reinforces the theme of her humanity and desire to understand and get close to others, a social predisposition she starts to appreciate in herself.

Bravery and tenacity: This is also a virtue, which Catherine identified through her seeds, and was glad to see it reinforced by others. At the same time, this same theme came out with a twist, expressed as: "Catherine is persevering to the point of being stubborn."

This last sentence seems like a critique, but it's actually great feedback. This comment allows her to see part of her Daemon's shadow. Be aware that every strength of your Daemon brings an excess with it, a potential imbalance, an overflow. Don't worry. Embracing your Daemon means enjoying its lights and working on its shadows. Don't think your Daemon needs to be perfect. Life itself will constantly ask us to confront, moderate, and transform its exquisite imperfections. In Catherine's case, her commitment and persistence can become stubbornness – something that could potentially limit her.

Reflect in Your Journal:
Become aware of your Daemon's shadow associating your most salient light and dark features. List them in your journal, following this suggested structure:

    Light feature _____   *Shadow feature* _____

In my case, this would be the analysis:

    Light feature: Curiosity   *Shadow feature: Insatiability*

    Light feature: Fierceness and   *Shadow feature: Vehemence*

    passion

    Light feature: Energy and   *Shadow feature: Impulsiveness*

    intensity

    Light feature: Determination   *Shadow feature: Imposition*

    Light feature: High standards   *Shadow feature: Inflexibility*

As you can see, attuning to our vital energy, talents, and virtues is a process of self-discovery. Catherine shows us the dedication with which we can approach this process. Our task with talents is to identify, cultivate, refine, enjoy, and offer them in service to others. Talents are a key component of our mission.

We need to give each talent its proper place and not be bound by them. Let's talk about a difficulty that can get in the way, using an example. Xiomara, a great friend, is excellent as a visual artist. Her mentor, a famous artist whom she trusted and admired, considered her the star pupil. This mentor was very surprised and disappointed when Xiomara said, "I don't want to keep studying art anymore, I want to switch to music." Although she has a great talent for drawing, her main passion is elsewhere. She wanted a more social environment, especially at work, and wanted to create music with others.

For Xiomara, it was a breakthrough to recognize this desire and then act on it. It was an act of emancipation to resist her tendency to please others and decide to do what made her feel happy and alive. At that moment, she followed her Daemon's instinct. She still draws and makes visual art in her journals in her free time and enjoys this talent, now in its proper place. Listen to your Daemon so that it can indicate the place your talent needs to occupy in your life and the way you want to offer it in service of your self-realization and world's benefit.

Virtues

The Daemon is the guardian of our gifts; our talents and virtues. When we are born, we are gifted with essential qualities, or virtues, that emerge naturally. Different from talents (verbs), virtues are nouns like courage, wisdom, love, justice, temperance, and transcendence. The Daemon wants these virtues expressed and protected and might instinctively get enraged if these virtues are overlooked or unappreciated. These are the deepest treasures that the Daemon guards.

We can learn to see virtues in ourselves and others, which is a way of honoring our true selves and keeping our Daemon nurtured and fulfilled. "Seeing" someone in this case is more than just looking at them. It means connecting with their essence. When I see the children at the Aldeafeliz ecovillage, I can perceive certain virtues expressed uniquely in each one of them. In Matías (7), I can see he is service-oriented and agile. In Mara (12), I see how creative and assertive she is. Juana (10) exudes harmony and tranquility. Emiliano (7) is loving and jovial. Mayna (11) is perceptive and sensitive. Lorenzo (8) is histrionic and savvy. Miguel (6) is generous and empathetic. Gabriel (4) is expressive and meticulous. Celeste (6) is curious and fun.

That which we can see in others is also within ourselves. All virtues exist inside of us, whether we see them or not. Some virtues are covered up by layers off personality. Other virtues are close to the surface, nat-urally expressed from a very early age without effort. Some of us have forgotten this. It's easy to forget about our own beauty, especially when we have an inner judge that tells us we're not good enough all day long. We shouldn't believe this judge, and instead we should pay close atten-tion to our virtues. What we pay attention to grows.

Let's remember the "Seeds" chapter. When we tell our stories, our virtues come through clearly. Eventually, we start to take notice and take ownership of them. Remember stories from your childhood and your adolescence. Michael Meade, author, storyteller, and mythology expert, tells us that the strangest stories from those periods often are the key to our virtues.[19] These gifts are interwoven in a story that wants to be told. Explore how these virtues are expressing themselves in your life right now and how they influence the twists and turns of your sto-ries.

Go back to your list of seeds, extract the virtues from them, and re-flect on them. Do you feel like they are your own? Could your virtues be expressed more? The Daemon knows which virtues are the most mean-ingful for you and feels proud of them. As I said before, your Daemon is the guardian of these virtues and needs them to be expressed and of-fered in service to others and to the world. If this is not the case and we have hidden virtues, there is malaise. Let's look at an example of this.

Catherine, whom we have been speaking about, remembered a seed that made her eyes shine. It was a story of how, as part of a training, she was given the challenge to be left alone in the middle of the woods in a foreign country. At first, she felt fear because it looked like she was all alone in a dangerous situation, without anybody to turn to. She al-most died of fright when poisonous bees seemed to be following her. She started running like crazy, then all of a sudden stopped and realized how absurd this was; nothing was after her.

She took a deep breath. After a while, she managed to put things in perspective, see the big picture of the situation (talent), and connect to a bravery inside that helped her calm down, sort the situation out, con-sider her options, and complete the challenge. Not only was she able to feel safe, but she also had a mystical experience, a sense of unity. She felt part of something greater as her heart exploded in infinite love for nature.

This was a transformative event in her life, a seed moment. The emotion with which she tells the story shows it. Catherine knows that what happened then changed her life forever. She decided to dedicate her life to environmental issues. But she hadn't paid much attention to the other important discoveries available with this story: her virtues. Together, we decided that two qualities of hers she expressed in that moment were *bravery* (which helped her to overcome her fear in an uncertain situation) and *wisdom* (which allowed her to understand and feel that she is a part of something bigger). Catherine noticed that, when she used her bravery to overcome her fears and her wisdom to connect to her surroundings, a deep feeling of contentment and unity emerged.

Catherine asked herself, "How much am I using these virtues today?" Unfortunately, her response at that time (2015) was, "Not much." She had been closed up in her office for years doing research for her doctorate degree. Using her bravery to be in the middle of nature and her wisdom to make sense of things is exactly what she was missing at that moment. Her Daemon was demanding experiences where her virtues could flourish so she could feel alive. This realization helped her get clear about what kind of work she would look for once she graduated. It also gave her new motivation, which is so necessary when searching for work you will feel passionate about.

We can harbor a belief about who we are and even be convinced that we already know ourselves. Like Catherine, we can have a fantasy of executing a life plan that sounds good in theory, one that our parents like, but in practice is not in line with our Daemon. There's no vitality, there's no happiness, there's only exhaustion. If we want to align with our life force, we really have to let go of the old maps of our identity and be willing to see ourselves with new eyes. This means letting go of our attachment to obsolete life projects and creating our new map based on who we really are, what is life-giving to us, what makes us vibrate, and from there, what makes us contribute with real passion.

When We Listen to the Daemon

Catalina, who we met in previous chapters, started to listen to her Daemon, which wound up opening her life to a surprising magic. One day (2015), I got a chat message from her that sounded like a whirlwind of passion. She said:

> "My End of Life doula project is finally getting off the ground! Everything is flowing. I've already accompanied thirteen people in their dying process. The last processes I have supported have been beautiful, magical. The last one was yesterday, and I can't describe the beauty...there was no pain, no tears. The patient and her family were able to let go, and when she died, all of the women in her life were around her, singing to her and praying for her. She died crowned with flowers. Every time this happens, I feel so thankful for life and for those who make me feel so fulfilled."

I was speechless. I breathed deeply and was able to feel her vitality, her love for life, how she contributed to the world in an authentic and brave manner, totally in line with what made sense to her soul. I allowed this particular and nurturing sensation that comes with living a life of purpose to invade me – a feeling of deep congruence. After a few moments of savoring this happiness, I told her, "How happy I am to hear from you. It brings me great joy that you are flourishing!" Like a waterfall of energy, she responded immediately:

> "Yes, I'm definitely flourishing! I'm living this cycle of life with lots of creativity. And surrounded by other women. The only thing I can tell you is that what we call 'death' is a moment of

infinite healing. More and more, I'm learning to channel new modalities, rituals, songs, and offerings."

"You won't believe it...It's my Daemon who is whispering them in my ear! It's a constant source of creativity! Like you recommended, I have my Daemon in my room, in my altar, I have it close to me and give it space to exist and be. This has been key, to know that there's something I can turn to permanently and communicate with. In my case, I didn't just draw it, but I also gave it its proper place in my life. I have several accessories I wear that connect me with it...and look! This is the most spectacular..."

There was a pause for several seconds. All of a sudden, an image appeared. She showed me a photo of her in front of an owl – a real owl. They looked as if they were connected, in dialogue. Catalina continued,

"...we met in Edinburgh! It was magical, I was doing the Harry Potter tour, and it appeared in front of me. I felt as if it were a signal. Since we saw each other, my creativity has been off the scale!"

Wow! How mysterious and magical Catalina's awakening has been! We can see how willing she was to open up to her imagination and connect with her Daemon. She put her ultra-rational Cartesian mindset aside and found something inexplicable, fantastic, and at the same time very palpable: her wild side. She was able to channel this energy in a very enlightened way; she responded to a necessity of life, occupied an important role, and put her talents in service of something spiritual. This deep connection to her gifts and to what life wants from her allows her to do something few people do: support others in their end of life by injecting spirituality into an otherwise tragic moment and into the whole family system for the sake of healing. Catalina is a great inspiration for the Life Re-Vision community:. We admire her authentic path, which she walks with so much sensitivity and bravery.

Susana also had an unprecedented awakening of her Daemon. When she came to the Life Re-Vision workshop, she knew that something had to change. She identified with my story of having broken into little pieces after a separation from a partner. Her life as it was no longer fulfilled her. She felt alienated by the expectations of her husband to start a family, and she was exhausted by her government job. Her research felt far removed from reality. The dreams she had had were crumbling, one by one.

The only remedy was to reconfigure her life. Susana understood that it was possible to reinvent herself, and she was willing to do so. She had already begun to take a leap into uncertainty: she separated from her husband, quit her job, and started to explore her passions. She started to listen to what made her heart beat – that which gave her life.

From this exploration, revisiting her bones and seeds, Susana remembered her passion for women's issues and poverty-related issues. Ever since she was young, she was interested in these topics and wrote articles and poems in her school newspaper, of which she was the managing editor. She loved to raise her voice fearlessly to reclaim her freedom and independence as a woman, rising above the debilitating chauvinism present in her birth city, Cali, Colombia. In one of her writings entitled "The Woman in Me," she proclaimed eloquently:

> "When I grew up, I found that the world I had imagined as a girl had been only a dream and a fantasy, and in order to find fulfillment as a woman, I would have to find some direction and goals for my life. I could put all my love into what was important and profound in order to be able to change the course of the world one day...

> "Women! This is still a patriarchal world that has made us the second sex...We are as free and independent as we decide to be...it is up to us...Women, you already know what your path is."

These bones and seeds gave her the strength and ability to listen to her calling: the desire to empower women, especially those who are economically disadvantaged so that they can have a real opportunity to get out of poverty. But to do her work she had to be in direct contact with these women. Her research couldn't just be theoretical. She had to be in the field, seeing the effects of her work for herself.

In a short time, she started to take action. She created an organization dedicated to feminine empowerment; the success it achieved in the first six months was extraordinary. The organization won a contract to perform some research in the United States and began a huge initiative with the Colombian government, which wound up being passed as law. To achieve this, Susana formed a team and generated lots of movement on social media that opened the doors to spheres of power very quickly. These results showed Susana that this was her path; there was no doubt about it.

"I'm like a lioness protecting my organization," she told me one Friday as we were having a coaching call. Although there had been ups and downs with her team, as would happen in any project, she expressed her conviction to me, "I no longer let myself be seduced by offers of prestigious jobs with high salaries." I could see that her life force and energy were committed to this cause, which gave her the stamina to get up in the morning and motivation to keep moving forward.

The Daemon that moves her – her lioness – can be felt when you talk to Susana. It's full of energy and makes you want to join her in her cause. After listening to her, you feel like anything is possible. It's the same Daemon that pushes her to do marathons and triathlons in cities all around the world. The same Daemon that gets her to go out for a spin on her bicycle in the middle of the day in New York, and that's the reason why she doesn't want fixed work hours. It's the same Daemon that takes her to far away lands on epic adventures when the irrepressible need to travel grips her. She told me that same day, "I need to take a break and change my environment for a while. I've decided to go horseback riding for two weeks on the steppes of Mongolia." That's what shows up when someone listens to their Daemon.

I want to give you another moving example about my dear friend Steven – may he rest in peace. One of Steven's great virtues was his generosity with other people, especially with the most needy. One doesn't forget virtues; they stay imprinted on one's heart even when that person dies. I remember that when we met, he was dissatisfied with his work life. He told me, "I want to dedicate myself to something where I help others."

As an architect working on luxury homes, he didn't enjoy himself. In that context, he didn't feel like his virtues were being fully expressed. He didn't believe that he was living up to his potential. He felt tired and bored. Clearly, this was a sign from his Daemon: stuck and bored. Steven needed to unleash his vitality; he knew that he needed to make a change.

One day, everything changed for Steven. He made a brave decision to come back to Colombia, his country of origin, and get involved in social causes. Once he was back in Colombia, he opened his heart and his house to the needy. When I visited him, his house was often full of indigenous people with their traditional clothes and musical instruments. Steven committed to helping out a particular indigenous community which had been displaced by violence, the Wounaan. To do this, he used his talents as an architect and as a public relations person. He built a house for them with funds that he raised among his friends and acquaintances in the affluent Jewish community. This changed his life so much that when the media published an article at his death, he was referred to as an "architect and social leader." I smiled when I read this because this role was much more in line with his Daemon.

It impressed me that in such a short time (five years or so), Steven made a complete change of his identity, to the point of being referred to with this new role as a social leader by the media. But at the same time, this doesn't surprise me. Steven was able to unleash his enormous generosity, expressed with all its force, in a context where it was so much needed.

At his funeral in the Jewish cemetery, a group of indigenous people came, which was the first time in history that ever happened there, according to the Rabbi. One of the indigenous leaders performed a special ceremony for him in his own language, expressing his gratitude for Steven's generosity. What happened after his death was really surprising. I will describe it in detail in the coda of this book because it's an example of a Life Re-Vision, step by step, carried out by the community.

This is my conclusion regarding our inner ecology: deep down, we all want to express and be recognized for who we really are. We want to feel alive, in connection with our greatest virtues, cultivating our talents and sharing those gifts unreservedly for the benefit of others.

As we saw with Steven, even if we only have a few years left in our life, that will be enough. If we connect with the Daemon, we can make the necessary changes to activate our real role in life and be remembered for that. We know that it's happening when we feel our vitality increase, a free expression of our virtues and an awareness and intentional development of our talents.

Look over your bones, seeds, and winds very well. From there, deduce your passions, talents, and virtues. You can start to see which changes you need to make in your life. Give space to your Daemon, listen and attend to it. Let it out of the cage. Let it grow.

To listen to your Daemon is to claim your freedom and answer your calling. Plato said that the Daemon is a genius protector that helps us fulfill our destiny. Claiming our freedom – as my friend Pablo, a philosopher and speaker, said – is one of the most difficult challenges of life. Sometimes we play the victim by using circumstances to try and excuse ourselves from not taking responsibility for our lives.

In the English language, there is a very interesting distinction: "fate" versus "destiny." Fate is something that happens to us, the cards we have been dealt. Destiny is what we do with those cards to give them meaning. James Hillman, the author of Soul's Code, says that the Daemon is the carrier of our destiny. This means that the Daemon takes the specific events that have happened in your life and lives them in its own way, without precedent. In the words of Hillman, "The Daemon is the carrier of our destiny. It is our gift, our fate, our genius, our calling, our soul. It motivates, protects, and invents us. It is totally unreasonable, a deviance, an oddity."[20] I appreciate this concept because instead of being ashamed of our peculiarities, we should trust in them.

The analysis of fate and destiny explains much of why my life is the way it is now.

Fate: I was born of a couple that split up when I was two. I was raised as an only child and lived a very lonely childhood. *My Daemon's response*: To inhabit the family territory intentionally, cultivate my relationship with my half-siblings, create community wherever I go, co-found an ecovillage with my friends to create another gigantic family with a common purpose.

Fate: I inherited a heavy load of social and family conflict, divorce, depression, and relationship chaos. *My Daemon's response*: To inhabit the personal development territory and become a life coach to develop relationship skills and respond to conflict in a different way. To marry a man also devoted to personal development.

Fate: I grew up in a context adverse to emotions, both at home and in school, a context that prioritized rationality and discredited the arts. *My Daemon's response*: To sing and compose, to connect with emotions and the arts in a healthy and creative way.

Fate: I was born in a relatively poor country, at war, that destroys its natural resources. *My Daemon's response*: to inhabit the territories of social innovation and sustainability and turn this into an opportunity to reinvent ourselves and tap into our true potential as a nation.

Reflect in Your Journal:
Your own Daemon has surely responded in creative, unique, and even strange ways (in the best sense of the term) to your life's circumstances (your fate).
Take a moment to analyze this in your journal using the same format:
Fate: _____ *Your Daemon's response*: _____

The Mission: Attuning to Our Inner Ecology in Three Steps

We've already gone over the steps to attune to the outer ecology and to formulate our vision. Now we are going to work on our mission related to our inner ecology, represented by our Daemon. The mission responds to the question, "What is the work that, when I do it, I feel fulfilled? What is the way I can respond to the needs of the world, while feeling happy? What is it that fills me with passion and meaning?" Attuning to our inner ecology consists of three steps: mapping our roles, connecting to our Daemon, and formulating our mission.

Our trusted source to consult about our mission is the Daemon. But the Daemon needs a master to direct its energy. Our Daemon, if it's open to listening, lights up when it hears the voice of the Wisdom Council. The vision that emerges from the Council will direct its force toward something bigger, more significant than our own impulses. This gives a higher purpose to the Daemon's creative force. This Wisdom Council's vision is a calling to activate your energy, talents, and virtues to serve a collective need, to contribute and take care of the world.

Listening to the voice of sages helps the Daemon get a clear calling beyond its own interests or immediate needs. When it receives this calling, a magic moment occurs. Imagine as if it were a scroll rolled up and tied with a burgundy colored ribbon when opened, the title "Mission" appears, and there's a map of a territory with a specific point where we need to go to find the treasure. This is the sensation of finding our mission. We now know what our role is in this territory and where to go to find the treasure.

This mission of the Daemon responds to the Wisdom Council's vision, and at the same time, elevates and uses one's unique gifts (talents and virtues). Remember the work with the bones, seeds, and winds, and the experience of connecting ourselves with the creative force and the virtues that we have. This work is our base to define a mission that is congruent with who we are, in line with our nature. This mission can be determined by mapping out our roles.

The mission can be composed of more than one role; it's not necessarily unidimensional.

It honors the multiplicity of talents that you wish to share with the world. In the book *Playing Big*, Tara Mohr talks about "the callings" that make up "the mission" as plural, in order to highlight that multidimensionality. They are callings to fulfill certain specific roles, which are yours to fulfill. You have the ability to make them work, and you are passionate about doing so.

Mohr mentions that creating space in your life for your callings will make all the difference in your happiness and energy levels – even if you only dedicate a couple hours per week to the subject, as is the case with my music. That doesn't mean that I put everything else aside for music, just that I opened up a space in my life for this passion. Since I honor that part of me, I feel more complete and have more energy for everything else.

Step 1: Map Your Roles

In the section "When We Listen to the Daemon," we saw how Catalina's life blossomed from the moment she connected with her Daemon and identified her passion. How did Catalina get so aligned with her passion? When she made her map of the end of life territory, her next questions were, "What is my role in this panorama? How can I contribute to the evolution of this territory?"

Progressively, the answers began to come forth. Seeing the current state of the end of life territory, she started to see opportunities that resonated with her being. Guided by intuition as well as her Daemon, a mysterious owl, lover of the night, she took step after step. Catalina is restless, reads a lot, and is always exploring subjects that interest her on the internet. After her dream where an owl mentioned the shaman of death, she familiarized herself with a compatible role that already existed in the territory: the end-of-life doula. She intuited that this was the role for her.

The end-of-life doula brings a particular perspective to the end of life territory. She sees death – when done right – as an enormous opportunity. The end-of-life doula offers holistic support for the patient and their family at the end of their life, keeping the needs of everybody in mind. The end-of-life doula facilitates processes of transformation for the patient and the patient's family. The doula aspires for all people to die in the middle of transforming encounters, rituals, and in reconciliation with others and with life, instead of in an impersonal hospital bed with exorbitant medical costs, estranged relationships, and people devoid of hope.

We can see with the case of the end-of-life doula (one specific role) that each role contributes to addressing an important need in a territory. Besides contributing to the territory, roles are something that fit us like a glove; we play them naturally and with gusto. For Catalina, death had always been something that fascinated her. Her Daemon, the owl, a night bird with large eyes, evokes a penetrating wisdom that illuminates in the middle of darkness. Not everyone can do that work.

With time, Catalina was able to clarify the other territories and roles her Daemon wanted to occupy to express its talents. At that time, she had a significant other and so she added a very important territory – that of family. She expressed that once her days in the peace territory as a researcher were counted, broader social issues no longer interested her. Now she was more passionate about family and community contexts.

Then, she connected with her wise ones – a list that already included wisdom on mourning, relationship consciousness, feminism, palliative care, spirituality, and community – and obtained new information. She also consulted her Daemon to see what excited her so much. Her trusted sources confirmed the roles she needed to develop in this moment of exploration and change she was living in: end-of-life doula, storyteller and speaker (in workshops and round tables)

Susana responded to a very different calling. Her Daemon is a lioness that activates the energy of others, injecting power. Her territory of women and gender absolutely needed her power. She knows that her strength is in empowering, using her talents to research and teach, and so her natural roles are leader, researcher, and teacher. These flow out of her without much effort. She learned to associate herself with people who complement her energy and help her to manifest her feminine empowerment vocation.

It's possible to identify the roles intuitively, like Catalina and Susana did. Yet sometimes the answer isn't obvious. We need a deliberate mapping process that can be supported with some tools. Navigating so much complexity requires a guided tour to assist with identifying roles.

There are tests that help identify occupations aligned with the natural orientation of our Daemon. As soon as I started my studies at Mount Holyoke, a small women's college in Massachusetts, I went to the Career Development Office. What a huge difference compared to my previous large university where I just felt like a number, a statistic! Here, I was able to find support to investigate who I really was. I was interested in many things but I had no idea what career to aspire to. I was studying biology, and I was pretty good at science, but something left me unconvinced that this was the right fit for me; something was missing, and I didn't feel completely fulfilled.

The career counselor with whom I met recommended I take a test called the "Strong Interest Inventory." The set of interests is divided into six typologies (the same categories as those of the calling cards, coincidentally). Each category is associated with a family of roles: realistic (building roles) artistic (creative roles), research (thinking roles), social (helping roles), entrepreneurial (persuasive or business roles), and conventional (organizational roles).

That test confirmed my intuition that I was not naturally inclined to investigate or work in the sciences. My strongest motivator came out as artistic, the second strongest was investigative and the third social. The test indicated that I was apt for creative expression in music or theater. Including the investigative and the social, I would do well with work that included an analysis such as supporting others (some sort of counseling), writing, and teaching. The test recommended a variety of occupations or roles, ones that are very much in line with what I'm doing now: coach, consultant, speaker, singer-songwriter, and writer.

Catherine also relied on this tool to clarify her roles. In transition while finishing her doctorate, she wanted to understand herself with fresh eyes and not just look for work that someone with her credentials should find. She wanted to take a break and inquire who she was and what she really liked and not feel forced to follow a career because of a past decision. She's conscious that she's made a number of decisions in her life not from a place of inspiration but from fear and in search of financial security. This has led to dissatisfaction and a feeling of distance from her real passions.

Catherine had already made an inventory of her talents, strengths and virtues, as we have seen. She then turned to studying possible roles. She found a test similar to the "Strong Interest Inventory" called the "Holland Code Test" she could take for free.[21] Her main categories came out as artistic and realistic. She also has a bit of social. This surprised her because she had been thinking about a future as a researcher and professor. At the same time, it was a relief to see these results because she hadn't felt fulfilled by her work as a researcher and assistant professor. She understood why she was feeling so tired doing her doctorate, dedicating most of her time to researching and writing. Trying to finish her doctorate had really been a great effort for her. Her Daemon, a slow moving feline but an infallible hunter, needed other activities to feel alive: creating, building, helping others.

Explore the Holland Code test using the link provided to clarify your role. What are your categories? Which of these flow naturally for you? Once we have our categories defined, for example "I am a researcher," we can explore them more specifically. What type of a researcher are you? What type of builder? That's how we can get to new and appropriate roles for your Daemon and for your territories.

It's important here to differentiate between what flows naturally and what you are passionate about from what you should do for status because of obligations or in order to compensate for low self-esteem. Tara Mohr invites us to observe how we define our roles: To meet an external expectation or because it really inspires and satisfies us?

Feel free to explore unexpected and apparently disconnected roles. The previously mentioned book *One Person / Multiple Careers*, talks about careers composed of multiple roles, separated by a slash. Real estate agent/singer-songwriter. Fundraiser/actress/mother. The author of this book has confirmed that people who opt for these composite careers feel more fulfilled.[22]

This book is full of practical advice for combining these roles effectively. Composite lives are increasingly common and are aligned with the Life Re-Vision methodology. This approach seeks to honor fundamental aspects of our identity, which make us feel alive while contributing our talents to benefit others.

Here's another recommendation: look for roles that are specific, and if you want, novel. As society changes, so do our roles. For example, an end-of-life doula is a relatively new role. Go over your bones, seeds, and winds. Listen to the sages of your territory. Look for something that inspires your imagination and fills your soul with happiness.

Reflect in Your Journal:
- *Do a preliminary inventory of your roles.*

Step 2: Connect with the Daemon

After using supportive tools and studying the topic of roles rationally, it's a good idea to let all of this go and confirm how it feels in your body, evoking the instinctive intelligence of your Daemon. Let's do a quick visualization that opens us up to other ways of asking the same question.

VISUALIZATION

Consult Your Roles with Your Daemon

Sit down comfortably in your seat. Put both feet on the ground and close your eyes. Breathe deeply three times. Feel your body. Imagine that you are in a natural setting, full of life and beauty. It's the right environment for your Daemon to feel comfortable. Feel the well-being and the energy of being in such a welcoming place. Look around and receive its beauty.

Your Daemon comes close to you, and you establish contact. Recognize and thank the presence of your Daemon in your life. It gives you vitality, your instinct for self-realization, and protects your virtues and your talents. It makes sure that you find your unique place in the world and that you express your potential to the maximum. After recognizing and thanking your Daemon, verify that it feels seen and acknowledged by you.

Take advantage of this moment to express regret for not always having acted with your Daemon in mind. Evoke moments when you have betrayed your own nature, when you have not honored your talents and virtues or have inhabited spaces that drain your energy. Bring to light the consequences you have experienced as a result. If you feel so inclined, tell your Daemon, "I'm sorry I haven't taken you into account." Observe its reaction.

Express to your Daemon that you are now ready to listen. You can say something like, "For me, it's important to keep you in mind because I feel alive when I do that, and that's how my full potential can be expressed." The next step is to ask your Daemon the following questions (as they apply to your case):

- *What aspects of the Wisdom Council particularly excite you?*
- *Are the roles I'm exploring appropriate for me?*
- *What other roles could I explore in order to fully use my virtues and talents?*
- *What other needs do you have to feel alive?*

Allow your Daemon to reply to these questions in its own way. It could be by responding directly, by putting images in your mind, or more abstract signals.

Receive what you get with gratitude without forcing anything. It could be that your Daemon is just beginning to trust you, so allow the communication to grow little by little. You can repeat this exercise later on when conditions may be better for obtaining a clear response.

When you have received a signal, no matter how abstract it may be, thank your Daemon and close this sacred connection space with some sort of gesture: a hug, a bow, whatever you feel is best. Go back to feeling your body, feel your feet on the ground, breathe deeply three times, and open your eyes.

This response can also come in a dream. In any case, when you receive the answer, make a note of it to show interest and respect for your Daemon's messages. That way, it will see that you are taking it seriously.

Step 3: Formulate your Mission

I encourage you to include your roles in your mission statement. Natalia did a similar visualization as above, and here's how her mission and her roles came out:

> *Mission:* To be able to contribute to the Colombian post-conflict process as a mediator and researcher. Mediation is a tool used to propose points of agreement between different parts of society and give space to different points of view. Research is an instrument to facilitate understanding of the Colombian armed conflict with a level of depth needed to overcome it.

Additionally, her connection with her Daemon indicated that she was living through an important time of transition and was being called to connect with the spiritual realm. In order to be a mediator and an agent of peace, she needed to cultivate her own inner peace and nurture herself from relationships that really filled her. She was moved as she listened to her inner sages directing her toward this inner path, which she now walks with lots of enthusiasm and curiosity.

Once Catherine discovered her talents and knew what categories of roles were good for her (artistic, realistic/building and a bit of social), she connected with her Daemon to consult which roles she was best suited for. The words that came to her were "congregator" and "creator." Understanding the space she was exploring, I suggested she also explore the roles of facilitator and designer, which match a few clear occupations including

- Facilitator of interdisciplinary spaces
- Designer of educational experiences

Catherine received my suggestion of roles to explore (facilitator and designer) and began investigating these roles until she felt they were for her. The mission she formulated was

> "To inspire others to connect to nature, community, and self in ways that are educational, fulfilling, and meaningful and that spark curiosity about other changes that could occur; and to do this through convening and facilitating conversations among thought leaders and designing hands-on, educational, and visual pieces."

Now it's your turn. You've already done a rational and intuitive exploration of your roles. Now you are ready to formulate a mission more connected with yourself.

If you have followed these steps, you now have elements for drafting your mission. Just as with your vision, you surely have a list of loose phrases, so you can start to organize this list thematically as well. Then, formulate a paragraph that captures the main ideas. Don't be a perfectionist. The mission will keep evolving. This is the first version.

Reflect in Your Journal:
- *Make a list in your journal of the elements of your mission.*

Let's Talk about Ecology

The Life Re-Vision workshops are a great place to shed light on people's key questions. Nicolas, a seventeen-year-old, didn't know what to study and came to the workshop at the recommendation of his father. At first, he was a little lost, but after listing his bones, seeds, and winds, and declaring that his territory would be sustainability, he surprised us when he shared his vision:

> "We need an ecological revolution that includes changes in the modes of production and consumption, the protection of water and other natural resources, the inclusion of new and sustainable materials, and changes in the industrial model."

Astonished, we kept listening. It seemed like he was channeling his sages. His clear mission was congruent with his vision:

> "My mission is to focus on the development of ecological projects, to fight for conservation of resources, to promote love for the earth, and to persevere in what I'm proposing, to execute these projects and not ignore my inner self."

Nicolas came out of the workshop with the clarity that he would study industrial design to plant his vision and mission in the territories of innovation and sustainability. His roles would be designer, activist, and caretaker.

In her workshop, years ago, Catalina shared her combined vision for all of her territories (peace, spirituality, and healthcare):

> "A world in which there is a balance between masculine and feminine energies so that there can be space for every living thing. All functions and missions exist in harmony and co-create as a tribe, a community. A world that's environmentally sustainable and socially just and spiritually fulfilling."

After sharing her vision, Catalina spoke about her role in achieving this vision, that is, her mission:

> "To recover and give a sacred place in our society to our cycles, our cyclical nature, and transformations – and more specifically, the physical transcendence known as death. To recover the idea of dying as a moment of transformation filled with community, healing, and liberation. To offer the possibility for every individual and every family to live this transition from a position of love and acceptance.

> "How? By supporting terminal patients and their families as an end-of-life doula. By participating in meetings and round tables where we talk about a dignified death as a speaker and storyteller."

It's not always easy to formulate our vision and mission. Andrea, a participant in the workshops, wasn't able to see her mission, even though she had a clear vision in the renewable energy territory:

> "To generate a safe, sustainable, accessible, and reliable energy matrix through the sustainable use of resources of each country, based on the best technology and with the purpose of improving the quality of life of the inhabitants in an environmentally sound way."

"And what is your mission?" I asked her. She said that she identified with everything that her vision implied. I seized this opportunity to explain an important aspect of the mission.

> "Declaring a mission is a way of recognizing that, in order to achieve your vision, you are going to need many people performing different functions. The mission defines what your par-

ticular function is so that you can enter into interdependence with others and see them as allies."

This helped her unravel things. To start, she said that her mission was to

> "Contribute from within my company to the lessening of greenhouse gas emissions, in line with the COP 21 agreement, by generating environmental awareness about sustainable technologies and by selling the proper technologies for thermal projects."

"How does it feel for this to become clearer?" I asked her.

"It feels uplifting. It's very different doing my job when I know now that it's part of my life's mission," answered Andrea.

I did a short Life Re-Vision workshop for a group of women of different age groups who went to the United States to attend a forum on women in business. When they got back, I guided them through the steps of the Life Re-Vision, and I invited them to share their visions and missions. Together, they helped each other to translate the learning experiences of the trip, in order to clarify their purpose in their territories. These are some of the visions and missions that emerged:

Alejandra (Business Territory)

Vision: Women who graduate from university need more awareness of the business opportunities that exist. Equally, relating to each other as women in the business world is often difficult.

Mission: I want to be a change agent creating a better environment so that women can enter the business world and have more solidarity with each other.

Roberta (Foreign Trade Territory)

Vision: The foreign trade sector is precarious despite all the potential we have here in Colombia because companies are all located in the center of the country, which makes transportation difficult. A dynamic foreign trade sector would positively impact employment, education, research, and innovation.

Mission: To land an influential job in this sector in order to strengthen this territory. Build gigantic hubs that offer relevant services for companies in coastal cities so that companies will want to relocate there and increase their exports.

Lariza (Higher Education Territory)

Vision: Education in universities is focused on technical knowledge and not in the integral development of people. There's a need for a huge army of coaches to support people's development in different dimensions of their lives.

Mission: As a coach, to be able to offer a more comprehensive education to young people so that they can develop in a more integral fashion and be able to plan their lives from deeper self-knowledge.

Carmenza (Education Territory)

Vision: To build a high-quality education system focused on literacy and provide empowerment for children and adolescents of the lower socioeconomic strata to resolve obstacles to their growth.

Mission: To be a social entrepreneur who achieves these goals so that children and adolescents can get a good education and be empowered to reach their potential.

In these examples, we see the intention with which these people inhabit their territories. Their commitment to honor the territory itself – through their contact with the Wisdom Council – translates to a vision. And at the same time, there is a desire to honor themselves as well – by being in contact with their Daemon – which translates to a mission.

They inhabit their territory with the goals of contributing, understanding their place and role, and moving in sync with what is there already. The intended contribution is illuminated by a clear sense of purpose, formulated in vision and mission. Through this way of inhabiting our territories, we get to an ecology of one's legacy. We feel like we are part of a system and become active contributors to the system, from a place of deep respect for its dynamics.

My Ecology

The Wisdom Council transmits accumulated wisdom about the ecology as well as the diversity and cycles of a territory. These sages could be real people that you know or perspectives that you begin to internalize. Here, I will refer to all of my territories combined: family, personal development, sustainability/social innovation, and music.

My Wisdom Council directs my work in all of my territories; it represents a wisdom that bridges worlds. It is these same sages who have guided me conceptually and energetically in writing this book, even though I don't directly know all of them. Although the specific people can change, the type of knowledge and wisdom has been the same for many years.

Historical Perspective: Spiritual paths, ancestral wisdom, and the world of rituals currently represented by

- Archetypal psychology and rituals: Carl Jung, James Hillman, Michael Meade, Clarissa Pinkola Estes
- Buddhism: Tenzin Wangyal Rinpoche, Joanna Macy
- Judaism: various Rabbis
- Ancestral wisdom: Ángeles Arrien, Jate Antonio

Collective Intelligence: The learning and co-creation spaces in which one experiments with new ways of being, interacting, and doing things that promote an integral perspective. People who take care of ecology and protect its diversity currently represented by

- Coaching and ontology: New Ventures West, Heidegger
- Society for Organizational Learning: Peter Senge

- Social innovation role models: ImpactHub, the Art of Hosting, Margaret J. Wheatley
- Social movements: Pachamama Alliance
- Farmers who take care of the land: Don Victor

Emerging Future: The spaces in which we practice visualizing the emerging future, which includes the art of "presencing," social entrepreneurship, the arts, theater, and music, when they are in service of transformation. Their current representatives:

- The Presencing Institute; Otto Scharmer
- Ashoka and social entrepreneurs; Wangari Maathai, Leonel Narváez
- The arts working together in service of social evolution

From the messages of these sages, my vision and mission came out as

> *Vision*: A whole generation of people define themselves and behave like change agents, expressing their genius and talent and using their creativity in service of a higher cause. This critical mass of enlightened and inspired leaders receives all the support they need in all stages of their evolution through the coordinated effort of networks and organizations, enabling a large-scale shift in consciousness.

> *Mission*: I am a visionary catalyst of personal development, social innovation, and creative expression as a master coach, leadership trainer, author and musician, and community builder through the design and facilitation of transformative experiences and through a body of work that inspires and empowers change agents, all in service of a sustainable, just, and fulfilled world.

This purpose was revealed as a result of my own Life Re-Vision in a process I honored and whose own rhythm I respected as I got to know myself and kept interacting and finding my place in the world. I have been sharing my vision and mission with the people around me and have found new allies and people as a result of sharing these goals. I invite you to do the same: formulate your vision and mission and start to spread the world with people with whom you think you have a common purpose.

Reflect in Your Journal: Declare Your Ecology
It's your moment to put words to your vision and mission. Using the prompts below and information that was revealed from your previous explorations, outline a paragraph for each one of them in your journal.

- *When I connected with my guides, I discovered that my vision is...*
- *When I connected with my guides, I discovered that my mission is...*

Giving Life to Your Ecology

To give life to your ecology, consider the following principles:

Dwelling. Heidegger speaks about learning to inhabit or "dwell" in our worlds or territories. He invites us to deepen our knowledge of them and commit to them, take care of them and potentiate them. Otherwise, if we do not "dwell," we have a strictly exploitative and utilitarian mentality and risk using the resources for our own benefit without worrying about the consequences for others, including future generations. This not only refers to natural resources but also to all the other treasures of these territories: the culture, relationships, people, and other species.

"Dwelling" is also different from being a simple consumer or even spectator. This particular moment in history offers us so many options for consumption and entertainment that it can anesthetize us and render us completely passive. Inhabiting a territory implies contributing, creating, responding to needs, being service-oriented, and staying open to what the territory requires of us. Inhabiting the territory implies going from being a consumer to being a caretaker or guardian.

Inhabiting our territories in this manner – as guardians and custodians of its treasures, of its ecology – contributes to making the world sacred again. We recover the magic and our sense of belonging, and develop a more organic rhythm to doing things without so much pressure.

Honoring interdependence. Each territory responds to certain needs of society. The name of each territory in general alludes to the need it is responding to (sustainability, personal development, social innovation, marketing, peace, etc.). In each territory, no actor does exactly the same thing. We all have our own unique way of doing things. Instead of seeing each other as competitors, it's more powerful to see how we can complement each other and realize the potential of our collaboration and collective endeavors. When we have a vision of our territory and know our own role, we can see how we need each other to achieve our vision; it's not possible to do it alone. This is where the consciousness of our interdependence comes in.

The consciousness of our interdependence invites us to a new type of relationship among each other. It's to know that we are united and looking for a common purpose: to generate well-being by responding to needs felt by a group of people. Knowing our role and the talents we have to offer motivates us to understand the roles of others and to appreciate our differences instead of seeing them as threats. When we let go of that irrational desire of wanting to fill all the roles and take care of everybody's needs (to be the hero!), we start to celebrate each other more and appreciate the richness of everybody doing their part.

Embracing interdependence dispels the myth of the "heroic leader" (the "Lone Ranger") who wants to save the world on their own. After a period of extreme individualism, we are now entering into an era that not only exalts the individual but also cares for the collective. We need strong individuals to bring together strong teams or communities who can achieve extraordinary results. This new orientation pushes us to listen to others, to get out of our own monologue. When we open up our perception, we start to feel the desire to help others to find their own roles so that they can perform them with passion and excellence in such a way that the collective results will be more compelling.

Many authors speak eloquently about this. Charles Eisenstein, in his book *Sacred Economics*, talks about the impoverishment of the soul when we don't recognize our connection and interdependence with others and nature.[23]

Parker Palmer, in *The Courage to Teach*, talks about the tendency in every discipline toward relationships and interconnection instead of seeing ourselves as isolated atoms in combat with each other.[24]

Therefore, choosing to inhabit a territory means entering in its network of relationships, ready to create quality relationships that are deep and alive.

Celebrating diversity. In my biology studies, I learned that diversity is what provides an ecosystem with resilience. This diversity could be internal or external. Inside of our guts, we have a diversity of microorganisms that protects us and strengthens our immune system. Outside, we count on people who represent different points of view and enrich us as they take us out of our comfort zones.

Life Re-Vision shows us other angles of diversity. Inner diversity is recognizing and honoring the different roles we are called to fill. Sometimes, we wind up in a state of inner conflict, rejecting a part of us that wants to express itself. Honoring our inner diversity is giving space for all the different roles in our lives and performing them harmoniously so that our multidimensional Daemon fully self-actualizes.

External diversity implies opening ourselves up to difference. One wise way of inhabiting our territories is celebrating and fostering a diversity of actors, perspectives, and experiences. This sounds easy, but our biology is also programmed to defend itself from what we consider to be "alien" and strange. Our first response when faced with diversity is often rejection. It's because of this that we need to be constantly opening our minds, hearts, and wills (as Otto Scharmer would say) to welcome differences and learn from them.

A recent article by Jess Rimington, who I mentioned in a previous chapter, confirms this challenge. She says that, within organizations that explicitly promote diversity and co-creation, very few people really put these values into practice. They prefer to keep their doors closed to new perspectives. This also happens at the individual level. We have so many ways of "protecting ourselves" from questioning our points of view by not interacting or listening to others or simply excluding them in many ways.[25]

Just as we have a tendency to exclude, we also have faculties to empathize with others and unite. We can use our "psychic muscles" to create bridges and favor fruitful exchanges between different actors and territories. At Aldeafeliz, we are very sensitive to this phenomenon. We know that it's more comfortable to keep ourselves isolated among similar people; it's much easier to plant a monocrop. But this doesn't enrich our purposes or enhance our common ground. We must constantly invite in other species, ages, and points of view to take part and contribute.

Fluid borders. The concept of territories doesn't have defined limits like those of a country. Territories are much more similar to bioregions, where the borders are fluid, there are lots of gray areas, and the territory changes gradually. For example, the marketing territory intersects with communication, which at the same time intersects with psychology, which intersects with health. The borders are in a way, arbitrary, and they keep evolving.

The notion of fluid borders keeps us open to new and unexpected interconnections. It also protects us from a damaging phenomenon that affects us from the industrial era: silos. The silo is a metaphor, but its original definition is a container for agricultural products. Each container is totally separate from the next. Most of us studied in institutions that separated their departments in that manner, like silos that didn't connect at all. This has generated myopias and limited ways of perceiving with narrow lenses from each silo.

In an interview with Lucero Zamudio, dean of the Faculty of Social Sciences at the Universidad Externado de Colombia, she said that the separation of disciplines has created a real "Tower of Babel" of knowledge and has taken us away from a more holistic understanding of phenomena. We need to go back to learning how to interconnect knowledge, starting with asking questions and solving problems in real life, rather than sterile abstractions or hypotheticals.

In the book, *The Silo Effect* by Gillian Tett, she talks about the paradox of our time: being technologically connected like never before and at the same time, being separated by silos. The author tells stories of organizations imprisoned by silos and others that free themselves from silos and transcend them. One can see the contrast, and it's very clear that today's challenges demand us to go beyond the limits of the silos. According to the book, silos taken to the extreme lead to fragmentation, bottlenecks of information, limited and blinded vision. At the same time, siloed perspectives blind us from seeing the interconnections; hence, we act myopically and in isolation, making for errors and missed opportunities. Transcending the silos allows for the creation of healthier relationships and mutual understanding, which opens doors to win-win solutions and innovation.[26]

However, silos are helpful and foundational to a point. Tett says that having a specific expertise can help resolve certain types of problems.[27]

This confirms the relevance of the Life Re-Vision model with its territories we commit to inhabiting, which gives us structure, belonging, and the possibility of going deeper.

The notion of fluid borders implies everybody still inhabiting their own territories without losing sight of others nor becoming too attached to rigid concepts, relationships, or theories of each territory. As the saying goes, "the map is not the territory"; the reality is much more complex than any map we could possibly have. Therefore, a humble openness to other ways of seeing the world and other relationships is not only enriching, it also shows us our blind spots and invites us to reimagine, redesign, and re-signify our territories as a dynamic process – just like that of life itself.

Responding to your calling. This Life Re-Vision path invites you to live a life of purpose, which in this case means having a clear vision and mission. But it's not enough just to be clear. It's also necessary to have commitment to carry out your purpose. After helping them identify their purpose, Tim Kelley, author of *True Purpose*, asks his students, "What percentage of your energy will you dedicate to achieving it?" It's a confrontational but realistic question, inviting them to take a step forward.

Responding to your calling implies a double dwelling: inhabiting yourself and inhabiting your world with the same devotion and commitment. In order to respond to your calling, you must constantly attune to your inner ecology and outer ecology, honor each one, and discover a meeting point that produces maximum fulfillment.

It's not always easy to respond to a calling. Sometimes it's not the most comfortable thing to do. But we can use everything that happens in life as an invitation to grow stronger. Michael Meade, author of *The Genius Myth*, tells us that everyone has an inner genius and that one's life should be dedicated to discovering it and offering it to the world – and that every event in our lives can awaken us to that reality.[28]

What practices can we turn to for support in responding to our calling and living a life of purpose?

> 1. **Stay connected to your Daemon.** To do this, you can carry out the following practices: visualizations, follow your Daemon's instructions, meditate, write in a journal, spend time in nature and wild places, and attend workshops and retreats to connect with yourself. Tim Kelley's book *True Purpose* offers several useful tools to consult trusted sources, which you can try as well.

2. Stay connected with your sages. In order to fully inhabit your territories and remain connected to your sages, you can carry out the following practices: get to know inspiring people and organizations in your territory, strengthen relationships, read continuously, go to workshops and conferences and on learning trips, practice attentive listening, and observe changes and trends in your contexts. Writing and teaching others are excellent ways of organizing your ideas and digesting what you have learned about your territories.

Closing of Ecology

The key ideas of this chapter are as follows. Many people lack a clear purpose. They are disconnected from others and from themselves, resulting in unhappiness and unrealized impact in their lives and those of others. A life of purpose has clarity of vision and mission. This requires attuning constantly to the inner and outer ecologies, which fills us with strength and wisdom.

To attune to our outer ecology, we follow three steps: mapping the territory, connecting with the wise ones, and formulating our vision. To attune to our inner ecology, we also follow three steps: mapping our roles, connecting to our Daemon, and formulating our mission.

Go out for a walk and reflect on your inner and outer ecologies and what you have learned in this chapter. Feel in your body how your life map is becoming more and more clear about who you have been and who you want to be in the future. Receive these benefits, take a note of your progress and of your increased ability to intuit what you are supposed to do.

Declaration for Closing Ecology:
When you are ready, declare the following:

I declare myself a guardian of my territories by means of understanding its ecology. I am now in contact with my inner and outer ecologies. I am attentive to the ways in which I can honor both of them, by clarifying my roles that honor my talents and respond to what the world needs.

Reflect in Your Journal:
- *What have you learned about yourself upon connecting with the inner and outer ecologies?*
- *Which ecology requires more attention from you? Who can help you do this?*
- *How does it impact your sense of purpose when you hear the wisdom of the territory?*
- *What effect does it have on your personal power to be connected to your Daemon and sages?*

Write and complete the following statement in your journal:

- *When I connect with my purpose, I discover or reinforce that...*

7

Fruits

It took me many years to see and embrace my musical side. From a very young age, I felt called to sing. Singing was a natural way to connect with my emotions and pure creativity – in essence, going beyond my mental structure. I told myself that there was no need to promote another album or yet another person seeking stardom through song. I rejected the prospect of using music to call attention to myself as "being special." I also feared that my musical expression could reinforce the image of the woman as a sexual object, which is easy to fall into and happens too often through performance. I wanted to be of service to something more meaningful, specifically a social cause or some concrete impact that one could say was worth it, as my sages indicated. For many years, I could not find the right place to engage my music – so I ignored my natural calling.

When I started to write this book and gathered my bones together, I received the instruction from my Daemon to pay attention to some songs I had written, and so I started practicing them. In the middle of my Life Re-Vision process, as I did my mourning and confronted my past, I had an idea that helped push my music forward. I noticed that my songs had a lot of similarity to my great-grandmother Mina's poems. In both cases, there was an evolution from the feeling of absence and abandon toward a light and fullness.

Many of Mina's poems only became known on the day of her death.

Performing them live would be a way of honoring her and, at the same time, give a place to my bones or creations. I felt Mina's support and strength at my back as I went through the process of producing the album. Every step I took felt like getting a band together (which I actually did one day on Facebook); there was a force pushing me from behind, telling me "everything will come out all right."

One year later, when my Daemon was ready, I released the music in the contemporary art gallery founded by my father. I received an unimaginable amount of support, including donations from the crowd-funding campaign that allowed me to finance the release. I couldn't believe how full the gallery was. It was a great accomplishment, and proof that if you really decide you want to do something, you can achieve it. But the most meaningful fruit I harvested was performing that concert for my mother's side of the family, the direct descendants of Mina.

The concert happened on family vacation. Every year for many years, my grandmother Julia invited us on a family trip. That particular year, it was a Caribbean cruise. My grandmother used her own funds for this, like the courageous and generous woman that she is. She did very well with her own company after divorcing my grandfather. When I proposed doing this concert, she reserved a private room on the ship to perform for my family on the open sea.

When the big day came, I introduced the event by telling my family they were the ideal audience for this concert. For the purpose of healing intergenerational wounds, we were in it together. I proceeded to narrate the threads that link my stories with those of Mina, and invited my aunts and female cousins, one after the other, to read one of Mina's poems out before each song. That day, my voice was freer than ever, my body loose and expressive. Uninhibited, I looked at each of my audience members. At times, I also looked out at the sea through the window. I felt at peace, fulfilled. I finished the last song in a state of ecstasy, of eu-Daemonia.

At the end, we all sat in a circle for a closing ceremony of this experience. There were fifteen of us including my grandmother, uncles, aunts, and cousins. Every one of them expressed what they experienced during the concert, which led to a unique conversation to share our stories about Mina and our own family history. More than one person expressed relief after finding out that they weren't the only one feeling those emotions of restlessness and of being an orphan. They understood that those feelings were part of the baggage transmitted from generation to generation that still needed healing.

To close, my grandmother offered some wise words:

> "Instead of focusing on our shortcomings and judging each other, we should see the positive. Mina obviously wasn't an angel: she had her lovers, a difficult character, and she drank a lot. But at the same time, she was an extraordinary woman. With only a fifth grade education, she was self-taught and ended up being a poet and a columnist at a newspaper. She was an opinion leader in her city of Cali. Her house was always full of luminaries and eccentrics. Mina was authentic, extraordinary, and at the same time, rebellious and impossible."

We all have lights and shadows. This was the main message for the family from my concert. I felt a big weight lift off my shoulders: the weight of judgment, of guilt. We also were able to talk openly about sensitive issues. This matriarchy has been like a tribe of Amazons – strong women warriors – with invincible shields. Talking about our emotions was unusual for us. The concert provided a safe space where we could share our feelings and express our truths without having a debate or fight. This opened up a new door to intimacy and to building better community between us, which is one of my life goals. I predict we will continue to see the repercussions of this in our family. As for me, I was left with a beautiful memory of a fruit offered in the territory of family. As I reflect on this, I also see how I contributed to creating a meaningful experience, and hence, this was worthy of my dedication.

What Are Fruits?

Once we are planted in territories, with the help of our sages, we can visualize the fruits we want to harvest. Fruits result from the fertilization between our vision and mission, the product of our inner and outer ecologies. Fruits are living and nourishing contributions to the territories we inhabit. These contributions are in line with the ecology and support the general flourishing of the territory. They open new possibilities for everybody and create a feeling of abundance, meaning, and cohesion. They allow for a great celebration of life itself.

The abundance that is generated can be called "euDaemonia" which comes from the word "Daemon." It's a state of harmony with our Daemon but also with the territories that host it and feed it. It's the specific happiness that comes from contributing in a way that uses our greatest talents, and at the same time improves the world in some way. In the book *The Great Work of Your Life*, Stephen Cope describes it in this way: "(Your Great Work) is born mysteriously out of the intersection between your Gift and the times."[1]

Parker Palmer says in his book, *The Courage to Teach*, that when we find our place in the ecosystem of reality, we can see more clearly which actions promote life and which do not. And, in the process, we participate more actively in bringing our own destinies and the destiny of the world into play.

The fruits we aspire to harvest contribute to an ecology of legacy, which is strengthened as we clarify our purpose (vision and mission). Visualizing our legacy – while at the same time being attentive to our creative impulses and the context that surrounds us – gives us focus and determination to be able to contribute powerfully, in a way that fulfills us and meets the world's needs.

The Ecology of Legacy

Imagine that your legacy is an attractive fruit basket you share with the world. As you taste each fruit, it is succulent, juicy, and delicious.

This basket is not only beautiful and nutritious, it also has an "organic product" seal, guaranteeing that it was produced in a regenerative way, honoring and replenishing the land. What does this mean? For your contribution to the world to be harmonious, make sure it is consonant with your inner and outer ecology. This is what we call "the ecology of legacy." In essence, our fruits also create seeds contributing to the territory.

Your legacy is the assembled set of your fruits: the big work of your life, as Steven Cope would call it. For your legacy to be ecological, each fruit should result from a fertilization of your vision and mission. The Wisdom Council, composed of the sages of our territories, informs our vision. The Daemon, the guardian of our talents and our creative force, defines our mission. Consulting these two sources of wisdom frequently helps create a legacy that is beneficial for you and for the whole planet. Fertilization implies that the Daemon and the Wisdom Council influence each other, that there's a dynamic exchange, a sacred accord. The Wisdom Council provides guidance that the Daemon receives and adheres to. At the same time, the Daemon will propose new and unique things, things that spring from our very instinct and passion, and the Wisdom Council will receive these suggestions when the time is right. The territory will evolve as a result.

Each will start to transform: the Daemon, the territory, and the sages of the territory. When this fertilization occurs between Daemon and the Wisdom Council, then fruits will emerge that are alive, ecological, and nutritious. The Daemon contributes its energy, our seeds enrich the fertile territory, and a fruit results that nourishes the whole ecosystem.

An organic or living fruit is sown with the consciousness of leaving an ecological legacy (that responds to our inner and outer nature). It's a fruit that grows out of a deep connection with the wisdom of the territories and the identity of the Daemon, its talents, virtues, and creative force.

Discerning Among Fruits

There are fruits that contribute to an ecological legacy they produce great happiness and create benefits in their territories; they contribute to life. These are living fruits. The opposite happens with exotic or bitter fruits. In order to start to visualize your fruits, it's a good idea to differentiate the living fruits from the bitter and exotic fruits, as well as to revisit our notion of what "failure" is (which, in the Live Re-Vision approach, we call an "unripe" fruit).

Exotic fruits. An exotic fruit is a fruit that can interest your Daemon but is not in line with what the territory needs. You've surely seen how the introduction of a non-native species (also called an "exotic" species) in an area can wreak havoc. In the mountains on the outskirts of Bogotá in the 1950s, pines and eucalyptus trees were planted everywhere. They grew quickly, provided wood and were considered pretty to some. However, over time, the ecology of this area was greatly impoverished and damaged. The exotic plants created more acidic soil, and the natural species of trees could no longer grow nor flourish. In some cases, the soil dried out completely. The landscape where these trees were planted did not resemble a majestic Andean ecosystem. It looked more like forested areas from Switzerland, Australia, or some other country. This dissonance disorients us and disconnects us from our ecological identity. Furthermore, the exotic species destroys the natural biodiversity and organic evolution, impacting many animals, insects, and other living organisms.

Whoever promoted the planting of these trees back then could be reflecting now on the damage they caused. This same reflection applies for people who, out of their greed and commercial impulse, introduced a product that creates havoc in people and in the environment (as is the case of the opioid epidemic in the US). But if we know, for example, that excess of sugar contributes to illness, that styrofoam is not biodegradable, that certain pharmaceuticals or agrochemicals have dangerous side effects, that spreading gossip can damage relationships, etc., then why do people keep on using, doing, and allowing it? It's a lack of awareness and an ignorance, a disrespect for our territories and their history, as well as natural evolution integrated with all living organisms.

Many mistakes are committed by planting exotic fruits that aren't compatible with the territory's ecology. Being exotic, they damage the natural balance and order of nature. The alternative for mutual growth is to attune to what already exists and to embrace what is emerging so we can collectively promote the common good. Consulting with the Wisdom Council will shed light on our misconceptions.

The unchecked impetus of our Daemon, often blind to what the territory really needs, is more common than we imagine. A Daemon run amok, full of greed and lust for status or power and empty and confused deep down, will wreak havoc in any territory. An obvious example: every day in Colombian newspapers, new cases of corruption and abuses of power are brought to light. We see people who over-produce and/or over-consume with no awareness or consideration; their "fruits" are new cars, gadgets, and clothes, and they aren't cognizant of the negative impact their habits or creations have on their territories or the negative impact on society. We recognize that deep down, these people aren't "bad;" they are unconscious of their roles as guardians of their territories and disconnected from sources of wisdom.

Bitter fruit. A bitter fruit is one that could be appropriate for the territory, but instead leaves us uneasy. We have seen many artists whose work is very much celebrated by the public and by the culture, but whose souls are malnourished. Sometimes they wind up taking their own lives.

This sounds like an extreme example, but suicide is the second leading cause of death today. There are people who are excellent at their profession, acclaimed by their colleagues, but inside they are dried out, decaying, unhappy. The fruits they produce are not in tune with their inner ecology, and this winds up sickening their body and soul. Or perhaps people simply aren't giving the best of themselves and end up contributing mechanically and soullessly.

One musician friend of mine faced this as she harvested a bitter fruit. I invited her to help me with vocal harmonies on two songs for my album. She accepted, and we got together to talk beforehand. She has a great musical talent, and there was no doubt that her territory was music. However, she told me about a recent experience that had left her empty. She wanted to become a star quickly and fell prey to a counter-wind in our culture. A producer wrote a song for her "that would compete with Shakira," launched a webpage with a stage name, and with the help of promoters, created strong visibility overnight due to dozens of radio interviews.

When she was being interviewed, she noticed that she didn't have any seeds to tell. Although her song was a hit, she felt that it had all been a facade. She realized that she had been too anxious to "extract" fruits from that territory without preparing the soil, planting the seeds herself, or caring for them. "I wanted an apple right then, and when I went to pick it, it was made of plastic. I couldn't even eat it. It didn't give me anything; it left me hungry." After this bitter fruit, she decided to let her album sit for a while. She is waiting to start another musical project, this time from an authentic place, connecting with her life's stories, her seeds, so that this accomplishment will have some meaning and nutrition for her soul.

Unripe fruit. Another category of fruit that's worth examining is the unripe fruit commonly referred to as "failure." These hurt, but they are different from bitter fruits. Oftentimes, these are fruits totally appropriate for the Daemon and the territory, completely aligned with the wise ones, but something was missing. Perhaps we aren't completely ready or the context wasn't ready. Certain conditions were missing for the fruit to be able to develop fully and, because of this, the fruit didn't ripen. Very likely, an unripe fruit causes disappointment. But these fruits aren't bad for you; they are still nutritious. Our western culture tends to demonize "failures" and turn them into taboos that nobody wants to talk about. Failures, like my friend Alan said in a workshop we taught together, "are proof that we have stepped out of our comfort zone and have opted to risk something." According to him, we should celebrate our failures because they demonstrate our courage.

Alan paints three concentric circles where the inner circle is the "comfort zone" then the "learning zone," and the outer circle is the "panic zone." "Failure puts us in the learning zone, and that's fertile ground for growing and maturing. There's no need to be afraid of failure; our failures should become our allies." Another friend, Mariana, promotes "failure dinners" – spaces where everybody talks about one of their failures and then uses this as a reason to celebrate what they learned from and how they grew from these experiences.

After a failure, it's probably the case that, if one knows how to take advantage of it, we have more awareness and maturity. The next time we offer something to the world, we will take additional elements into account to make it more timely. The process of attuning more and more with our inner and outer worlds is necessary and sometimes messy. It can hurt. Mistakes are part of the path, and they are proof that we are still "on the move." When we take risks and are willing to fail, we become more attuned to our purpose and direction. In this way, our actions are increasingly powerful.

A little while ago, I tasted an unripe fruit – it was not easy to digest. I was invited to be a leadership lecturer at a university in a master's program on sustainability. In the opening ceremony, the organizers offered me the opportunity to sing with my band, including the song "*Esta Tierra*" ("This Earth"), which was very much in line with the theme of the program. At first they were going to give us forty minutes. We rehearsed profusely and prepared a set for an entire month. The day before, they told us that they hadn't been able to obtain permission for us to perform, but that I could still sing two songs with voice and guitar only.

Disappointed and angry, my Daemon made a transgression: not adhering to their "stupid rules." I just had to include the whole band, who were very excited about this opportunity to perform and had been preparing for a month. I opted for singing a single song with everybody: my voice, a guitarist, and everybody else playing small percussion instruments. (In my mind, they were fine.) In that way, I'd give everybody the opportunity to be on stage. The song was well-received by the audience, and we had a fantastic celebratory dinner afterwards. However, the organizers did not agree with my decision to include the band, and because of some miscommunications around the use of the microphone and the resulting complaints from the university authorities, they let me go from the team altogether.

When I reflected on this *faux pas*, I noticed that this fruit wasn't timely, even if it was in line with my Daemon and with what I believed the territory was ready for and needed. Academia is crying out to become more interdisciplinary and involve the arts. But obviously I didn't bring that forth in the best way. Also, the conditions weren't right for my Daemon. Too many constraints turn my Daemon off. However, I grew stronger from this situation. I understood that in order to visit a different territory – in this case, education – I needed more understanding of what it entails and whether I am up to following its rules and codes of behavior.

The territory of academia has very different values from the territories of social innovation and personal development to which I was accustomed. I and the territories I inhabit value bravery and creativity, while not necessarily valuing strict obedience – so I rebelled and ignored what the education territory expected of its inhabitants. In my territories, "We don't ask for permission, we ask for forgiveness." In most cases, this is rewarded, but not in the education territory, as I found out. *Ouch!*

I noticed that teaching at a university was not a priority for me at that time. I had let myself be seduced by the prestige of the role, without being willing to understand and adapt to that context. It's unlikely that my Daemon would find fulfillment under those strict rules. It's too unwieldy. I had accepted the opportunity lightly, not knowing many of the codes of the territory, leading to an unforeseen outcome: a painful unripe fruit. I cried, I expressed my indignation in writing, but in the end, I saw that what I needed to do was to reflect on my priorities.

I invite you to discern between live fruits, exotic fruits, and bitter fruits. If we project fruits for our lives that are disconnected with our inner ecology or the outer ecology of the territories, we will be disappointed at the time of harvest. Like Stephen Cope says in his book *The Great Work of Your Life*, "When a life is founded on self-betrayal, the habit of self-betrayal proliferates until we are at peril of not remembering who we are at all."[2] This includes betrayal toward ourselves or the world, which leads to losing our drive and direction.

The disorientation happens gradually, and we may not notice until we have a rude awakening. At first, we give ourselves over half-heartedly, with a vague sensation that something's not quite right. We start to disconnect from ourselves and from the world, we stop listening to signals, we become stubborn or zombies, and eventually end up in despair and downfall. We are empty and hungry for a life with meaning, belonging, and contribution. The consequences are disheartening – in essence, we are disconnected from who we are.

This is the panorama of harvesting exotic or bitter fruits. Some thinkers have called this state "alienation." What do you think of these phrases from Eric Fromm?

> "Modern man is alienated from himself, from his fellow men and from nature. He has been transformed into a commodity, experiences his life force as an investment, which must bring him maximum profit obtainable under existing market conditions.
>
> "The danger of the past was that men became slaves. The danger of the future is that men may become robots."[3]

Fromm adds that a healthy society is one in which individuals are constantly giving new birth to themselves. When we cultivate and sow these bitter or exotic fruits that do not fulfill us or contribute to the world, we become enslaved or roboticized, and we lose our essence, diminish our vitality, and are blinded to our wisdom.

Unripe fruits are something else entirely. If you have the sour flavor of an unripe fruit in your mouth, don't flagellate yourself too much. I also need to remind myself of this; I'm too hard on myself at times. Breathe deeply and have patience because soon the conditions will be "ripe" for your gifts to be well-received in the worlds that need them. All of these experiences provide the opportunities to see ourselves, understand what motivates us, and get more in tune with our Daemon and our territories. This reflection will fine-tune our ability to nurture our fruits into ripeness, generating euDaemonia in the next harvest. At that time, you will be able to tell a new story, turning the "unripe" fruit into a seed with a happy new and fruity ending.

Let's Talk about Fruits

In the Life Re-Vision workshops, the participants, after having lived the whole process of bones, seeds, winds, and territories, share the fruits that will guide their paths in the coming years.

Claudia sees herself as a designer, host, caretaker, and ambassador of her main territory of communication. Claudia shared that: "My wise people tell me that everybody needs to come to the communication territory to be nurtured. Why don't they come more often? What are people doing at this moment to learn more about communication? My wise people tell me that most problems stem from a lack of good communication, which at the same time depends on being vulnerable and talking about our feelings honestly." Her fruits were the following:

- Doing research to find out what people do to learn about communication in their daily lives.
- Summarizing and illustrating visually the essential messages of the territory.
- Creating a laboratory or virtual space for learning about communication.
- Creating an exhibit with sculptures and pictures about vulnerability.

María Teresa, an inhabitant of the sustainability territory, heard from her wise people that it's necessary to simplify the topic of sustainability. She explained: "There's so much information out there that people don't even know where to start. Nobody gets involved because nobody knows how. It's difficult for the average businessperson to contribute to the cause. My mission is to facilitate people in companies to get motivated and equipped to act sustainably by creating tools for them." Her fruits are consistent with this mission:

- Designing sustainability guidebooks. The guides are one way of sharing lessons learned. When I look at my bones, almost all of them have been guidebooks. For example, a bio-commerce guidebook for companies. I've always felt it flowed for me to make guidebooks because they show that the issue really isn't that complicated, you do this and you do that. I connect it with my talent for seeing the big picture and finding solutions.
- Designing action plans, for example, plants for adapting to climate change, rural development plans.
- Creating a blog. This will be my way of disseminating the guidebooks. I feel bad about knowing so much and not sharing it more widely. I want to share simple things, tips that clarify what sustainability means.
- My permaculture project. I want to have an ecologically-friendly farm that will be an inspiration to others. I've dedicated myself to helping others, but I want to invest in my own project.
- Financial independence. Obtaining the freedom to focus on my own projects.

Ricardo, an inhabitant of the human development, organizational and technology territories and a spreader of the agile wind for many years, shared this vision: "We need for the next generations to change this world by breaking the current pattern and model of development." His mission is to energize change agents by offering them tools and learning spaces. He noticed that some ecosystems in the technology territory lack vision, they are guided by competition and therefore, they are producing exotic fruit. He felt a need to find inspiration and to distance himself from some teams and projects. He desired to redirect his focus by visualizing the following fruits:

- Supporting organizations as a consultant and co-creating contexts of abundance with collaborative and experimental cultures and great purposes, not with economic gain but in a way that benefits everyone.
- Designing models for building agile schools, using the principles of this culture of abundance and collaboration.

Sandra, who spent many years in her work as a mother in the family territory, felt she needed a new professional dimension to herself. Frustrated, she told us, "I don't have any bones. I need to start to build my own legacy, and my fruits will help me to do that." However, all the ideas she had for professional projects or jobs didn't convince her. It was like she was trying to force herself to enter a professional territory, but her Daemon wasn't ready.

She concluded that what was needed was patience. Her children are still young, and her energy was still totally within the family territory. The fruits that interested her all were within this territory:

- Compilation of recipes, some of which my mother gave me, to remember the delicious food she made.
- Reading books to enrich myself and be able to inspire my children.
- A small home garden to share with my kids.
- Making my own jams and marmalades from the garden.
- In the long term, a farm and a house in the country, where we can all get together as a family. Eventually making more jams there.

I responded to the above:

> "I've seen the impact that country spaces have in the family territory many times. Families come together in these places, and they bond. The recipes also have a huge impact. I have many memories associated with family recipes. What you are planning as fruits is very wise."

Sandra realized that this was a moment to value her belonging to the family territory. Her sister Carolina, also present at the workshop, recommended, "This is a time for learning, while your children are small. It's like fertilizing the land for a professional career, which will come later. Be patient." Sandra breathed in, looking more relaxed, and decided to enjoy this moment of her life.

There were people in the workshops that weren't ready to formulate their fruits yet. Gloria, who had been inhabiting the peace territory with great commitment and has lived and seen very difficult things, was still in a period of grieving. She told us,

> "I don't have any fruits right now. The first thing I learned is that I have to quit my current job. Secondly, I have to connect with myself. Thirdly, I want to go back to school. I have some ideas of what I could explore. My wise people tell me peace should be built from the ground up. We need to involve communities. It's necessary to go against the grain, but in this country, that's dangerous. On my part, I need to prepare emotionally for that and then act. I need to use my passion and drive to make a difference, but I need time to recover."

I respected where she was and her insight on not taking on fruits at this time. Each person who undertakes the Life Re-Vision process has their own rhythm. She will carry out the next step when she is ready. We can know intuitively when someone needs time and space to digest things instead of offering questions and suggestions.

In another workshop, María Pía shared a very clear list of fruits. She inhabits the human rights territory. Her fruits are finishing two documents on Colombia's public policy on human rights that she has co-authored. But it's not as simple as it looks. A lesson came up for everybody: the need to negotiate with the Daemon on the conditions of her day-to-day life and the call from her sages for a new approach in the territory.

Her sages told her it was essential to finish the documents; the whole country has invested many years in this, and the fruits need to be culminated. But that same time, her sages also communicated that these policies need to shift from a centralized approach to a territorial approach in order to impact the greatest number of people. They can't just stay as words on a piece of paper in an office. Her Daemon coincides with this directive. It needs to be out in the country, hands-on, and participating in the implementation of these policies in daily life. It wants to be more in contact with nature and people.

Sometimes it's necessary to negotiate and to make conscious concessions with our Daemon in order to create the conditions for it to thrive. Connecting with our Daemon as well as writing down our fruits will assure we have the intention and the energy to focus and work on our fruits. Every day that passes where we don't listen and don't make an agreement with it, our Daemon becomes weaker and starts to sicken, which will cost us dearly down the road.

María Pía realized this one time. In the workshop, a volcano of emotions coming from her Daemon exploded because it had become increasingly hard for her to keep working at her desk job. María Pía needed to negotiate with her Daemon so that it could accept staying a few more months in the office while the documents got finalized. She calmed down when she declared that, after finishing the documents, her next fruit was to experiment with living in the countryside, where she would put into practice the policies she formulated at the community level.

Once she had this clear, her eyes began to shine. She now had a new possibility in her soul toward which she could orient herself. While she implements a pilot program based on the human rights policy she drafted, she will transform her lifestyle in order to give the Daemon the space and habitat it needs. She walked away with a big smile and an open heart full of courage because of this new roadmap.

Carolina came in needing a kind of sabbatical from her territories, needing to focus her fruits in a territory of enrichment: personal development. She doesn't necessarily see herself inhabiting that territory permanently, but she needs to take a good amount of time there, like a wandering traveler. She had recently lost her mother, so she was grieving as well as needing to take a break from her busy life in her other territories.

Her Daemon wants her to focus on developing healthy habits: meditating, going on exploration journeys, having deep conversations, and reading. What makes her Daemon (a dinosaur) feel alive is participating in workshops and learning new things. It also loves cooking, drinking coffee with friends, and "talking about issues that concern me." She very happily made a list of her fruits in this territory of enrichment:

- Start a women's circle.
- Go on journeys and make photo albums of them.
- Start a personal journal.
- Organize and participate in personal growth workshops.

I thought she was going to finish her list there, but curiously, once she finished this list of enrichment fruits, she found herself wanting to contribute to the territories she currently inhabits and contributes. All of a sudden, she started to talk with great energy about the projects she will be part of in her two territories of social innovation and organizational development. She listed them in a detailed and convincing manner, as if they were coming out of her guts. Obviously, her Daemon had become excited about her working again.

What we saw with Carolina is similar to what happened with María Pía. When her Daemon felt heard, it got excited and allowed for a new future plan. Instead of turning into a demon like an upset Daemon usually does (with resistance and despair), it found its groove. In both cases, it communicated its needs clearly and provided the forward momentum for a greater plan to emerge. We can see how important it is to listen to our Daemon. When we do, it will give us the best it has, which is its energy and passion.

We had another opportunity to see the effect of an upset Daemon and learned how, by listening to it, the Life Re-Vision journey turned around. María came to the workshop because she felt that her leadership was not finding a favorable environment for expressing itself fully. Her Daemon, a lioness whose enormous face and hair occupied the whole page, gives us clues about how the force of her personality and the impetus that it has can contribute and make itself heard. She concluded that the best thing to do was to leave her current organization and get a master's degree, so that she could later find a better context for her talents and growing leadership.

We had a conversation about accepting her Daemon *as it is*. Some Daemons seem bigger than life for us, but they are powerful forces that push us for increased visibility and leadership. Instead of being critical of ourselves because of this, what we need to do is find a way to satisfy the needs of our Daemon by nurturing it and offering it the right conditions for flourishing.

For example, besides living in the territory of education (as a life coach, counselor, and economist), where she now feels a bit suffocated, Maria's also an artist. She decided that, while working on her master's degree, she's going to satisfy her need for visibility and self-expression by painting. This gave peace to her Daemon.

The interesting thing was that Patricia, who had been very quiet until this point, suddenly identified with the same need for leadership that María had. As if a volcano had erupted, she started to speak with a forcefulness that she didn't have the day before:

> "I also miss my leadership strength! I hadn't noticed how much I did! And I can see that I've been slowly shrinking since I started with the foundation. I started with a very interesting position,

but the environment there is very hostile. I've had to make con-cessions on many fronts...to the point where I stopped being the leader I was before.

"This has created tremendous discomfort in me, lots of unease, and lots of dissatisfaction. I want to learn to recognize when I do things to please others, but it costs me my well-being. Now I'm no longer willing to do that. I want to invest time in my personal development in an integral way. I've invested a lot in my career, and now I want to be my authentic self again. Maria, if you hadn't said anything, I wouldn't have noticed any of this. Confronting this is a part of my Life Re-Vision."

The group took a deep breath with her. It was a moment of strength and honesty, a moment of succulence (as I call them) that touched every one of our beings. Her Daemon, a bird with multicolored wings, was obviously enraged and until this moment had not been able to express itself. When she thought about her fruits, just like Carolina, her wish was to spend some time in the personal development territory enrich-ing and renewing herself. She included an athletic plan, a well-planned diet, new spiritual practices, and some activity in the world of art. Ba-sically, she needed a "first-aid plan" for her Daemon, who just couldn't take it anymore.

Carolina asked her what she was thinking of exploring in the art world for her Daemon. This is how Patricia responded:

"Anything but quiet! I'm tired of being quiet! I need a space where I can express and be myself. I need to find myself again and have more clarity about who I am."

Carolina, who is also a talented coach, observed,

"Patricia, you have a different voice today. The projection of your voice is radically different. You had given up so much that you had switched yourself off. Today, it's like you woke up an energy, a life force. It's great that the group was able to catalyze this by being a mirror for you."

After everyone had time to reflect on their fruits, I asked Patricia about her fruits in the enrichment territory of personal development. She shared them with gusto and with a tone of urgency:

- I want trips; I want to see lots of new cities!
- I want health and wellness: to run many kilometers and have an excellent food plan!
- I want to mentor people, help them, I don't know how or who yet!
- I want to have a reading club, a film club, where we can create conversations!
- I want an organic garden!
- [She clarified her artistic activity.] I want to go back to my fla-menco dance classes!

Making this list brought her soul back to her body. Just like Carolina and María Pía, Patricia learned how to listen to her Daemon, who talked with great force. Afterward, she felt a great relief in her chest. Once again, the same phenomenon occurred. Patricia unleashed her Daemon and hence started to connect with her other territories again. She was able to release the burden that prevented her from feeling pas-sion for her work.

Carolina was inspired by Patricia and helped her see a possible next step:

"You've gotten so much experience at the foundation that you now have the opportunity to pass that on to others. Soon your client will no longer be the foundation but rather the whole sustainability territory, full of NGOs that can benefit from your knowledge. This is leading to something new, for you wanted to reconnect with your leadership. Now it won't have to be about fighting with the bottlenecks that happen inside an organization, but rather you can graduate to another role, that of facilitator. You can go out and facilitate a workshop, help people formulate their knowledge management strategy, and then support the implementation process – solving the challenges that you have lived and overcome yourself. You have a huge opportunity here; you know the sector, you know the issues."

Upon hearing these words, Patricia opened her eyes, visibly excited. I concluded,

"This new and powerful possibility can help you over-come your daily struggles, knowing that you won't be there forever, but that it's something transitory that is helping you prepare for what's to come."

This was a good negotiation between Patricia and her Daemon. From this workshop, Patricia saw the possibility of making the most of this difficult time at her organization to learn about the difficulties that exist in her type of role. In due time, she will quit her job and start an independent consulting practice. That made sense to her.

In individual sessions, people undergo a much more detailed process of defining their fruits. Catherine, who clarified her vision, mission, and roles in the last chapter, came to a coaching session to explore her fruits. She was exploring roles as a facilitator and designer. While she had many ideas, she didn't know where to start.

To get her creative juices flowing, I gave her an exercise that had previously helped me, to identify what gave me passion. This exercise can be done at any moment in your Life Re-Vision. I learned it from the book titled, *How to Think Like Leonardo Davinci* by Michael J. Gelb. It's the "hundred questions" exercise. As indicated by the name, the task is to formulate 100 questions that currently are on your mind that you are genuinely curious about. Some of her questions were:

- Since when did I lose my enthusiasm for life? Is it connected with not spending time in nature?
- Why are open air spaces so often excluded from education and science, for example, which tend to focus a lot on laboratories?
- Why aren't there beautiful open spaces around the settlements where economically disadvantaged people live?
- Why are so many towns so insipid and boring?
- Why do we forget about our seniors?
- At what moment did we become so focused on consumption?
- How can one teach people that life is more than this?
- What would it be like to live in a society that values culture and nature over business and money?
- What would happen if there were native forests and edible species in public spaces?
- What would happen if we expanded the role of the library beyond that of reading?
- How could we design green and forested spaces that are edible as well as educational?

We can see how her fruits originated from these questions:

- Formulate and implement a project of edible forests around public libraries in low-income areas involving children and seniors.
- Plan and facilitate a meeting between designers, landscapers, permaculturists, and silviculturists, which aims to exchange ideas about new ways of designing green areas that include edible species, ecological, and social justice considerations.
- Design a toolbox for the facilitation of outdoor educational experiences.
- Design a web page where I can show my projects and creations.

Collective Organic Fruits

In August 2014, I was invited to the two-year anniversary of ImpactHub in Bogotá. ImpactHub is a fruit in the social innovation territory: a co-working space for social innovators where they receive support, training, opportunities, and the possibility of joining a network of people that inhabit the same territory, which promotes synergies and collaboration.

On this occasion, they wanted to recognize everybody who was involved in its creation. It was a happy and lovely get-together. Stories (seeds) were told of its creation and the positive impact it had in the lives and initiatives of its users.

The ImpactHub didn't consolidate overnight. First, a group of people tuned into the wind of co-working spaces, visited other similar spaces and then started to talk to opinion leaders about the relevance of this idea for Colombia. It took four years to understand the model, assess whether the Colombian context was favorable, then join the global network that had conceived the idea and the brand, and create an agreement and a unique expression of the model in this setting.

Step by step, the project began to materialize in Bogotá, Colombia. At first, it was all about building community and achieving a common language and a collective purpose, which was captured in a Change Manifesto. I was part of this incubation stage. We organized events and mechanisms to get to know the needs of this emerging community, defined five principles we would be guided by, and did experiments to bring these principles into action. Eventually, a group drafted a business plan, and a steering committee took on its implementation. Many hands were involved in its coming into being. The work of Paula, who was the main flag-bearer of this project, was essential. The fruit of the ImpactHub is full of the nutrition of all those years of incubation, where the social innovation territory was carefully fertilized with the collective Daemon of its founders.

My Fruits

When I did my Life Re-Vision, I had the opportunity to recognize my fruits; those contributions that are alive, contribute to the ecology of the territories, and at the same time are nourishment for everybody's Daemons. Unlike the bones, which are individual relics, often buried and forgotten, fruits are living food for many and form a part of the collective ecology of the territories. Bones can turn into fruit if we breathe life into them and share them in our territories in order to inspire others. Also, fruits turn into bones after we have shared them; they become part of our beautiful set of sacred objects or relics.

In the music/arts territory, my first music album became a fruit when I dusted it off and recorded my songs and shared them with my family, as mentioned at the beginning of the chapter. Other fruits that I aspire to contribute to this territory are an established band, a history of concerts and new albums, and a body of work that is artistic and consciousness raising.

In the social innovation territory, my most important fruit is the Aldeafeliz ecovillage, where we hope to build a trans-cultural maloka, a compendium of beautiful, sustainable buildings that function as a learning center for social technologies, aiming to strengthening a culture of change agents at an international level. Other fruits include my work on Ecobarrios and the soon-to-be published book about these kinds of initiatives around Latin America.

In the personal development territory, which became "human and organizational development," I aspire to keep supporting individuals and organizations, as indicated in my mission. An important fruit is this book, together with the Life Re-Vision workshops, which are turning into the Re-Vision Ecosystem and Academy. My work as an Integral Coach® will hopefully lead to many leaders trained and supported globally. I hope to write other books and design new workshops to have many more stories to tell about transformations at the individual and collective levels.

Declare Your Fruits

What could your fruits be? What can you visualize growing in your territories? This is the moment in which you recognize your current fruits, as well as visualize those that are to come. Remember that, in order for them to be living fruits, you need to connect with your inner and outer ecology. In the words of Otto Scharmer: "The principle of 'do what you love' needs to be complemented with the other principle of profound immersion in the world, particularly on the world's edges, with the practice of always being in dialogue with the universe."[4]

The fruits are the realization of the vision and mission through tangible and intangible achievements in our territories. Fruits are at the intersection of your creative force (represented by the Daemon) and the needs of the world (represented by the wise people). Fruits are the result of you consciously inhabiting your territories, listening to your wise people, and getting to know them and yourself well, in order to contribute something that can be celebrated or shared with others.

It's possible that for some time, we simply visit territories and nourish ourselves, but we don't live there; we don't offer fruits. For example, some people who don't really know what they want can visit the personal development territory to nourish themselves, or the art territory, or any other without generating fruits there. If you're not ready to formulate your fruits, there is no need to force it. Listen to your Daemon and its current needs and the winds carrying your seeds.

When we do the work of connecting within ourselves and with the world, there is a moment when an intention is awakened, a desire to contribute from our soul to the soul of the world. As Michael Meade says eloquently in his book *Fate and Destiny*, "In becoming aware of one's natural gifts the need to give something to the world becomes stronger than the hunger to consume it." How do you want to use that creative force you have to contribute to others?

To harvest fruits, you need clarity, commitment, and perseverance. Fruits require planting and caring for – sometimes for many years – as if they were a child. The implications of formulating a fruit can be scary.

It can also be that a fruit we declare now can take years, even decades, to harvest. I invite you to declare your fruits, and even if they are too big, to incubate them patiently. Trust that the tools, support, and skills to accomplish this will come to you at the right moment.

It's never too late to visualize completely new fruits. There's an infinity of possible fruits, as we saw in the above examples. When we think of fruits that are alive and in line with our being, we feel fulfillment and inner abundance. They aren't sown out of obligation or the need to prove anything but rather from the knowledge that we have a unique contribution to the symphony of life, as Michael Meade says, coming from a great generosity and desire to take care of territories together. Fruits are part of our legacy and a manifestation of our destiny. The same author says that accomplishing our destiny brings us to euDaemonia.

Fruits are the culmination of our Life Re-Vision journey, which starts with bones, seeds, winds, territories, and ecology. Fruits represent the new possibilities that propel us forward. Envisioning the fruits we will harvest creates clarity, focus, and priorities. Remember what the philosopher Heidegger said that human beings are oriented toward possibilities. In the absence of meaningful possibilities, we will wilt. Additionally, human beings are called to serve. Fruits are a conscious way of projecting future possibilities that invite us to contribute to others' well-being, naturally filling us with joy and meaning.[5]

I encourage you to be honest with yourself and visualize an exciting future that will have you come alive. Offer yourself the opportunity to live in euDaemonia. Visualizing your fruits is an invitation to aspire, to dream about the legacy that you want to leave. I offer you this short visualization to enter into this exploration.

VISUALIZATION

Visualize Your Fruits

Close your eyes. Breathe deeply, exhaling through your mouth three times.

Imagine your territories as fertile grounds, full of vegetation, from which you can reap an abundant harvest. This came about as your Daemon, together with the Wisdom Council from every territory, gave you guidance and you listened, allowing you to sow the right things at the right time. You acknowledge your Daemon and your Wisdom Council, and then you acknowledge yourself for attuning to your inner and outer ecologies.

Today you are ready to harvest these fruits and celebrate the abundance with your community. At the same time, you can visualize what comes next; you are in a virtuous cycle of visualizing and manifesting. You can now see new fruits that you dream of harvesting for you and for the world – which your intuition tells you are a response to what is needed now. Your chest explodes with joy! Feel this! This is the future you are creating and are living into!

Reflect in Your Journal:

It's now your turn to name your fruits. Go out for a walk if you need fresh air or perspective. Read your vision and mission. Reflect on what would bring you joy and fulfillment, and fulfill your mission while contributing to your territories.

Write what comes to you in your journal. See your Daemon in front of you when you write your fruits. The Daemon is the carrier of your destiny. It acts from passion and not from fear or shoulds. Take advantage of that strength to give everything you have to the world. Write the list of fruits for every territory for the next five years using the following model:

Fruit_____Territory_____

Giving Life to Your Fruits

Planning a New Planting Cycle

In order to plan for organic, living fruits in line with our inner and outer ecologies, it's useful to have moments of reflection and reconnection with our trusted sources. After any harvest (including an exotic, bitter, or unripe fruit), it's a good idea to center ourselves and reflect on where we are going. It's helpful to acknowledge the good work and fruits you have already harvested as well as those that are neither visible nor celebrated as of yet.

Susana came to a coaching session exhausted and shaken because of some disappointing events that happened with her team in the last project they did together. She felt that something radical needed to change; she was ready for something new. I invited her to do a visualization for the end of a cycle.

VISUALIZATION

Harvest and End of Cycle Feast

Close your eyes. Breathe deeply, exhaling through your mouth three times.

Imagine that your guide is with you – a being that represents deep wisdom and vision – and also your Daemon, which represents your life force and your wild instinct. In the company of these two beings, you are going to have a harvest feast. You're going to celebrate all the fruits that came from this cycle; from well-done, generous, passionate, and hard work. You have full baskets that you want to share with others so that they can know about this huge harvest.

Visualize a full fruit basket in detail. See its colors, shapes, and smells. Feel the special abundance of this harvest, which we call euDaemonia. It's a harmony between your Daemon and the territories that feed it. It's time to celebrate!

With your guide and your Daemon, you will send invitations to people who should know about your harvest. In this harvest you can include fruits from every area of your life, from every territory.

All kinds of people begin to arrive. Those who supported you, those you have supported. Everybody is happy for you, for everything you have harvested. You feel proud of your harvest. It is robust and meaningful. Your fruits have genuinely touched the lives of people who have shown up and are grateful. Receive all their energy, their strength, and their gratitude for what you have done.

Imagine how you like to celebrate: with a glass of wine, good food, or dancing. Bring those elements with maximum happiness and abundance. This is YOUR life harvest! You've received a huge dose of love from your community, and you feel acknowledged, satisfied, and grateful. You now decide to say goodbye to your guests and end the celebration.

When everybody has left, you go back to the company of your guide and your Daemon. You thank them for all their guidance, and you thank yourself for attuning to your inner and outer ecology. Your Daemon now wants to rest, and you satisfy that need fully.

You and your Daemon go into a state of hibernation. It could be in a cave or in a comfortable and relaxing place that evokes total, deep rest. You allow yourself to fully let everything go. Connect with the stillness of your body. Connect with the silence of this moment, feeling the empty space in which to be, to relax. There is nothing pressing upon you at this moment, absolutely nothing. Feel this time as a deeply renewing gift.

Little by little, the time to wake up approaches. Enjoy the last moments, breathing and feeling your body. Register what it feels like to do nothing.

You suddenly realize that your Daemon is licking or kissing your hand to get your attention. It's already awake, and it invites you to go somewhere. You follow it to a well. It jumps in first and invites you to do the same. The water's temperature is perfect: not too cold, not too hot. Just right.

As you plunge into the water, you feel like you're being reborn. You feel a refreshing sensation in your whole body, in every cell. When you are ready, you climb out of the water, and you lie on the ground for a while. You feel the sun's rays on your skin. You rest for another moment, enjoying this new energy.

I stop here and ask Susana if she wants to go on to the next stage. In this case, she doesn't. It was important for her to rest some more. She needed to take more time to renew herself before planning a new planting cycle. These hibernation periods are critical to restore our energy.

Since she still had the flavor of unripe fruit in her mouth, Susana appreciated the celebration. She needed to acknowledge everything that she had done and gain perspective after a very rough stage. She noticed how much she was longing for a vacation, in order to get away from everything and get ready for a new planting cycle.

There's no need to force things. Sometimes the best thing is to rest and renew oneself so that your capacity to Re-Vision your life can return.

Catalina, who we have heard from in other chapters, was ready for a new planting cycle. She had already gotten to a feeling of euDaemonia and felt abundant with her baskets full of fruits. After having celebrated in real life with her community, she took some time to reflect on what is to come. In a session with me, she revised her list of sages and submerged herself in a visualization that included the one just shared above and went one step further. After having rested be-side the well (where the visualization above leaves off), I invited her to get up and meet her guide.

VISUALIZATION

Ending the Rest and Starting a New Cycle

Breathe deeply. Be conscious of different parts of your body. You are starting to awaken the intelligence of your body, your heart, your soul, relaxing more and more. The sun fills your entire body with light, which illuminates your whole be-ing. You are completely renewed.

You now get up and walk to a very beautiful place, like a sanctuary. In that place, together with your guide and your Daemon, you convene with your Wis-dom Council. There's a circle of chairs around you, a fire pit in the center.

Your wise people start to arrive, one by one. You will engage in a conversation about what is needed in your territories right now. It doesn't matter who says what; the combination of their energies and their collective intelligence starts to generate a list of instructions of what needs to happen in all your territories.

Connect with their energy and their wisdom. When you feel that these people start to talk through you, open your eyes and write things down. Channel their wisdom. Write down the messages you receive.

Catalina took all the time she needed to connect with her sages. After twenty minutes of silently incubating their messages, she under-stood that her fruits in the new planting cycles:

- Learn about Tibetan Buddhism to understand its perspective on death better.
- Engage in a more rigorous routine of spiritual practices includ-ing meditation and fasting.
- Make a documentary about her work as an end-of-life doula.
- Design and facilitate a workshop on the knowledge she has ac-quired in this end-of-life work.

- Write an article explaining a new theory she has on death, from her own experiences.

This list of fruits felt fresh and in line with her being in that moment. It didn't come from a "have to" or "should" place but rather from an enthusiasm to do work that's truly hers to do. She feels the vibration of her Daemon, who wants to carry out these tasks and contribute to benefit her territories. It's an inspired plan for starting a new cycle.

Telling a New Story

Your Life Re-Vision journey will allow you to constantly reinvent yourself – to be the author of a new story for your life and for the life of your territories. I'm going to share with you the model for the animation company Pixar, that helps us write new stories.

Once upon a time...

Every day...

One day...

Because of this...

Because of this...

Until finally...

You can tell your story on two levels: your own personal story and the future story of your territories. I'll share with you my example below.

New Individual Story

Once upon a time...a woman with multiple interests scattered about, not knowing how to focus her energies and her talents.

Every day, she would try to focus on important things but ended up doing busywork. She said she was committed to her music, her creative expression, and her grand changemaking visions, but in reality, she devoted her time to what the world threw at her on a given day. What often motivated her was a vague sense of anxiety and the struggle to make a living. She also incessantly checked her email and social media to get a sense of connection, out of an inner emptiness. She often felt internally hungry and craved some sexy new job, activity, or lover that would make life more juicy and complete.

One day, she decided to go on a personal journey of transformation that she entitled her "Life Re-Vision." This journey involved collecting her creations, her essential stories, defining her major influences or winds of change, and finding the right terrain to plant herself and blossom into fruits she would share with her entire community.

In this journey she learned to honor herself and her essence, letting herself be fully known and opening up to fully knowing others. She learned to appreciate her creative manifestations, giving them their proper place in her life, enlivening her life force and creative spirit. She learned to honor her learning path, providing sense and meaning to her major decisions. She learned to recognize her proper place in the world, where she could give her best. She saw her most important talents and could envision the best way to share them with the world.

Because of that, an unconditional love was unlocked in her unlike anything she had ever experienced before. Her actions started to spring from a place of inspiration, inner abundance, and joy. She felt free and present to then access unprecedented levels of energy.

Because of that, she was drawn to express this overflowing fulfillment through her music and her body, spontaneously engaging in creative expression. She tuned in to herself and chose activities that were truly meaningful, letting go of the nonessential. She engaged in practices that brought out the best in her. She was able to have a healthy relationship with technology and social media. She saw the best space and learning environment for her to be in and the best way for her to learn. She then made some choices about stepping into that learning environment.

Because of that, her bountiful inner state inspired others in forming multiple relationships of support and intimacy. Her family and community actively started to reach out and learn about more sustainable, creative, and transformative ways of living. They started to get involved in her ecovillage, the Re-Vision Ecosystem and Academy.

Until finally, her affiliations led to a system of contribution where livelihood needs were met. Exchanges of knowledge and resources freely flowed from community to community. She inspired and pollinated innumerable people, organizations, and networks with the most novel ideas about human and organizational transformation, co-creation, and social innovation. She was able to see the connections between her different ecosystems, and her life started to feel like an integrated whole. She clearly found her place in the system – in the big mess – and was able to focus her energy to address the key levers of change in her field. She was able to significantly contribute to the creation of a culture of changemaking in the world!

New Collective Story (The Re-Vision Journey Dream)

Once upon a time, there was a world that had lost its true north. People moved at a frenetic pace, consumed by senseless preoccupations, with no empathy for themselves, the suffering of others or of nature.

Every day, we were driven by our busyness, distractions and automatic behaviors that led to a lack of balance and complete exhaustion. We convinced ourselves that we were "fine," attached to our accumulation of achievements and objects, masking a void inside. This disconnection generated symptoms of individual and collective disease. The cumulative effect of these attitudes brought about three big crises (environmental, social and spiritual), which provoked poverty and violence internally and externally. The challenges were so great that we were demoralized and felt overwhelmed to take any action.

One day, each of us decided to listen; we could no longer ignore the signals. Certain challenges shook us in our lives at individual and collective levels, offering an opportunity to look at ourselves in the mirror as individuals and as a human species. A critical mass of citizens interrupted the collective slumber and started shaking the world to also see.

Through confronting our pain, we activated compassion for ourselves and others. We practiced forgiveness and reconciliation within ourselves and with others, so our hearts opened. A large number of individuals inspired by greater hope embarked on a Re-Vision Journey, each in their own way, reinforcing a movement of people living purposeful lives, willing to be in service to a greater cause. One by one, each individual declared "I am a change agent" – a clear and powerful declaration taking responsibility for their part in resolving the planetary crisis.

Because of that, a collective awakening happened. An attitude of "blessed unrest" (as Paul Hawken calls it) spread everywhere, which enabled us to be alert and empowered. Although we were well-aware of the magnitude of the crisis, we knew that in the current historic moment, more than ever, we had all the tools to resolve it.

We were able to keep this attitude without burnout, by practicing meditation, self-care, healthy eating, conscious movement, and having regular contact with nature. We started living integral lives, deepening our mindfulness, opening to learning and growth, letting go of obsolete ways of thinking and behaving, stepping out of our comfort zone, and being authentic and coherent with our values. We learned new ways to communicate with more vulnerability and an open heart, and by listening deeply, which cultivated strong and nourishing relationships.

Because of that, we saw it was possible to heal the damage caused by our blindness, promoting a restoration of our relationships, communities and ecosystems. We adopted new practices based on an ethos of care. Relationships of trust, generosity and co-creation flourished everywhere. This led to the creation of countless communities of support and common purpose where true cohesion was felt.Education became a priority – an education based on values and relationships, with an emphasis on identifying and cultivating each person's talents and developing the mindfulness necessary to transcend fear and live from love.

The opportunities for education and personal development multiplied, elevating consciousness at all stages of life, and disseminating the knowledge and tools to live this global transition. New rituals were performed everywhere to reconnect internally, with others and with nature. We recovered a sense of the sacred and developed a more spiritual view of life, creating a unity of us as an integrated, interconnected whole.

Until finally, a whole generation was defined and behaved like change agents, forming a true culture of altruism and empowerment in service of a regenerative, just and fulfilled world. A flourishing system of support (in coordination between organizations and movements) responded to the needs of change agents at all stages of their evolution: from their inspiration to contribute, having multiple transformative experiences, incubating, growing and scaling up new initiatives, all the way to generating systems change. Each change agent responded wisely to their inner call and to the needs of our time. There was a constant revision of social and economic structures that are oppressive or obsolete, in favor of appropriate new models, adapted to the local circumstances, and responding to needs effectively. The systems of production and consumption became more regenerative and just, and the most promising social innovations scaled up and became the norm. In this process, everyone was led by a greater purpose and a calling from the soul, propelled by genuine passion and a joy of serving others, filling the hearts and minds of people and spreading fulfillment all around.

Until finally, the great transition or great turning signaled a new beginning: a time of integral awakening for collective flourishing, – a new era for humanity – with a central commitment for the care of our souls, our communities and our planet.

Learn to Celebrate

Walking the Life Re-Vision path by taking every step consciously will lead to a new chapter of your life. Give yourself a moment to recognize and appreciate your journey so far. Hopefully you feel more rooted in life, and aspire to fruits that will nourish you and the world. All fruits are collective, since they are contributions to a territory. I invite you to commit to celebrating each and every fruit, and acknowledging every meaningful step. Don't just celebrate in your imagination, do it with your tribe when it's the right time. I'm not talking about celebration for its own sake, but rather with substance and purpose. The story of my concert with my family is an example of how sharing a fruit can become a celebration in favor of life itself, which inspires others to sow their own fruits, harvest and share them.

The person who taught me the importance of celebration was one of my great mentors, Guillermo Cuellar (RIP). He told me that if you want to have a creative life, it's important to celebrate every time you break free of the patterns of survival and fear, toward experiencing new things, even if they don't turn out well. If you don't celebrate, you wind up falling into thinking that "what I do doesn't matter" and fall back into survival and fear. Celebrating is to say "everything I do with the intention of fulfilling my purpose is valuable progress."

Aldeafeliz takes celebration seriously. As I write this, we are in the middle of reconstructing our *cusumy*, or *maloka* (a ceremonial space with a thatched roof, as mentioned elsewhere in this book). At this point we are already thinking about the great feast. In January of this year (2017), we performed a ceremony to celebrate a collective fruit, the first cocoa harvest.

Cocoa of life, cocoa of love,
Cocoa that sweetens and feeds passion
Open our consciousness toward expansion
Deepen the roots of our heart.

We started with this song, intoned by Yuluka, a member of the ecovillage, gardener, dancer, and activist. Later, Tatiana, another ecovillage resident and facilitator of social technologies, told us:

"Nine years ago, we planted these cocoa trees. The harvest just started; these plants produced fruit and today we are reunited, and we will share it. They've already been dried and fermented. Together we will perform the whole preparation process, from toasting the beans, grinding them and making the hot chocolate, to drink in the afternoon as is the custom in this region, with melted cheese inside and with pandebonos, almojábanas and arepas (assorted Colombian baked goods)."

"Bravo!" we all shouted and everybody applauded with enthusiasm. On the table, we put the potluck of snacks to be served with the hot chocolate. When the hot chocolate was ready, filling our senses with its delicious aroma, we toasted together to everything the cocoa represented: many years of persevering through thick and thin to build community. In spite of all the challenges, we kept our commitment, dreaming together and learning from each experience. We celebrated that, more and more, Aldeafeliz is offering fruits to the world, a world that comes to learn how to build ecological communities through committed individuals by means of reinventing themselves – "Re-Visioning" – themselves and co-creating.

Cocoa is such a symbolic fruit on so many levels. Its botanical name means "food of the gods." In order to harvest it, you need a long-term vision, since their fruit-bearing cycle has a minimum of five years. This teaches us to be persistent and patient when we plant fruits in our territories. Abundance will soon come. Your constant Re-Vision is a good way to fertilize the ground.

Cocoa is the fruit being promoted in Colombia to replace the "exotic" fruit of coca, which has produced so much mayhem by financing a painful war, but one which is hopefully now coming to an end. We hope that this fruit contributes to the wellbeing of people in the country as a substitution for coca crops, and in the building of peace.

Closing of Fruits

The main ideas of this chapter are the following: achievements that are not in tune with the ecology will produce inner and outer impoverishment. There are accomplishments that make you feel empty, they don't have aliveness nor generative qualities, and produce a sensation of bitterness. Visualizing our legacy, being attentive simultaneously to our creative impulses and the context that surrounds us, gives us focus and determination to achieve living and needed contributions that help ourselves and the world.

To conclude this chapter, I invite you to write your fruits on colored index cards. Write fruits that will guide your next several years. Keep them visible, hopefully somewhere where you will see them every day.

Go out for a walk and reflect on your fruits and what you learned in this chapter. Feel how the map of your life is slowly imprinting in your body: that which you have been and what you want to be in the future. Receive these benefits. Notice the progress in your greater ability to intuit what you need to do. When you're writing what you learned in your journal, notice that you have more clarity about your future. The only thing we have done is to open space, ask certain questions and connect to new sources of energy and wisdom.

Also, realize the importance of your unique and incomparable role that nobody else has. You have a calling to which only you can respond, and that calling will give meaning to your life. Life itself needs you to discover it, communicate with it and manifest it, first with yourself, and then with the world. Everybody is enriched as a result.

Declaration for Closing Fruits

When you are ready, declare the following:

I can now visualize my fruits that I want to nurture and harvest in each of my territories, respecting my inner and outer ecologies, in this way inspiring and directing my day-to-day actions toward a clear purpose.

Now reflect:

- *How do you feel after having formulated your fruits? What motivates you most?*
- *How does that help in driving and focusing your daily actions?*
- *What are the first actions that you want to take?*
- *What kind of support are you going to need?*

8

Incorporating Your Life
Re-Vision

The Habit of Re-Visioning

We're going to close this journey with an invitation: Make Life Re-Vision a habit. This habit consists of a series of practices that help digest the past and design the future constantly to achieve what this process promises: connection, meaning, direction, belonging, and contribution.

Life Re-Vision is immersed in a field that is starting to gain prominence: life design. The most popular class at Stanford University in 2016 was "Design Your Life" offered by the department of design. This book aims to be a contribution to everyone's personal development, and especially in the realm of life design. It aims to awaken and use our creativity to design our lives, including various symbols and elements so that our design is holistic, pragmatic, and poetic.

To finish, I'm going to share with you some practices that help make this Re-Vision a habit in your life.

Life Re-Vision Practices

Designate a place for your bones. Starting here is important because being conscious of your physical relics, artifacts, trophies, and sacred objects gives you great satisfaction and the recognition that you already have a legacy. Giving your bones an appropriate place in your physical space will give you pride as well as promote meaningful conversations with whoever visits your spaces, providing an opportunity to share your seeds (the next practice). Take your creations seriously. Start to identify your talents. Listen to the messages from your Daemon about what you should do with each of your bones. Follow its instructions, take action, and get the necessary support.

Share your seeds. When we identify our essential stories, or seeds, a deeper channel of connection opens up between us and others. These seeds show your essence, your virtues. When you share your seeds, you are strengthening yourself and accessing a deeper sense of meaning in your life. Engaging in intimate conversations about seeds creates a bond with others where you find commonalities and are inspired by each other. This builds true community. Take advantage of special occasions to tell your stories, get to know others, and let others know you in this way. Write your seeds down. Record them – preserve them in some way. You will be grateful you did.

Let yourself be blown by winds. We are surrounded by information and all types of influences, but each person tunes into specific winds, or ideals, that reflect their values and shift their trajectories. With these winds, we see that we have a clear sense of direction, and this gives us confidence and trust in our path. These positive influences constantly push us forward, driving us to keep dreaming and exploring so that we can eventually inhabit our territories. Take note of what's calling you. Keep learning and exposing yourself to new ideas so that the winds keep you engaged in what is present, what is evolving, and what supports your flow and movement toward who you are becoming and where you will contribute.

Inhabit your territories. There are times to explore and visit territories (realms of action and conversation), but eventually we are called to plant ourselves in certain worlds in order to actively contribute to their development. Identifying these territories simplifies our lives, optimizes our efforts, and directs our energy toward a more focused and conscious cultivation as opposed to a haphazard one. These territories show us that we are not alone, that we are a part of systems and of broad collective endeavors. We develop a sense of belonging, and we notice that together we can achieve a greater impact once we get to know the ecology of the territories. Get to know your territories more. Explore them, discover them and commit yourself to being their guardian.

Know the ecology of your territories. Every territory has its language, its logic, its players, its role models, and its trends. Opening up to this breaks the individualistic paradigm that many of us grew up with: we think we are alone and unique in the world, so we act in an isolated, disconnected way. When you consult your Wisdom Council, you attune with the cycles, structures, and processes of your territories and assure that your contributions will be wise and timely, guided by a clear vision. That's how you direct the creative force of your Daemon. Open the channel to receive the wisdom of your territories and your Daemon. This will inspire a legacy in tune with your being and with what the world needs.

Direct the creative force of your Daemon. Listening to the Wisdom Council supports you in having a clear vision. This vision skillfully directs the creative force of your Daemon, using its energy, talents, and virtues for a greater purpose. See your imperfections as part of this vital and wild force – the Daemon – and learn to channel it. Clarify your roles and your mission, and from there you can visualize and nurture your fruits.

Visualize and nurture your fruits. A shared fruit is more satisfying than one consumed alone. Because of this, fruits are planted in territories where you are in the company of others who share the same purpose: to respond to a need in a wise manner. Visualizing, planting, and harvesting fruits will bring a great abundance and fullness to your life – euDaemonia – a satisfying sense of harmony resulting from alignment with our inner and outer ecologies. Visualize your fruits, and this will give your life focus.

Strive for coherence. One of my mentors, Jeffrey Davis says, "We need coherence. It's a fundamental element of meaning. We want the past, present, and future to be coherent with each other. We want parts of a story to show coherence. We want parts of a business to be coherent. We love for things to be coherent." When we are conscious of our bones, seeds, winds, territories, and fruits, we leave a certain legacy, one that exudes coherence and a correspondence, as the poet Baudelaire calls it. Think about it and consider coherence as part of your definition of success.

Review your definition of success. Behind our actions are ideals, and these ideals have to do with what success means for all of us. Sometimes, this notion of success is conscious; other times, it isn't. Sometimes it's our own, and other times it's inherited from others, like our parents, the media, and our education. Shaking off your borrowed dreams and discarding other people's maps is liberating. It allows you to listen to what you really value, what gives you happiness, and what success means for you. Clarifying what success looks like is a big step in your process of defining yourself and your identity. From that clarity, you cannot live someone else's life – only our own. That's how you can find fulfillment.

Commit to self-care. In order to give the best of ourselves, we need to take charge of ourselves at every level: physically, emotionally, mentally, spiritually, economically, socially, and environmentally. This implies paying attention to our needs and creating habits that keep us awake and energetic as much as possible. This also means keeping your Daemon happy. This Life Re-Vision journey invites you to a series of practices around rest, proper eating, walking, meditation, visualization, and writing in a journal, providing constant personal hygiene on every level. Find out what other habits you want to incorporate into your life to be in great shape. Share those habits with other people, and build community that way.

Build community. Years ago, in college, I was told this story:

> "There once existed a community of brothers and sisters in a monastery in a faraway town amidst the mountains. They had a history of peacefully living together, but in current times, discord was starting to reign and the community threatened to disintegrate. They called in a sage to help maintain the community. The sage came and observed every member of the group. After a long moment of reflection they said, 'The messiah, the messenger of truth, is among you. I cannot tell you who it is, but to assure your salvation, you must treat each other as if your neighbor were the messiah.' Being a very faithful and committed community, the brothers and sisters did what the sage told them to do. Over time, the community regained its strength, people trusted each other again, and love reigned."

This story always makes me wonder, "What would it be like if we treated each other like that, with such reverence?" This type of relationship seems to be the grounds for building true community. Whatever community means to you, I encourage you to invest your time and energy in fostering deep and meaningful relationships around a common purpose. This will fill you with vitality, growth, and constant enrichment – belonging and contributing to a bigger conversation than your own.

Connect to the biggest conversations. We can spend our whole lives talking about trivial things, or we can promote topics that fertilize our constant flourishing and fruit-bearing. Life Re-Vision has helped you identify what's important to you and your territories. Make the most of every encounter with the people in your life to broaden and deepen these topics for you. Explore them. Listen to your wise people and your Daemon. You don't need any fancy protocols for this; you can do it anywhere, at any time. Make your next conversation a meaningful one.

Closing Questions

The purpose of Life Re-Vision is to offer you a journey that enhances your sense of connection, meaning, direction, belonging, and contribution. Take a few moments to close your Life Re-Vision with these questions:

- To what degree do you have a better connection with your creative force?
- With what else have you connected?
- To what degree do you have more meaning in your life and in your stories?
- To what degree do you have a better sense of direction and clarity of where you're going, and have you declared your main influences?
- To what degree do you feel a greater sense of belonging to the territories you choose to inhabit?
- To what degree do you have more clarity about the contributions you want to make in the world?
- What actions have you taken or would you like to take in that direction?

Next Steps

Congratulations! You've finished your Life Re-Vision journey!

You now have a first version of your bones, seeds, winds, territories, ecology, and fruits. You've taken a step forward in the story of your life. We could say that you are starting a new cycle. In order to mark this accomplishment, you can take these three steps:

1. **Craft your life matrix.** This is the same as drawing your new map. In previous pages, you've seen examples of this life matrix, which in a very simple way gives you a clear structure that can guide you.

2. **Physically or virtually involve your community.** To enhance the relevance and potency of your journey, share it and receive feedback from your community or tribe. It helps them comprehend that Life Re-Vision is a transition ritual, which, when you involve others, gains more strength and transformative power.

3. **Celebrate your fruits.** Your community or tribe will be very happy to support you in celebrating the harvest of the fruits you planted in your Life Re-Vision, which I hope will be many and will give you a deep euDaemonia. You will know the way you best like to celebrate. I hope that you share with me a memory of your celebration because your euDaemonia is mine as well.

On the Re-Vision Academy website,[1] you will find more information about taking these three steps. I invite you to join one of our virtual courses to live this journey with others, feeling fully supported by community. Meanwhile, concentrate on finishing the exercises in this book, and you will be ready to share this work and strengthen your relationship with yourself and your community.

Thank you for undergoing this exploration! I wish you blessings in your path.

9

Coda

Find Completion

We never know when our last moment will be. If we postpone important things, we may never get the chance to do them. The death of Steven Heller, among many other lessons, showed me the importance of not leaving matters pending, and of taking care of them in time.

The last time I saw him was when I listened to "the call for completion." I found out he had a new girlfriend, and I knew that was a milestone in our story: to acknowledge and support each other in this new stage of our lives, each one with a different partner, now as friends. I had coffee with him and congratulated him on his new girlfriend. I told him about Carlos, my then-boyfriend, and we remembered some of our learning experiences together and noted how they were helping us with our new partners. He showed me his new apartment, and I told him about the house in Aldeafeliz that I had bought. We celebrated each other's successes. Some days later, we saw each other by surprise at the synagogue, now each one of us with our partners. We all hugged each other and expressed affection. This last encounter was warm and magical; I felt a deep completeness. Since he left this world, the memory of that last moment together brings me great happiness. Constantly looking for completeness is a principle of Life Re-Vision, since it's the recognition of how sacred each moment is and that we don't know how long we are going to be here.

A Sign of Life

In March of 2015, a month after that last time we saw each other at the synagogue, my friend Alfonso called to tell me that Steven had been killed. I was silent at first, until a desperate tear slid down my face. I went into deep mourning. The pain of losing him as a friend and of the world losing such an incredible person overwhelmed me with grief. For various reasons, this pushed me to write a book on Life Re-Vision.

Steven (RIP) was murdered by a group of young people so they could steal his bicycle in a rural area very close to Aldeafeliz. Clearly, these young people lacked goals in life that would orient them toward more constructive activities. I think that a large part of society has lost its direction since we no longer create sufficient support structures so that everyone, including young people, feels a sense of purpose and connection with themselves.

The death of someone close to use reminds us how fragile life is. Connecting with our strength, clarifying our purpose, and achieving our dreams should not be postponed for a "tomorrow" that may never come. Steven had always been supportive of my writing. He'd be very happy to see me manifesting this dream.

Steven saw me voraciously writing in my journals every day and reading one book after another. He never stopped telling me, "Stop over-preparing. You're ready to share your message right now with the world." This was hard for me because I didn't yet see what my message would be since I belonged to so many worlds and had so many interests. It was precisely the Life Re-Vision process that began to give me clarity about my place and my message, which gave me strength and confidence to express myself.

The ways in which we have processed Steven's death as a community or tribe has been a reflection of the Life Re-Vision process. Like the Babemba tribe does, after his death, his friends and family started to collect and share Steven's stories in order to remember his spirit. The first meeting we had was in the house of his best friend, Alan, to cook vegetarian recipes Steven liked and share stories about him.

That night, his friends told stories about the most memorable moments they had with Steven, full of laughter and nostalgia. We talked about "the no plan day" they had with Alan, where they went from one place in Bogotá to another, with no plans allowed. They played billiards, went to the market, got lost in the crowds, and discovered new unknown places. The two friends concluded that it had been an unforgettable day. This reflected Steven's adventurous explorer's spirit. He was open to the virtues of his city and trusted the community and people living in it.

His cousin Claudio told us about how he helped him connect to the present moment. Claudio was going through a rough time, with no peace of mind. Steven took him to the beach in the middle of the night and asked him to follow his lead: take off his shoes and feel the contact with the elements. They sat down in the sand together with their feet in the water and looked at the stars. "Feel all the sensations. Experience what it is to be alive," he said. This was unforgettable for Claudio. He talked about the connection Steven had with nature, his spirituality, and his special affinity for water.

I remember once that we went out to an art exhibit in Bogotá and there was a homeless person next to his car. Many people would be afraid to have someone looking like that get close to them: someone with torn clothes, bad hygiene, and an insistent attitude. Steven, without thinking twice, told him, "I'm going to give you a chicken today." Across the street, in a chicken parlor, he ordered a whole bird and reserved it for the man. I will never forget the look of happiness on the man's face. This was one of a million such gestures on the part of Steven – from his great generosity, to his sense of social responsibility – coming from the Jewish concept of *Tsedaka*. The root of this word is *justice*; we don't give out of pity but out of a sense of justice to our neighbors.

We kept on remembering Steven's seeds, a type of collective catharsis to preserve his memory, celebrating his spirit and infusing ourselves with him. His stories are a fundamental part of his legacy, as they capture his essence.

As we were revealing his life stories (seeds), we were gathering his physical relics, artifacts and works he left behind (his bones). A few days after his death, my instinct was to make a little altar in the Mexican Day of the Dead style to celebrate Steven's life. I put all the objects that reminded me of him there. I gathered pictures, the box where he gave me the engagement ring he made, a painting with a reflection on love he had given me, a book on the energies of water, and a blueprint of a house and cultural center for the Wounaan indigenous people. At the ecovillage, a yarumo tree he gave me has been planted, which is now gigantic.

With these stories, relics, and objects, we could see and appreciate who Steven was. The house he was building for the Wounaan and the blueprint he had designed shows his social awareness and his sense of aesthetic and desire to celebrate and protect our cultural patrimony (wind). Other bones that characterize him, like his investments in the colonial neighborhood La Candelaria in Bogotá, show his passion for architecture and the historical identity of cities with his processes of urban renewal (wind). His travel journals, full of questions and drawings, show his artist and explorer's soul (wind).

In an important meeting with forty of his friends at the Bogotá ImpactHub branch, an inventory of his works, projects, and dreams was carried out collectively. The place where we met shows the connection Steven had with the world of social innovation (territory).

The community of people present there was a reflection of the diversity of his interests; it included indigenous people and people involved in interculture (territory). We felt called to know and preserve his legacy by helping complete the projects he had started. It was as if everybody had absorbed a spark of his Daemon in order to keep fertilizing and watering his seeds.

Steven's list of projects in development left us very busy. He was very ambitious and generous, connected with the ecology of his territories. We spread the different projects out among ourselves; teams were formed and goals were set. This helped to channel the pain of his death and the love we had for him into a constructive purpose. The tribe got interconnected and mobilized to take collective action around Steven's vision.

In the following months, fruits from that fertile meeting at the ImpactHub were harvested. In his memory, a documentary was made called *Se Adoptan Sueños* (Dreams Adopted) that shares anecdotes about Steven and his ideals, which inspired many people. A web page on his legacy was brought into being (www.stevenheller.org) through which funds were raised for his projects. The "Entre Paréntesis" (In Brackets) Foundation, which he co-founded, activated its mission to promote intercultural understanding and raise awareness of indigenous communities. Thanks to this collective work, the Wounaan house and cultural center was funded and completed. The repairs of the roof he had started in a senior care home that had been damaged in a hailstorm were also funded and completed. A massive tree-planting happened on a piece of land where Steven and his girlfriend had envisioned an ecological project. Surely there were even more things I am not accounting for.

There are other dreams still pending. Many of us remember an initiative he visualized and described with lots of excitement. He wanted an artistic installation with the word "welcome" in all the indigenous languages that exist in the country displayed at the arrival areas of every airport in Colombia. For him, it was important that Colombians learn about the cultural richness that exists within our borders and that indigenous people feel proud of their tradition, with the goal of preserving them and that others recognizing, affirming, and respecting this history and legacy.

Steven's death showed me that at any moment in life we already have a physical legacy, relics that represent us. There are already various objects charged with our essence. I saw how Steven's friends and family did the work of gathering his bones as part of the mourning process and commemorating his life.

I reflected on how death can surprise us at any time and how our loved ones cannot possibly feel called to consolidate our relics and contributions until that moment. However, why wait for death for this to happen? How can we take ownership of our tangible and intangible legacies in this life? What can we do to harvest the richness of our lives so far and build community around our purposes? Part of what we need is clarity and strength, and this is precisely what this Life Re-Vision process aims to give you – to help you connect with your creative force, to make your purpose and place in the world clear, to strengthen your tribe, and to call others together to help you do this and then celebrate together with you.

BIBLIOGRAPHY

Alboher, M. (2012) *One Person / Multiple Careers: The Original Guide to the Slash Career*. New York, UnitedStates: Warner Busi- ness Books.

Arrien, A. (1999) *Las cuatro sendas del chamán: el guerrero, el sanador, el vidente y el maestro*. Madrid, España:Gaia Ediciones.

Baldwin, C. (2010) *Storycatcher: Making Sense of Our Lives through the Power and Practice of Story*.California, United States: New World Library.

Becker, E. (2007) *The Denial of Death*. NewYork, United States: Simon & Schuster.

Booker, C. (2005) *Basic Plots: Why We Tell Stories*. London, England: Bloomsbury Publishing.

Bridges, W. (2004) *Transitions: Making Sense Of Life's Changes*. Massachusetts, United States: Da Capo Press.

Brown, B. (2010) *The Gifts of Imperfection*. Minnesota, United States: Hazelden.

Buckingham, M., Clifton, D.O. (2001) *Now, discover your strengths*. New York, United States: Simon & Schuster.

Burnet, E., Evans, D. (2016) *Designing Your Life: How to Build a Well-Lived, Joyful Life*. United States: PenguinRandom House.

Cope, S. (2012) *The Great Work of Your Life: A Guide for the Journey to Your True Calling*. New York, UnitedStates: Random House Publishing Group.

Eisenstein, C. (2011) *Sacred Economics: Money, Gift, and Society in the Age of Transition*. California, United States: North Atlantic Books.

Estés, C.P. (2011*) Mujeres que corren con los lobos*. En M.A Meni- ni (Trad.) Barcelona, España: Ediciones B (Trabajo originalmente publicado en 1992).

Flaherty, J. (2010) *Coaching: Evoking Excellence in Others*. Abingdon, England: Routledge (3ª Ed.).

Gelb, M. (2006). *Atrévase a pensar como Leonardo Da Vinci: siete claves para ser un genio.* España: Punto de Lectura.

Grant, G. (2017) *Beyond Gridlock: The Power of Conversations in a Polarized World.* Oakland, CA, United States: Berrett-Koehler Publishers.

Hillman, J. (2013) *The Soul's Code: In Search of Character and Calling.* New York, United States: Random HousePublishing Group.

Jacobsen, M.E. (2000) *The Gifted Adult: A Revolutionary Guide for Liberating Everyday Genius.* New York, United States: Ballan- tine Books.

Kaptchuk,T.J. (2014) *The Web that has No Weaver: Understanding Chinese Medicine.* New Jersey, United States:BookBaby (2ª Ed.).

Kelley, T. (2009) *True Purpose: 12 Strategies for Discovering the Difference You Are Meant to Make.* California, United States: Transcendent Solutions Press.

Kumar, S.M. (2005) *Grieving Mindfully: A Compassionate and Spiritual Guide to Coping with Loss.* California, United States : New Harbinger Publications.

Lapsley, M. (2014) *Reconciliarse con el pasado.* Bogotá, Colombia: San Pablo.

Mariotti, S. (2014) *The Young Entrepreneur's Guide to Starting and Running a Business: Turn your Ideas into Money.* En D. DeSalvo (Ed.) New York: Crown Publishing Group (3ª Ed.).

Meade, M. (2012) *Fate and Destiny: The Two Agreements of the Soul.* Colorado, United States: Mosaic Multicultural Foundation.

Meade, M. (2016) *The Genius Myth.* Colorado, United States: Mosaic Multicultural Foundation.

Mohr, T. (2014) *Playing Big: Practical Wisdom for Women Who Want to Speak Up, Create, and Lead.* London,England: Penguin Publishing Group.

Moore, T. (2009) *Care of the Soul: Guide for Cultivating Depth and Sacredness.* New York, United States: HarperCollins.

Narváez, L., Armato, A. (2010) *La Revolución del perdón.* En L.A. González (Trad.) Madrid, España: Editorial San Pablo.

Palmer, P.J. (2012) *The Courage toTeach: Exploring the Inner Landscape of a Teacher's Life.* New Jersey, UnitedStates: John Wiley &Sons. Pullman, P. (2007) *Luces del norte: La brújula dorada.* En R. Berdagué (Trad.) Barcelona, España: Ediciones B.

Riveros, E. (2015) *Focusing: desde el corazón y hacia el corazón: Una guía para la transformación personal.* Bilbao, España: Desclée de Brower.

Rosenberg, M.B. (2006) *Comunicación no violenta: el lenguaje de la vida.* En E. Falicov (Trad.) Buenos Aires,Argentina: Gran Aldea Editores (1ª Ed.).

Scharmer, O., Kaufer, K. (2013) *Leading from the Emerging Future: From Ego-System to Eco-System Economies.* California, United States: Berrett-Koehler Publishers.

Stein, M. (2015) *The Principle of Individuation: Toward the Development of Human Consciousness.* NorthCarolina, United States: Chiron Publications.

Stroh, D.P. (2015) *Systems Thinking for Social Change: A Practical Guide to Solving Complex Problems, Avoiding Unintended Consequences, and Achieving Lasting Results.* Vermont, United States: Chelsea Green Publishing.

Tett, G. (2016) *The Silo Effect: The Peril of Expertise and the Promise of Breaking Down Barriers.* New York, United States: Simon & Schuster.

Vogl, C. (2016) *The Art of Community: 7 Principles for Belonging.* Oakland, CA, United States: Berrett-Koehler Publishers.

Weller, F. (2015). *The Wild Edge of Sorrow: Rituals of Renewal and the Sacred Work of Grief.* Berkeley, CA, United States: North Atlantic Books.

Weisman,A. (1998) *Gaviotas: A Village to Reinvent theWorld.* White River Junction, VT, United States: Chelsea Green Publishing.

Acknowledgments

First and foremost, I want to thank my family. My husband, Carlos, has been an enormous loving, nourishing, and healing support in my life. This book is born from the hearth of our home and marriage, from the platform of a stable and growth-enhancing partnership. I also want to thank my mother who has empowered me from an early age and given me opportunities to expand my work through her foundation and work with women around the world. I want to thank my father who has inspired me to live a creative life, the life of an artist, and Cathy who taught me from an early age to take care of my body and role-modeled the nurturing principle. I want to thank my siblings Julian, Sophie, and Emiliano who have engaged with this work and allowed me to experience true brotherhood/sisterhood.

Second, I want to thank my teachers and mentors who believed in me and have encouraged me to own my true path and calling. James Flaherty, Sarita Chawla, and other coaches at New Ventures West supported me in creating a foundation and path of integral development in my life and thus becoming the person I am today. Guillermo Cuellar (RIP) was my angel, creativity maven, and spiritual father, who magically created the field for finding my soul mate. Jeffrey Davis mentored me in writing this book with his amazing program "YourCaptivatingBook." Gabriel Grant and Mark Boyce incubated my dreams for seven years at the Byron Fellowship weeklong, where I became a transformational leadership trainer, and my purpose community at Global Purpose Leaders, who have helped me find my place in the world of purpose practitioners.

Third, I want to thank the Re-Vision Ecosystem. The first group of mentors of Life Re-Vision who believed in this work were my muses: Catalina Mahecha, Cecilia Castro, Ivonne Hernandez, Natalia Baquero, Lizdany Gomez, Angélica Virguez. Finally, I want to thank all the other mentors, allies, collaborators, and participants of my workshops, in particular Juliana Luque, Stella Strazdas, Marleth Morales, Camilo Valero, Andres Lievano, Paola Henao, Angélica Pena, Carlos Gil, Camila Reyes, Juan Daza, Claudia Sandoval, among many, many others for their trust, support, and for opening up their hearts and lives in the sacred space of the Life Re-Vision conversation.

Endnotes

Introduction

[1] William Bridges, *Transitions: Making Sense of Life's Changes* (Massachusetts, United States: Da Capo Press, 2004).

[2] Bridges, *Transitions*.

[3] Ángeles Arrien, *Las cuatro sendas del chamán: El guerrero, el sanador, el vidente y el maestro,* (Madrid, España: Gaia Ediciones, 1999).

[4] Arrien, *Las cuatro sendas del chamán.*

[5] Brené Brown, *The Gifts of Imperfection* (Minnesota, United States: Hazelden, 2010).

Chapter 3

[1] Christina Baldwin, *Storycatcher: Making Sense of Our Lives through the Power and Practice of Story* (California, United States: New World Library, 2010).

[2] S. C. Diwaker, *Religion and Peace* (Mathura, India: All India Digamber Jain Sangh, 1962).

[3] Leonel Narváez and Alessandro Armato, *La Revolución del Perdón,* trans. Luis Alberto González (Madrid, España: Editorial San Pablo, 2010).

[4] Charles Eisenstein, *Sacred Economics: Money, Gift, and Society in the Age of Transition* (California, United States: North Atlantic Books, 2011).

[5] Baldwin, *Storycatcher.*

[6] Rainer Maria Rilke, *Letters to a Young Poet* (San Rafael, California: New World Library, 1992).

[7] Christopher Booker, *Basic Plots: Why We Tell Stories* (London, England: Bloomsbury Publishing, 2005).

[8] Baldwin, *Storycatcher.*

[9] Baldwin, *Storycatcher.*

[10] Baldwin, *Storycatcher*.

[11] Michael Lapsley, *Reconciliarse con el pasado* (Bogotá, Colombia: San Pablo, 2014).

[12] Charles Vogl, *The Art of Community: 7 Principles for Belonging* (Oakland, CA: Berrett-Koehler Publishers, 2016).

[13] Francis Weller, *The Wild Edge of Sorrow: Rituals of Renewal and the Sacred Work of Grief* (Berkeley, CA: North Atlantic Books, 2015).

[14] Sameet M. Kumar, *Grieving Mindfully: A Compassionate and Spiritual Guide to Coping with Loss* (California, United States : New Harbinger Publications, 2005).

Chapter 4

[1] Baldwin, *Storycatcher*.

[2] Tara Mohr, *Playing Big: Practical Wisdom for Women Who Want to Speak Up, Create, and Lead* (London, England: Penguin Publishing Group, 2014).

[3] Diana Uribe, *Historia de las Independencias* (Madrid, Spain: Aguilar Publishing, 2013).

[4] Jane Goodall and Jennifer Lindsey, *Jane Goodall: 40 Years at Gombe* (New York: Harry N. Abrams, 1999).

[5] Bernardo Toro, "Paradigmo del Cuidado," posted March 26, 2015, TED video, https://www.youtube.com/watch?v=0dhUju6Acak.

[6] Jeremy Rifkin, "The Emphatic Civilisation," RSA Animate, posted May 6, 2010, https://www.youtube.com/watch?v=l7AWnfFRc7g.

[7] Rifkin, "The Emphatic Civilisation."

[8] Borja Vilaseca, *El Sinsentido Común* (CreateSpace Independent Publishing Platform, 2020).

[9] Edgardo Riveros, *Focusing: desde el corazón y hacia el corazón: Una guía para la transformación personal* (Bilbao, España: Desclée de Brower, 2015).

[10] Baldwin, *Storycatcher*.

[11] Baldwin, *Storycatcher*.

Chapter 5

[1] Martin Heidegger, *Being and Time*, trans. John Macquarrie and Edward Robinson (New York: Harper & Row, 1962).

[2] AJ Robinson, Symphonic Strategies (website), accessed November 3, 2021, https://symphonicstrategies.com/.

[3] Toro, "Paradigmo del Cuidado."

[4] Geoffrey Wagner, *Selected Poems of Charles Baudelaire* (NY: Grove Press, 1974).

[5] Marci Alboher, *One Person/Multiple Careers: The Original Guide to the Slash Career* (New York: Warner Business Books, 2012).

[6] Danielle Laporte, *The Desire Map Experience: A Guide to Creating Goals with Soul* (Colorado, United Stated: Sounds True, 2014).

[7] Alboher, *One Person/Multiple Careers*.

Chapter 6

[1] Parker Palmer, *The Courage to Teach: Exploring the Inner Landscape of a Teacher's Life* (New Jersey, United States: John Wiley & Sons, 2012).

[2] Palmer, *The Courage to Teach*.

[3] Ken Wilbur, *A Brief History of Everything* (Boston, Massachusetts: Shambhala Publications, Inc., 1996).

[4] Rosario Cordoba, "Sin coordiación no hacemos nada," Semana (website), February 28, 2014, https://www.semana.com/rosario-cordoba-habla-de-competitividad-innovacion/379022-3/.

[5] Maria Popova, "Wisdom in the Age of Information" (video), Future of StoryTelling, accessed November 3, 2021, https://futureofstorytelling.org/video/maria-popova-wisdom-in-the-age-of-information.

[6] Katrin Kaufer and Otto Scharmer, *Leading from the Emerging Future: From Ego-System to Eco-System Economies* (California, United States: Berrett-Koehler Publishers, 2013).

[7] Robinson, Symphonic Strategies.

[8] David Peter Stroh, *Systems Thinking for Social Change: A Practical Guide to Solving Complex Problems, Avoiding Unintended Consequences, and Achieving Lasting Results* (Vermont, United States: Chelsea Green Publishing, 2015).

[9] Heidegger, *Being and Time*.

[10] Stroh, *Systems Thinking for Social Change.*

[11] Palmer, *The Courage to Teach.*

[12] Clarissa Pinkola Estés, *Mujeres Que Corren Con Los Lobos*, trans. M. Antonia Menini (Barcelona, España: Ediciones B, 2011).

[13] Mary-Elaine Jacobsen, *The Gifted Adult: A Revolutionary Guide for Liberating Everyday Genius* (New York: Ballantine Books, 2000).

14 Ted J. Kaptchuk, *The Web that Has No Weaver: Understanding Chinese Medicine.* 2nd ed. (New Yord: McGraw Hill, 2000).

[15] Philip Pullman, *Luces del norte: La brújula dorada*, trans. Rose Berdagué (Barcelona, España: Ediciones B, 2007).

[16] Michael J. Meade, *The Genius Myth* (Colorado, United States: Mosaic Multicultural Foundation, 2016).

[17] Meade, *The Genius Myth.*

[18] Donald O. Clifton and Marcus Buckingham, *Now, Discover Your Strengths* (New York: Simon & Schuster, 2001).

[19] Meade, *The Genius Myth.*

[20] James Hillman, *The Soul's Code: In Search of Character and Calling* (New York: Random House Publishing Group, 2013).

[21] "Holland Code Career Test," Truity (website), accessed November 2, 2021, https://www.truity.com/test/holland-code-career-test.

[22] Alboher, *One Person/Multiple Careers.*

[23] Eisenstein, *Sacred Economics.*

[24] Palmer, *The Courage to Teach.*

[25] Jess Rimington, "Presentation at SOCOP by Jess Rimington and Joanna Levitt Cea," Vimeo, posted 2015, https://vimeo.com/143929407.

[26] Gillian Tett, *The Silo Effect: The Peril of Expertise and the Promise of Breaking Down Barriers* (New York: Simon & Schuster, 2016).

[27] Tett, *The Silo Effect.*

[28] Meade, *The Genius Myth.*

Chapter 7

[1] Stephen Cope, *The Great Work of Your Life: A Guide for the Journey to Your True Calling* (New York: Random House Publishing Group, 2012).

[2] Cope, *The Great Work of Your Life.*

[3] Erich Fromm, *The Art of Loving,* 1st ed. (New York: Harper, 1956).
[4] Kaufer and Scharmer, *Leading from the Emerging Future.*
[5] Heidegger, *Being and Time.*

Chapter 8
[1] Re-Vision Academy (website), accessed November 2, 2021, https://www.re-vision.academy.